100 Science Fiction Films

BFI Screen Guides

Barry Keith Grant

A BFI book published by Palgrave Macmillan

First published in 2013 by
PALGRAVE MACMILLAN

on behalf of the

BRITISH FILM INSTITUTE
21 Stephen Street, London W1T 1LN
www.bfi.org.uk

There's more to discover about film and television through the BFI. Our world-renowned archive, cinemas, festivals, films, publications and learning resources are here to inspire you.

Palgrave Macmillan in the UK is an imprint of Macmillan Publishers Limited, registered in England, company number 785998, of Houndmills, Basingstoke, Hampshire RG21 6XS. Palgrave Macmillan in the US is a division of St Martin's Press LLC, 175 Fifth Avenue, New York, NY 10010. Palgrave Macmillan is the global academic imprint of the above companies and has companies and representatives throughout the world. Palgrave® and Macmillan® are registered trademarks in the United States, the United Kingdom, Europe and other countries.

Designed by couch
Cover image: *The War of the Worlds* (Byron Haskin, 1953), © Paramount Pictures Corporation
Set by Cambrian Typesetters, Camberley, Surrey & couch
Printed in China

This book is printed on paper suitable for recycling and made from fully managed and sustained forest sources. Logging, pulping and manufacturing processes are expected to conform to the environmental regulations of the country of origin.

British Library Cataloguing-in-Publication Data
A catalogue record for this book is available from the British Library
A catalog record for this book is available from the Library of Congress

ISBN 978-1-84457-457-5 (pb)

Contents

Acknowledgments

During the writing of this book, I have benefitted enormously from discussions with several friends and colleagues, especially Sherryl Vint, Malisa Kurtz and Denis Dyack. Once more I am deeply grateful to Rebecca Barden, Senior Publisher, and Sophia Contento, Senior Production Editor at BFI Publishing. Again both have been enormously supportive and a pleasure to work with. Although Rebecca is moving on to a new position, I hope that we will be able to work together again in the future. Michael Brooke was wonderfully thorough in his copyediting, catching my embarrassing mistakes. Rob Macmorine at Brock University helped with technical matters. All have helped in different ways to bring this book to fruition.

Introduction

Once upon a time, sometimes seeming as if in a galaxy far away, the science fiction film was a marginal rather than mainstream genre. Indeed, while the term 'Science-Fiction' was used as early as 1851,[1] it didn't enter common usage as a generic category until the 1930s, when editor Hugo Gernsback used it to describe the type of fiction that he was publishing in his pulp magazines such as *Amazing Stories* and *Wonder Stories*. Then, with the end of World War II, seemingly all at once came the Atomic Age, the Cold War, waves of UFO sightings, accelerated social and technological change – and in the cinema, the science fiction genre burgeoned. Postwar anxieties translated well into science fiction's hypotheses, as films such as *The Thing from Another World*, *The Day the Earth Stood Still*, *Invaders from Mars*, *The War of the Worlds*, *The Beast from 20,000 Fathoms*, *Gojira* and *Invasion of the Body Snatchers*, all discussed in this book, clearly attest. The 1950s provided, to borrow a phrase from H.G. Wells, a glimpse of things to come, for just two decades later, science fiction blockbusters such as *Close Encounters of the Third Kind*, *Star Wars*, *Superman*, and *Star Trek: The Motion Picture*, also discussed in these pages, dramatically changed Hollywood.

Where Westerns once rode tall in the saddle across the movie landscape, now it is the speculative genres of science fiction, horror and fantasy that dominate popular cinema. Once the mainstay of Hollywood studio production, the Western declined dramatically after the revisionist and parody Westerns of the 1970s precipitated by changing social values. During the studio era, film series, which depend on the repetition of box-office success to continue, were about singing cowboys and talking mules, Oriental detectives and crusading doctors, Tarzan and the Bowery Boys; but apart from *Harry Potter*, the supernatural teens of *Twilight* and the seemingly unstoppable James Bond films, the big franchises of recent years have included the *Star Wars*, *Star Trek*, and *Alien* films, all science fiction. In his introduction to the volume on the Western in the *Screen Guides* series, Edward Buscombe has noted that 'For many decades the Western occupied a central position within the American film industry. From around 1910 until the beginning of the 1960s, films in the Western genre made up at least a fifth of all titles released'.[2] Yet the inversely changing fortunes of the Western and science fiction genres is no coincidence, for the more technological society becomes, the more science fiction cinema seems central to our collective experience.

Indeed, many science fiction movies are like Westerns, with space becoming, in the famous words of *Star Trek*'s opening voice-over, the 'final frontier'. James Cameron's hugely successful *Avatar* is just one example, albeit perhaps the best known. *Battle Beyond the Stars* (1980) is a remake of *The Magnificent Seven* (1960), itself a remake of Akira Kurosawa's *The Seven Samurai* (1954), while *Outland* (1981) is a version of *High Noon* (1952) set on a space mining station instead of a frontier town. In the vast wilderness of space, heroes and villains wield stun guns instead of six guns, space cowboys fly customised rockets instead of riding horses, and, as movies like *Enemy Mine* (1985), a remake of the pro-civil rights Western *Broken Arrow* (1950), show, aliens easily serve as the swarthy Other in the place of Indians. In *Star Wars*, George Lucas designed the scene where Luke Skywalker finds his aunt and uncle killed and their homestead destroyed by storm troopers as an homage to the scene in John Ford's classic Western *The Searchers* (1956) in which Ethan Edwards (John Wayne) discovers the charred and defiled bodies of his brother's family after an Indian attack.

While the conventional appearance of the cavalry to save the day in, say, Ford's 1939 *Stagecoach* seems dated to many contemporary viewers, essentially the same convention has enthralled contemporary spectators watching Han Solo come back for the final showdown with the Death Star in *Star Wars*. In other words, some of the ideological myths that inform the Western carry on within a different genre, one with a technological iconography rather than a pastoral one, because it is more related to our daily experience. Originally Westerns developed just as the American frontier was disappearing; now, because we are more likely to be familiar with computers than horses, and more likely to visit the new frontier of cyberspace than what remains of the wilderness, the classic Western has been largely replaced by the science fiction film.

In retrospect, perhaps the ascendance to dominance of science fiction as a film genre was inevitable. For Christian Metz, the chronological development in early film history from the Lumière brothers, who held the first public film screening in 1895, to Georges Méliès (director of the earliest film discussed herein, *Le Voyage dans la lune*, from 1902) marks an evolution of 'cinematography to cinema' – that is, from a conception of film as a recording tool to an artistic medium.[3] But it is perhaps more accurate to say that cinema is simultaneously Lumière and Méliès – that is, science and fiction – for the film image is at once a concrete, scientific record of things in the real world (the Lumières' 'actualities') and a selected account of that world (Méliès's 'artificially arranged scenes'). Further, the motion picture camera, that unblinking machine, always open to showing that which is placed before it, suggests that the cinema is an ideal medium for conveying the 'sense of wonder' that science fiction critics have argued is central to the genre. Damon Knight defines this sense of wonder as 'some widening of the mind's horizons, no matter in what direction', an apt description of what Siegfried Kracauer has called the camera's 'affinities' with the real world.[4] It is also, accordingly, a phrase that turns up on several occasions in this book.

As a medium, cinema displays three such affinities that are also central to the genre of science fiction: space, time, and the machine. In cinema, narration proceeds by manipulating time and space, elongating and condensing them. Indeed, the techniques for achieving spatial and temporal distortions for dramatic and expressive purposes constitute the foundation of classic narrative cinema (although such manipulations are central to documentary and experimental cinema as well). The camera, the recording apparatus itself, seems capable of moving through both dimensions at once. Terry Ramsaye has noted how much the cinema resembles the description of travelling through time in H.G. Wells's first novel, *The Time Machine*.[5] Significantly, Wells's book was published in 1895, the same year in which film history is conventionally said to have begun with the Lumières' first screening. (After Wells's book was published, inventor Robert William Paul applied for a patent for a machine that would provide simulated voyages through time as described in Wells's novel. The machine was never built, and it would be decades before anyone truly understood that cinema was itself a time machine.)

The machinery of cinema, like the Constructors in Stanislaw Lem's novel *The Cyberiad* (1967), is capable of imagining and 'building' (through special effects) other machines infinitely more sophisticated than itself. Thus science fiction film has relied heavily on special effects (a tendency itself symptomatic of the genre's concern with technology), and explains the attention given to them in this book in the discussion of films from *Le Voyage dans la lune* to *Avatar*. It is therefore understandable that for many viewers the value of (that is to say, the pleasure derived from) science fiction movies is determined by the quality (often synonymous with believability) of their special effects. To be sure, sometimes nothing destroys the pleasure of a science fiction movie for viewers more than seeing the 'seams' in a matte shot or glimpsing the zipper on an alien's bodysuit. Special effects are 'filmic moments of a *radically* filmic character',[6] seeking to depict the (as yet) unreal as realistically as possible – to engage 'our belief, not our suspension of disbelief', as Vivian Sobchack puts it.[7] We marvel at special effects images at once for their fantastic content and for the effort of their realisation. They announce the powers of cinema.

Special effects show us things that either do not exist in the real world or things which the camera cannot capture. In doing so, they mobilise what Darko Suvin has influentially called science fiction's 'cognitive estrangement', which for him is the genre's uniquely defining quality.[8] According to Suvin, with science fiction our attention is returned to reality because of its very distortion: that is to say, in order to appreciate the 'What if?' premises of science fiction tales, we must attend to, if not question, the physical, technological and possibly ideological givens of the real world. Numerous critics and scholars, following Suvin, have argued that the appeal of science fiction is for this reason primarily cognitive.

Yet at the same time, others have argued that in film the genre's primary appeal has been the kinetic excitement of action – that 'sensuous elaboration' which Susan Sontag famously describes as 'the aesthetics of destruction … the peculiar beauties to be found in wreaking havoc, making a mess'.[9] This pleasure is itself visualised in the 'bird's-eye view' shot in Alfred Hitchcock's 1963 (science fiction?) thriller *The Birds*, as the viewer is placed with the hovering birds looking down in seemingly satisfied contemplation of the avian apocalypse they have just wrought upon the town below. The conflation of the science fiction and action genres since the 1980s is proof of this aspect of science fiction's appeal, and at least one subgenre of the science fiction film, the apocalyptic film, is founded on the promise of scenes of mass destruction. In these films, from *When Worlds Collide* (1951) to *2012* (2009), we eagerly await the climactic scenes of mass destruction inevitably showing the collapse of the landmarks of western civilisation like the White House or London Bridge.

Of course, most science fiction movies offer the pleasures of both speculation and spectacle, and the best ones, including all one hundred discussed in this book, are, to use Jules Verne's phrase, *voyages extraordinaires* in one way or another. The range of science fiction films covered includes many of the most important examples of both aspects of the genre. They were also chosen to provide (allowing for the imbalance noted at the outset) a historical spread from the beginning of film history to the present. I have also endeavoured to include films representing the various types or subgenres of science fiction film – such as alien invasion, space opera, extrapolation, utopia and so on. And despite the overwhelming and inevitable dominance of Hollywood, I have sought to provide a wide geographical sampling, with films from Great Britain, Canada, New Zealand, Australia, Japan, South Korea, South Africa, Germany, the Soviet Union and France among those discussed.

In order to be as inclusive as possible given the constraints of one hundred titles, I limited the number of films included by any one director to three (as with Steven Spielberg, John Carpenter and Paul Verhoeven).

Clearly directors such as Jack Arnold, Roger Corman, David Cronenberg, Byron Haskin and Stanley Kubrick are deserving of greater representation, and I particularly regret not being able to include discussions of such personal favourites as Arnold's *It Came from Outer Space* (1953), Corman's *Attack of the Crab Monsters* (1957) and *Not of This Earth* (1957), Haskin's *Robinson Crusoe on Mars* (1964), Kubrick's *Dr. Strangelove or: How I Learned to Stop Worrying and Love the Bomb* (1964), Carpenter's *Starman* (1984), Cronenberg's *eXistenZ* (1999) and *Crash* (1996), as well as such other clearly worthy films as Saul Bass's *Phase IV* (1974), Andrei Tarkovsky's *Stalker* (1979), Nicholas Meyer's *Time After Time* (1979), Robert Altman's *Quintet* (1979), Alex Cox's *Repo Man* (1984), Terry Gilliam's *Twelve Monkeys* (1995) and Andrew Niccol's *Gattaca* (1997), to name only a few. In most cases where science fiction films have been sufficiently popular to launch a series or sequels (*Alien*, *Back to the Future*, *Frankenstein*, *The Invisible Man*, *Jurassic Park*, *Mad Max*, *The Matrix*, *Planet of the Apes*, *RoboCop*, *Star Trek*, *Star Wars*, *Superman*, *The Terminator*), I have focused on the first film for being foundational.

Aelita (*Aelita: Queen of Mars*)
USSR, 1924 – 111 mins
Yakov Protazanov

One of the first Soviet movies, and the first feature film to depict space travel, *Aelita* was directed by Yakov Protazanov, one of the founding figures of Russian cinema. *Aelita* began a tradition of socialist space fiction from the Soviet Union and its satellites, with movies from *Cosmic Voyage* (1936) to *The Silent Star** (1960) to *In the Dust of the Stars* (1976) that embrace a Marxist worldview and critique the decadent West, while its imaginative design elements influenced the look of subsequent space operas including Fritz Lang's *Frau im Mond** (1929) and the *Flash Gordon** (1936) and *Buck Rogers* (1939) serials. However, *Aelita*'s significance comes not only from its science fiction elements – which are, ultimately, rather minimal, the rocket looking as though it was inspired by Jules Verne and the trip to Mars seeming to take no time at all – but also from how it contextualises those elements within its narrative of daily life in post-Revolutionary Russia.

The film's narrative shuttles between scenes in Moscow in 1921 and on Mars. Some of the former scenes, particularly the exteriors, have a documentary quality, while the Martian scenes are highly stylised. Los (Tseretelli), an engineer in Moscow, dreams of travelling to Mars. His marriage begins to break down, and his wife Natasha (Kuindzhi) finds herself beginning to succumb to the seductive blandishments of the opportunist Viktor Erlich (Pol'), a refugee who has been billeted in Los and Natasha's apartment. Meanwhile on Mars, Queen Aelita (Solntseva), who has been watching Earth through a powerful new telescope in the Radiant Tower of Energy, falls in love with him. Los is driven by jealousy to the point that, when he thinks that his wife has been unfaithful, he shoots Natasha. He then travels to Mars on a spaceship that has secretly been constructed, along with an aspiring detective, Kravtsov (Il'inskii) and Gusev (Batalov), a Bolshevik soldier, who quickly leads a proletarian revolution of slave workers against the ruling Elders. Aelita permits the revolution, on the assumption that the Elders will be overthrown and that she will assume power. Los kills Aelita, whom he imagines as his wife, to prevent her from realising her plan – and then wakes up, realises that his Martian adventure has been a dream or fantasy, and returns home to reconcile with Natasha. In almost Godardian fashion, the film suggests that the personal is also political.

On one level, the film seems obvious socialist propaganda, with the workers' revolution extending beyond Earth to elsewhere in the solar system. From this perspective, to become a good citizen, a comrade of the revolution, requires recognising and disowning fantasy for pragmatic action in the real world. Yet its implications are in fact more ambiguous. *Aelita* may be seen as a reminder of how the revolution may serve the interests of a few rather than the many – a possible comment about the Russian Provisional Government of 1917 or even about Lenin himself.

Moreover, the scenes of daily city life in the film – such as Natasha doing housework in the cramped apartment kitchen, the various peoples' committees doing their work, and especially the scene of the secret

DIRECTOR Yakov Protazanov
SCREENPLAY Aleksei Faiko, Fёdor Otsep, based on the 1923 novel by Aleksei Tolstoi
DIRECTOR OF PHOTOGRAPHY Emil Schünemann, Yuri Zhelyabuzhskii
MUSIC Valentin Kruchinin
ART DIRECTOR Isaak Rabinovich
MAIN CAST Nikolai Tseretelli, Yuliya Solntseva, Igor Il'inskii, Nikolai Batalov, Vera Orlova, Valentina Kuindzhi, Pavel Pol', Konstantin Eggert, Yuri Zavadskii
PRODUCTION COMPANY Mezhrabpom-Rus

party where the characters, with some food and drink as encouragement, wax nostalgic about the 'old days' – while presented with such loving detail, depict an existence of privation and hardship sufficiently difficult to drive Erlich to steal food rations, Los to imagine killing his wife, and Gusev, the restive proletarian revolutionary, to want to flee domestic life. In addition, the film's fantastic Martian sets, featuring deliriously Constructivist spaces with Escher-like stairways, and flamboyant costume designs, with astonishingly ornate headgear, plastic midriffs and umbrella slacks, offer a stark contrast to the drab realities of post-revolutionary Russian life in the terrestrial scenes and provide an imaginary excess that is itself an opposition to the growing sentiment toward Socialist Realism, which would become official state policy in 1932.

Alien
US/UK, 1979 – 117 mins
Ridley Scott

Essentially a haunted house story set in outer space – the promotional tagline for the film was 'In space no one can hear you scream' – Alien is, like such films as Frankenstein* (1931) and Videodrome* (1983), an especially effective combination of science fiction and horror elements, most notably because of the eponymous extraterrestrial, with its double set of jaws, designed by Swiss artist H.R. Giger. Directed by Ridley Scott (Blade Runner* [1982]) and written by Dan O'Bannon (Dark Star* [1974]), it generated three sequels – Aliens (1986, directed by James Cameron), Alien³ (1992, directed by David Fincher) and Alien Resurrection (1997, directed by Jean-Pierre Jeunet) – and two prequels, hybrids of two franchises – Alien vs. Predator (AVP, 2004) and Aliens vs. Predator: Requiem (2007) – as well as a novelisation by Alan Dean Foster (who also novelised John Carpenter's The Thing*, 1982), comic books, action figures and toys, video games and a board game. Prometheus (2012), also directed by Scott, was initially conceived as a prequel, but in the end also places the events of Alien in a much wider, but only minimally explained, cosmic narrative.

In the plot of Alien, a commercial mining vehicle with a crew of seven, the Nostromo, receives an emergency signal and travels toward a desolate planet to investigate. Exploring the planet's surface, they find an alien spaceship where an alien life form bursts from its eggshell and attaches itself to the face of one of the crew, Kane (Hurt). Following a debate about quarantine protocol, Kane is admitted to the ship. He awakens and initially seems unharmed, but shortly thereafter the alien, having sloughed off its initial body and burrowed within Kane's host body, bursts through his chest and escapes into the ship. The crew searches for the alien, whose acidic blood burns through metal, throughout the dank ship, a plot point inspired in part by the earlier It! The Terror from Beyond Space (Edward L. Kahn, 1958). One by one, the crew is killed by the alien, as in a slasher film, while science officer Ash (Holm) turns out to be a cyborg embedded with the crew and programmed to protect the unknown lifeform at their expense by the Company that runs the mining operations. In the climax, sole survivor Ripley (Weaver) battles the alien alone, programs the ship to self-destruct, and escapes in the shuttle only to find the alien in it. She manages to eject the alien from the craft, after which she enters a sleep pod for the journey home.

Alien established Sigourney Weaver as a star (she is also featured in Galaxy Quest* [1999] and provides the voice of the computer in WALL-E* [2008]), and her character Ripley became the connecting link between the films in the series. Ripley, like Linda Hamilton's Sarah Connor in Cameron's Terminator 2: Judgment Day (1991), was also the focus of debates about whether female action heroes are progressive representations of women or merely contain them within a masculine sensibility. The alien itself is ambiguously gendered, monstrous in part because it possesses both masculine and feminine qualities. As well as its concern with the representation of gender, Alien was also innovative for its depiction of space flight as blue-collar drudgery rather than noble scientific exploration with gleaming futuristic technology, a

DIRECTOR Ridley Scott

PRODUCER Gordon Carroll, David Giler, Walter Hill

SCREENPLAY Dan O'Bannon

DIRECTOR OF PHOTOGRAPHY Derek Vanlint

EDITOR Terry Rawlings

MUSIC Jerry Goldsmith

PRODUCTION DESIGN Michael Seymour

MAIN CAST Sigourney Weaver, Tom Skerritt, Veronica Cartwright, Harry Dean Stanton, Ian Holm, John Hurt, Yaphet Kotto

PRODUCTION COMPANY Brandywine Productions, 20th Century Fox

visual representation that informs the film's critique of the capitalist exploitation of the working class crew, which is regarded as expendable.

In 2003, 20th Century Fox invited Scott to re-edit *Alien* for the DVD box set of the four films. Then, thinking it was too long, he recut it again, the resultant 'Director's Cut' eliminating about five minutes of original footage and adding approximately four minutes of deleted footage, making it about a minute shorter than the theatrical version. To complicate matters, the studio released the Director's Cut in cinemas that year. Scott claims not to consider one version more faithful to his 'vision' than another.

Alphaville, une étrange aventure de Lemmy Caution
France, 1965 – 99 mins
Jean-Luc Godard

Even when working with genre conventions in his early films – the gangster film in *À bout de souffle* (1959), the musical in *Une femme est une femme* (1961), the war film in *Les Carabiniers* (1963) – Jean-Luc Godard had no interest in making conventional movies, and *Alphaville*, Godard's sole venture into science fiction (apart from the apocalypticism of *Weekend*, 1967) is no exception. While the narrative is formulaic, combining a series of conventions from several genres (science fiction, film noir, crime films), Godard's imagery is dense with references to history and cultural texts and often anti-illusionist. If Godard's *nouvelle vague* colleague, François Truffaut, failed to make a completely satisfying interpretation of Ray Bradbury's *Fahrenheit 451** (1966) the following year, Godard succeeds in making a Brechtian science fiction film with social satire and critique.

Pulp-fiction secret agent Lemmy Caution (Constantine), a character originally created by British writer Peter Cheyney and which Constantine had already played in many films (he also reappears as Caution in Godard's later *Allemagne 90 neuf zéro* [*Germany Year 90 Nine Zero*, 1991]), travels to the dystopian, technocratic world of Alphaville – a night's drive through 'sidereal space' in his Ford Galaxy. He poses as a journalist from the 'Outlands' with a secret mission to neutralise the mastermind of Alphaville, Professor von Braun (Vernon), and destroy Alpha 60, the super-computer that controls the city and its people, imposing its logical orientation on all aspects of social organisation. Individualism has been all but eliminated in the logical world of Alphaville. Thus in Alphaville emotion is forbidden, and anyone who reveals emotional behaviour, such as weeping, is arrested and executed in public spectacles.

Von Braun's daughter, Natacha (Karina), is assigned as Caution's escort, and when Caution falls in love with her, his emotions introduce an element of the unpredictable into the equation, causing Alpha 60 to malfunction. Caution defeats the computer by providing poetic answers (several are quotations from the poetry of Argentinian writer Jorge Luis Borges) to its factual questions. Killing von Braun, he escapes with Natacha, who, as they are leaving the city, begins to rediscover words that have disappeared in Alphaville. The film concludes with the two driving away to the Outlands in Caution's Ford as Natacha haltingly learns to say the words '*Je vous aime*' ('I love you') – the same words that, beyond the grasp of totalitarian reason, are written on a furtive note which initiates Winston and Julia's forbidden relationship in *Nineteen Eighty-Four** (1984).

As is typical of Godard's early work, the story is merely a pretext for an investigation of a variety of artistic, philosophical and political issues, including the nature and function of art, the power of language and the relation of ideology and culture – issues that came increasingly to the fore as Godard's career grew more overtly political in the late 1960s. The film anticipates Godard's subsequent abandonment of narrative in favour of a more experimental approach, encouraging viewers to question how film images signify, thus positioning us in direct opposition to the citizens of Alphaville, who are outlawed from asking 'Why?' Because Alpha 60 is omnipresent and omniscient in Alphaville, the computer's voice periodically acts as a

DIRECTOR Jean-Luc Godard
PRODUCER André Michelin
SCREENPLAY Jean-Luc Godard
DIRECTOR OF PHOTOGRAPHY Raoul Coutard
EDITOR Agnés Guillamot
MUSIC Paul Misraki
PRODUCTION DESIGN Pierre Guffroy (uncredited)
MAIN CAST Eddie Constantine, Anna Karina, Akim Tamiroff, Howard Vernon, Valérie Boisgel, Michel Delahaye, Jean-Louis Comolli, Jean-André Fieschi, Christa Lang, Jean-Pierre Léaud
PRODUCTION COMPANY Athos Films

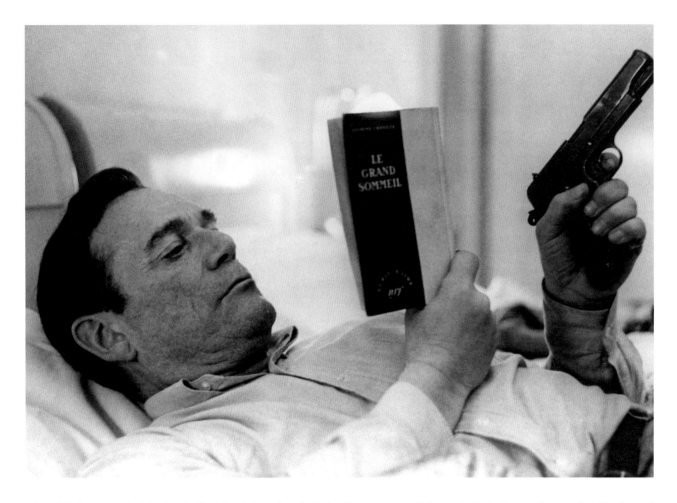

voice-of-God narrator. And despite the film's futuristic setting, Godard uses no special effects and no sets, but only actual locations in Paris, the city's modern (at the time) glass and concrete architecture convincingly signifying its dystopian vision. The seemingly endless corridors of office buildings through which Raoul Coutard's camera tracks indicates just how impersonal the world had already become.

Just as the brutally violent Lemmy Caution disturbs the rational regime of Alphaville (Godard had originally considered titling the film *Tarzan versus IBM*), so Godard disrupts the comfortable flow of classical narrative cinema. As Godard himself has remarked, he is interested not in the illusion of reality but in the reality of the illusion. In *Alphaville*, Godard, ironically, uses science fiction in an anti-illusionist way, anticipating Guillaume's clever argument in Godard's later *La Chinoise* (1967) that the Lumière brothers made fiction films and Georges Méliès (*Le Voyage dans la lune** [1902]) made documentaries.

Altered States
US, 1980 – 102 mins
Ken Russell

Long regarded as his country's cinematic *enfant terrible*, Ken Russell is a director whose outrageous and excessive style violated British cinema's decorum from the late 1960s onwards. Although he directed only one other film with science fiction elements – his second, *Billion Dollar Brain* (1967), based on Len Deighton's novel about a super-computer – most of Russell's work can be described as fantastic. His films characteristically feature a flamboyant *mise en scène* and a 'kino-fist' approach to editing frequently incorporating shock effects. His imagery often concentrates on sexuality and the body, bespeaking both desire and disgust. These qualities suggest that Russell's work has a greater affinity with horror than science fiction – explicit in *Gothic* (1986), about the genesis of Mary Shelley's *Frankenstein*, and *The Lair of the White Worm* (1988), a somewhat campy treatment of the novel by Bram Stoker – although some might argue that all of his films are in some sense horror films. Based on the only novel by Paddy Chayefsky, a writer known for his realist teleplays during the 'Golden Age' of American television in the 1950s (he also wrote *Marty* [1955] and the original screenplays for *The Hospital* [1971] and *Network* [1976]), but here credited as Sidney Aaron because of disputes with Russell, *Altered States* is a psychedelic science fiction story about a psychologist's experiments with psychotropic drugs that is perfectly suited to Russell's bold style.

Professor Edward Jessup (Hurt), seeking to explore the origins of alternate states of consciousness, begins experimenting with an extract of hallucinogenic peyote that he receives from a tribal shaman in Mexico in combination with extended isolated sessions in a sensory-deprivation flotation tank (a briefly popular fad at the time of the film's release). In his experiments, Jessup experiences increasingly intense psychological visions of the human race's primitive past, and then begins to physically devolve as well. At one point he temporarily regresses to a primitive feral hominid and exults in a hunt for animal flesh (at night in the zoo). Soon his episodes of devolution become spontaneous and beyond his control, and he eventually regresses to a shapeless blob of protoplasm that was the very beginning of life. In the climax, in what may be the only 'happy ending' in Russell's *oeuvre* (although it is consistent with Chayefsky's novel), as Jessup seems on the verge of regressing into primal protoplasm completely, he grasps the hand of his wife Emily (Brown), who pulls him back to his human form. Until this point, Jessup's scientific perspective kept him emotionally aloof from his family, which he regards as constraining – nicely depicted by Russell in subjective images of the family's cramped apartment – but now he professes his love for Emily. It is love, the film sentimentally insists, that makes us fully human.

Russell's films are filled with imagery of ineluctable mortality ('not damp – DECAY!' as Julian Sands's Shelley shrieks in *Gothic*), of all the natural shocks to which flesh is heir, and *Altered States* is no exception. Jessup's hallucinatory montages depict the simultaneous desire and dread of the body and sexuality that is characteristically Russell: kissing Emily intercut with Jessup being smothered by a snake, or Emily and Jessup

DIRECTOR Ken Russell
PRODUCER Howard Gottfried
SCREENPLAY Paddy Chayefsky (as Sidney Aaron), based on his 1978 novel
DIRECTOR OF PHOTOGRAPHY Jordan Cronenweth
EDITOR Eric Jenkins
MUSIC John Corigliano
PRODUCTION DESIGN Richard McDonald
MAIN CAST William Hurt, Blair Brown, Bob Balaban, Charles Haid, Thaao Penghlis, Miguel Godreau
PRODUCTION COMPANY Warner Bros.

turning to stone statues that erode in a sandstorm (an image also used earlier by Russell in the '1812 Overture' sequence of *The Music Lovers* [1970]). Looking for answers to what he perceives as life's meaninglessness, Jessup is, as Emily calls him, a 'Faust freak – you'd sell your soul to find great truth', thus suggesting Jessup as another mad scientist figure exploring areas where man was not to go. But Jessup is also very much in line with other Russell protagonists. Russell specialised in the biopic, focusing on artists as romantic visionaries, and *Altered States* is about a hunger artist of sorts. 'Everybody's looking for their true selves', observes Jessup at one point, and his quest, like that of Tchaikovsky in *The Music Lovers* or the sculptor Henri Gaudier-Brzeska in *Savage Messiah* (1972), is to find his, not in music or stone but in his very DNA.

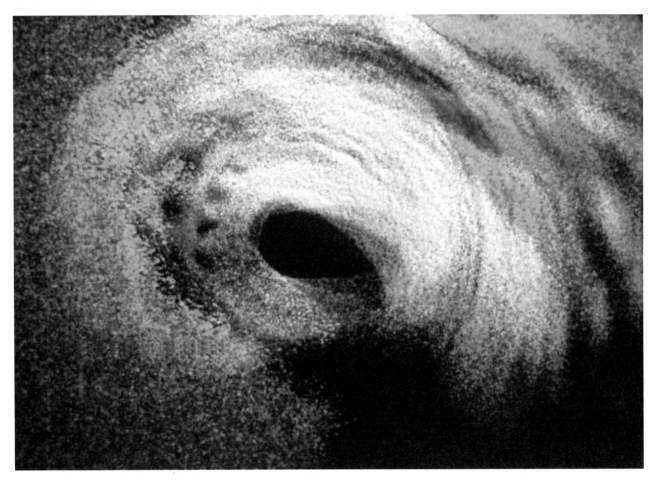

Avatar
US, 2009 – 162 mins
James Cameron

With its straightforward pro-ecology and anti-militarist and capitalist message, *Avatar* struck a chord with appreciative audiences, breaking numerous box-office records on its way to becoming the highest-grossing film of all time, surpassing writer-director James Cameron's own *Titanic* (1997). Made on an enormous budget that exceeded $300 million, it boasted new 3-D technology to present a convincing depiction of the lush alien world of Pandora. In it Cameron (*The Terminator** [1984], *Aliens* [1986], *The Abyss* [1989], *Terminator 2: Judgment Day* [1991], writer of *Strange Days** [1995]) pastiched numerous earlier works of science fiction to re-energise the myth of alien noble savagery for the digital age. Because of its astonishing commercial success, Cameron has contracted with 20th Century Fox to make two sequels.

In 2154, humanity has moved into space in its continuing search for natural resources. Particularly sought after is the mineral from Pandora, a moon in the Alpha Centauri system, known (puzzlingly) as unobtanium. Pandora's atmosphere, poisonous to humans, is inhabited by the Na'vi, a race of indigenous, blue-skinned humanoids who live in harmony with nature and pose an obstacle to the Resources Development Administration (RDA), intent on mining unobtanium. To win the hearts and minds of the Na'vi, RDA employs scientists in a programme headed by Dr. Grace Augustine (Weaver) that uses Na'vi-human hybrids called avatars, operated by genetically matched humans. In his avatar form, Jake Sully (Worthington), a paraplegic former soldier, meets Neytiri (Saldana), who introduces him into her clan. The Na'vi's spiritual gathering place, the giant Hometree, is also the site of a particularly rich deposit of unobtanium, so Sully agrees to provide intelligence to the leader of RDA's military operations, Col. Quaritch (Lang). But over time, Sully comes to embrace the Na'vi ways, including its pantheistic reverence of nature, and falls in love with Neytiri, prompting him to take up their cause and lead them in their fight against the human invaders who would blithely despoil their world. In the end, successful in defeating the Terran imperialists, Jake is able to stay in his avatar identity permanently.

A white fantasy of going native, *Avatar* recalls Westerns such as *Dances with Wolves* (1990) and science fiction tales such as Edgar Rice Burroughs's John Carter novels: in each, a white man accepts the more 'primitive' lifestyle of the Other and becomes a hero in their world. Other works that explore similar concepts as the film include some of the stories by feminist science fiction writer James Tiptree, Jr (Alice Sheldon), especially 'The Girl Who Was Plugged In' (1974) and 'We Who Stole the Dream' (1978); the *Noon Universe* series of novels by Russian writers Arkadii and Boris Strugatskii, which contains a green world called Pandora inhabited by an intelligent species, the Nave; and Ursula Le Guin's work, especially *The Word for World is Forest* (novella 1972, novel 1976), about a harmonious alien race living on a dense forest world invaded by colonising 'yumens'. *Avatar* similarly decries militarism, capitalism, imperialism and racism, making its ideas explicit in, for example, the gung-ho caricature of Quaritch and the Na'vi ability to neurally connect with animals and plants through tendrils in their hair.

DIRECTOR James Cameron
PRODUCER James Cameron, Jon Landau
SCREENPLAY James Cameron
DIRECTOR OF PHOTOGRAPHY Mauro Fiore
EDITOR James Cameron, John Refuoa, Steven Rifkin
MUSIC James Horner
PRODUCTION DESIGN Rick Carter, Robert Stromberg
MAIN CAST James Worthington, Zoë Saldana, Sigourney Weaver, Stephen Lang, Michelle Rodriguez, Giovanni Ribisi, Wes Studi, Joel David Moore
PRODUCTION COMPANY 20th Century Fox, Dune Entertainment, Ingenious Film Partners

While much of the plot is derivative, *Avatar* nonetheless succeeds in immersing the spectator into the complexly realised world of Pandora, largely through Cameron's own pioneering 3-D techniques that enable the moving camera to give physical depth to Pandora's elaborate ecology. Two production designers were involved in the film: Rick Carter (designer of several films for Steven Spielberg, including *Jurassic Park** [1993] and *War of the Worlds* [2005], as well as the two *Back to the Future** sequels) and Robert Stromberg (who has provided visual effects for numerous science fiction television series and films, including *The Road** [2009], Steven Soderbergh's version of *Solaris* [2002] and the visually stunning *Sky Captain and the*

World of Tomorrow [2004]). *Avatar* also made use of state-of-the-art motion capture techniques to provide the Na'vi with a complete range of facial expressions equalling that of the actors in the live action images. The film was nominated for nine Academy Awards including Best Picture and Best Director, winning three, for Best Cinematography, Best Visual Effects and Best Art Direction, an indication of – ironically, given its message – *Avatar*'s emphasis and reliance on technology. (The *Avatar: Special Edition* DVD contains an additional nine minutes of footage, including an extension of the sex, or 'bonding', scene, while the Extended Collector's Edition contains a further six minutes.)

Back to the Future
US, 1985 – 116 mins
Robert Zemeckis

Writer/director Robert Zemeckis has specialised in high-concept, benevolent fantasy with such films as *Who Framed Roger Rabbit?* (1988), *Death Becomes Her* (1992), *Forrest Gump* (1994), *Contact* (1997), *The Polar Express* (2004) and *A Christmas Carol* (2009), and *Back to the Future* is no exception. A family-friendly film that plays with the conundrums of time travel stories, it also provides an appealing fantasy for youthful viewers who easily identify with the plucky teenaged protagonist who is hip enough to give his parents life lessons. Unsurprisingly, *Back to the Future* became the most successful film of the year at the box office and created a franchise consisting of two sequels – *Back to the Future Part II* (1989) and *Back to the Future Part III* (1990) – as well as an animated television series and several video games. Even US President Ronald Reagan, referenced *in* the film, himself referenced *Back to the Future* in his 1986 State of the Union Address.

The story centres on 17-year-old Marty McFly (Fox), who accidentally travels back in time from 1985 to 1955 in an enhanced 1981 DeLorean automobile invented by the eccentric Dr. Emmett 'Doc' Brown (Lloyd). Marty meets his mother Lorraine (Thompson) as a teenager, and she becomes romantically interested in him instead of his father George, thus threatening the meeting of his parents, their subsequent marriage and Marty's birth. Marty finds and convinces the younger Dr. Brown of his real identity, and Doc manages to harness lightning to the DeLorean to provide the necessary electrical power to return Marty to 1985. But first Marty must convince George (Glover), a nerdy loner, to ask Lorraine out on a date so that they will eventually fall in love and so on. Needless to say, all ends well, even to the point that when Marty returns to his present he discovers that his family is no longer a bunch of losers, while Biff Tannen (Wilson), the bully who had tormented George through high school and then as his supervisor at work, is now a labourer doing work for the McFlys. Along the way, Marty even becomes the inspiration for future rock star Chuck Berry, giving him his distinctive sound.

The time-travel premise affords ample opportunity for humorous contrasts between the supposedly more innocent 1950s and the 1980s, the time when the film was made and its narrative present. Thus, for example, Lorraine calls Marty 'Calvin Klein' because that is the name sewn in his underwear, and her mother scoffs at the very idea of anyone having two television sets. Doc Brown at first disbelieves Marty's story that he is from the future: when Marty replies, in answer to his question, that Ronald Reagan is President in 1985, the incredulous Doc retorts, 'And who's Vice-President? Jerry Lewis?'

The two sequels, like the second and third films in *The Matrix** trilogy (1999–2003), were filmed simultaneously and released several months apart. Each begins by overlapping with the end of the previous film, in the manner of serials like *Flash Gordon** (1936). In *Part II*, Doc Brown appears the next morning in the DeLorean, now sporting futuristic trappings such as a 'Mr. Fusion' nuclear engine that resembles a kitchen blender, and whisks Marty and his girlfriend Jennifer (Elisabeth Shue) to 2015, twenty years into the

DIRECTOR Robert Zemeckis
PRODUCER Neil Canton, Bob Gale
SCREENPLAY Robert Zemeckis, Bob Gale
DIRECTOR OF PHOTOGRAPHY Dean Cundey
EDITOR Harry Keramidas, Arthur Schmidt
MUSIC Alan Silvestri
PRODUCTION DESIGN Lawrence G. Paull
MAIN CAST Michael J. Fox, Christopher Lloyd, Crispin Glover, Lea Thompson, Thomas F. Wilson; Claudia Wells, Marc McClure, Wendie Jo Sperber
PRODUCTION COMPANY Universal Pictures, Amblin Entertainment, U-Drive Productions

future, to prevent his future son from becoming involved with Biff's grandson Griff (Wilson). When the elderly Biff realises the situation, he surreptitiously takes a trip in the time machine back to 1955 and gives his younger self a sports almanac so that he can bet on winners for the next 45 years, resulting in a radically changed history that sees Biff become wealthy and corrupt and the town a hellish den of depravity, as in Frank Capra's *It's a Wonderful Life* (1946). Again, Marty and Doc successfully manage to set history back on its proper course. *Part III* finds Marty back in the frontier of 1885, where he has come to rescue Doc, who is trapped there, this time enabling a genial genre hybrid and play with the conventions of the Western, including a chase by Indians in Monument Valley and a showdown at high noon on Main Street in the style of Sergio Leone.

The Beast from 20,000 Fathoms
US, 1953 – 80 mins
Eugène Lourié

Based on Ray Bradbury's moody short story 'The Fog Horn', *The Beast from 20,000 Fathoms* was the first and one of the best examples of that popular science fiction subgenre of the 1950s, the giant dinosaur film. Made for under $200,000, it grossed more than $5 million and set the narrative as well as budgetary template for the cycle of giant monster films to follow, including the foundational Japanese *kaiju eiga*, *Gojira** (1954), which it inspired, and the later *Cloverfield* (2008), written by Drew Goddard (*The Cabin in the Woods** [2012]). *The Beast* fleshes out Bradbury's slim tale of a dinosaur drawn to the sound of a lighthouse foghorn out of loneliness, explaining it as a prehistoric creature awakened from its long slumber in the Arctic by an atomic explosion and returning to its ancestral habitat, now occupied by New York City.

The film was ably directed by Eugène Lourié, who had also worked as a production designer for Jean Renoir (*Les Bas-fonds* [*The Lower Depths*, 1936], *La Règle du jeu* [*The Rules of the Game*, 1939]), Charles Chaplin (*Limelight* [1952]), and Samuel Fuller (*Shock Corridor* [1963], *The Naked Kiss* [1964]). Lourié also directed the admirable *The Colossus of New York* (1958), and was responsible for the production design of two other science fiction movies, *The Giant Behemoth* (1959), which he also wrote and directed, and *Crack in the World* (1965). As he did with *Beast*, Lourié also worked on the special effects for both of these films. The excellent miniature sets through which the creature stomps in stop-motion animation were created by Ray Harryhausen, in his first feature as special-effects head. His later credits include the effects for *20 Million Miles to Earth* (1957) and the legendary *Jason and the Argonauts* (1963).

In her famous essay on science fiction movies, Susan Sontag wrote that they provide 'an aesthetics of destruction' – 'the peculiar beauties to be found in wreaking havoc, making a mess' – and *Beast* certainly delivers this guilty pleasure. The film provides exciting scenes of the eponymous Rhedosaurus's attack on New York as it flattens vehicles, damages skyscrapers and causes crowds of people to flee in panic. A policeman is lifted in the air by the creature's powerful jaws, his legs kicking, and then swallowed. 'This is full-scale war against a terrible enemy such as modern man has never before faced', explains the news announcer during the post-rampage montage.

Such scenes would become obligatory in later monster movies, some of which even include a variation of *Beast*'s climax, itself harkening back to the shooting of *King Kong* (1933) on the Empire State Building, in which the dinosaur is vanquished amid the Cyclone roller coaster at Brooklyn's Coney Island amusement park. The Venusian Ymir of *20 Million Miles to Earth* is felled with bazooka fire in the Roman Colosseum; *Gorgo* (1961), also directed by Lourié, is killed in Piccadilly Circus; and the giant octopus of *It Came from Beneath the Sea* (1955) threatens San Francisco's Golden Gate Bridge. The roller coaster climax of *The Beast from 20,000 Fathoms* may be understood as the potential guilty pleasure of trashing a landmark, like seeing the White House explode in *Independence Day* (1996) or Big Ben crumble in *Mars Attacks!** (1996), but it

DIRECTOR Eugène Lourié
PRODUCER Hal Chester, Jack Deitz
SCREENPLAY Lou Morheim and Fred Freiberger, adopted from the short story 'The Fog Horn' (1951) by Ray Bradbury
DIRECTOR OF PHOTOGRAPHY Jack Russell
EDITOR Bernard W. Burton
MUSIC David Buttolph
PRODUCTION DESIGN Eugène Lourié
MAIN CAST Paul Christian, Cecil Kellaway, Paula Raymond, Kenneth Tobey, Lee Van Cleef, Donald Woods
PRODUCTION COMPANY Warner Bros.

is also a reflexive metaphor for the way popular movies such as *Beast* provide us with a series of coordinated and controlled thrills, anticipating Steven Spielberg's *Jurassic Park** (1993) forty years later. The film's explanation for the creature's appearance was also picked up by numerous other movies such as *Them!** (1954), and makes the beast another thinly veiled metaphor for nuclear anxiety during the height of the Cold War. Even the blood of the creature is radioactive, the drops from its wounds making soldiers ill as they track it through the streets of the city in one especially suspenseful sequence.

Blade Runner
US/Hong Kong, 1982 – 117 mins
Ridley Scott

Although it did not do well when first released – in part because it was up against *E.T.: The Extra-Terrestrial**
at the box office – *Blade Runner*'s reputation has since grown from cult favourite to the point that it is
considered by many to be one of the greatest science fiction films ever made. In the tradition of Mary
Shelley's *Frankenstein* (1816), the film addresses issues of science, morality and religion in a narrative about
genetic engineering, here set slightly in the future. Its superb production design pioneered the tech-noir style,
influencing many later films such as *Ghost in the Shell** (1995) as well as videogames and the concurrently
developing genre of cyberpunk literature. Its combination of futuristic and 'forties style elements,
technological innovation and decaying environment, reinforced by Vangelis's score, which incorporates both
classic and synthesiser sounds, creates an appropriately dark mood and establishes the link between the
world of the film and our own.

The film is set in the year 2019, when the technology of genetic engineering has become widespread
and large corporations are making androids known as replicants for dangerous work on the 'off-world'
colonies, where much of the population has already gone to escape a polluted, over-crowded Earth. Virtually
indistinguishable from actual human beings, they are banned on Earth, but a group of four new generation
Nexus-6 replicants made by the Tyrell Corporation – Zhora (Cassidy), Leon (James), Pris (Hannah) and their
leader, Roy Batty (Hauer) – have escaped to Earth and are hiding in Los Angeles, where retired police officer
Rick Deckard (Ford), a hunter of renegade replicants known as a 'blade runner', reluctantly agrees to take on
one more assignment to find and 'retire' them. At the corporation's headquarters he meets Tyrell's assistant,
new model replicant Rachael (Young), who is initially unaware that she is a machine, and she and Deckard
fall in love even though he knows that she is not truly human. Deckard retires Zhora, Pris and, with Rachael's
help, Leon, although in a final violent confrontation with Roy, he is no match for the more powerful replicant.
However, as the desperate Deckard is about to plunge to his death from a tall building, Roy lifts him to safety
just as his life-functions expire at their predetermined time.

The film ends, depending on the version, with Deckard and Rachael leaving his flat together in the lift
or driving through a lush landscape. Seven different versions of the film have been shown, beginning with
the original test print (113 mins), the negative response to which resulted in the changes made for the US
theatrical version (the one most widely seen, known as the 'Domestic Cut'), which included the studio-
imposed final scene of the couple driving away and a voice-over narration by Deckard evocative of classic
hard-boiled detective noirs. Both elements were removed for 'The Final Cut' 25th Anniversary Edition DVD in
2007, the only version over which director Ridley Scott (*Alien** [1979], *Prometheus* [2012]) had complete
control. Regardless, the question of whether Deckard is human or a replicant has been a subject of much
debate, the textual ambiguity of the film on this matter consistent with the film's vision of a thoroughly

DIRECTOR Ridley Scott
PRODUCER Michael Deeley
SCREENPLAY Hampton Fancher,
David Webb Peoples, based on the
novel *Do Androids Dream of Electric
Sheep?* (1968) by Philip K. Dick
DIRECTOR OF PHOTOGRAPHY
Jordan Cronenweth
EDITOR Terry Rawlings
MUSIC Vangelis
PRODUCTION DESIGN Lawrence G.
Paull
MAIN CAST Harrison Ford, Rutger
Hauer, Sean Young, Edward James
Olmos, M. Emmet Walsh, Daryl
Hannah, William Sanderson, Brion
James, Joanna Cassidy, Joe Turkel
PRODUCTION COMPANY The Ladd
Company, Warner Bros., Shaw
Brothers

postmodern future in which it is impossible to discern the difference between the human and the imitation, the natural and the artificial.

Blade Runner brought the work of author Philip K. Dick to the attention of Hollywood, initiating a string of film adaptations of his work including Total Recall* (1990, 2012). Dick, who was wary of Hollywood, died shortly before the film's release (it is dedicated to him), but had expressed enthusiasm for it, including the special effects by Douglas Trumbull (who was responsible for the effects in 2001: A Space Odyssey* [1968] and Silent Running* [1972], which he also directed). One of Blade Runner's screenwriters, Hampton Fancher, aware of William S. Burroughs's unfilmed treatment for an adaptation of Alan E. Nourse's novel The Bladerunner (1974), thought the title provocative enough to use, despite little similarity between the two narratives other than them featuring a dystopian future.

Born in Flames
US, 1983 – 80 mins
Lizzie Borden

Lizzie Borden is an independent film maker whose films *Born in Flames* and *Working Girls* (1986) were important contributions to the feminist cinema of the time. Her chosen name, alluding to the alleged axe murderess famous from 1890s American folklore for killing her parents, is indicative of the violently confrontational style of her work. Strongly influenced by feminist theory and the political cinema of Jean-Luc Godard (*Alphaville** [1965]), both films were highly controversial. *Born in Flames*, made on a minuscule budget of $40,000 and edited over a period of five years, explores questions of racism and sexism, and the role of media in shaping the discourse of such political issues, in a near-future alternative Socialist Democracy in the United States. Its unorthodox and somewhat distancing style is a challenge to spectators, just as the various women within the film struggle to reach political insight and take collective action.

The film shows a normative world characterised by the oppression of women on the personal and political levels, and the attempts of women, straight and gay and of different colour, to work together. Set in New York City ten years after the peaceful Socialist Democratic revolution, the plot focuses on two feminist groups who communicate to the wider public on pirate radio stations. One group, on 'Radio Regazza', is led by a radical white lesbian, Isabel (Bertei), the other, on 'Phoenix Radio', led by a more moderate black woman, Honey. Despite the Revolution and its stated goals of equality, the old sexism of patriarchy seems to continue as women construction workers around the city are laid off as a result of a government policy giving employment priority to men with families. Their political concerns become more urgent when an important political activist, Adelaide Norris (Satterfield), is arrested and shortly thereafter dies under suspicious circumstances while in custody, the police claiming that she had committed suicide as a political protest. As well, the Women's Army led by Hillary Hurst (Hurst), which both Honey and Isabel at first refuse to join, is growing larger and more militant. When a woman is being raped on the street, a contingent of Army women appears on bicycles blowing whistles and chasing the rapists away, showing the potential efficacy of united action.

Three young editors of a Socialist-sponsored newspaper – one of whom is played by director Kathryn Bigelow (*Strange Days** [1995]) – are supportive of the developing events and eventually get fired because their feminist sympathies put them at odds with the party's rhetoric of solidarity. Both radio stations are destroyed in suspicious fires, but Honey and Isabel join the Army and come together to broadcast from mobile vans. The film concludes with a group of terrorists from the Women's Army forcing their way into a television station where they interrupt a broadcast by the President in which he proposes legislation that would pay women for doing housework, and then (chillingly, in retrospect) bombing the antenna on top of the World Trade Center in a blow against the empire of mainstream media.

Born in Flames's style is inseparable from its politics. Structurally, it alternates between minimally narrative sequences, mostly of women's groups' meetings or radio broadcasts, and montages of women in

DIRECTOR Lizzie Borden
PRODUCER Lizzie Borden
SCREENPLAY Ed Bowes
DIRECTOR OF PHOTOGRAPHY Ed Bowes, Al Santana
EDITOR Lizzie Borden
MUSIC The Bloods, Ibis, Red Crayola
MAIN CAST Honey, Adele Bertei, Jean Satterfield, Florynce Kennedy, Becky Johnston, Pat Murphy, Kathryn Bigelow, Hillary Hurst, Sheila McLaughlin, Marty Pottenger, Bell Chevigny, Joel Kovel, Ron Vawter, John Coplans

daily contexts, thus establishing connections between theory and practice, the political and the personal. From the beginning, the Women's Army is under investigation by FBI agents and, tellingly, during the first third of the film we only hear the agents' voices but do not see them, a stylistic choice suggesting the pervasive power of patriarchy. The male voices function like narrators, providing background exposition from a clearly biased perspective in context of what we actually see on the screen, prompting viewers to question their authority and reliability. Overall, Borden's rough mockumentary style, including her use of non-professional actors and banner newspaper headlines, recalls the 'imperfect' aesthetic of Third Cinema, a contemporary political film movement in South and Central America that sought alternatives to Hollywood and European art cinema, both traditional bastions of male expression.

A Boy and His Dog
US, 1975 – 91 mins
L.Q. Jones

Harlan Ellison's 1969 book *A Boy and His Dog* consists of a series of stories beginning with the short story of the same name, and includes an expanded novella in his collection of short stories, *The Beast that Shouted Love at the Heart of the World*, published later the same year and which also served as the basis for the film, and *Vic and Blood*, a graphic novel illustrated by Richard Corben (who also illustrated the poster for Brian De Palma's cult horror musical, *Phantom of the Paradise* [1974]). As the title of this post-apocalyptic black comedy suggests, it mocks the typical heartwarming boy's own tale of a youngster and his faithful pet.

The story takes place in the American southwest in 2024, after the nuclear destruction of World War IV. The few male survivors compete for resources, including food and women, in the desert wasteland. One of these young men, Vic (Johnson), is aided in his search for women to rape by an intelligent telepathic canine named Blood (voiced by Tim McIntire, who also provided the music for the film), who uses his enhanced senses of smell and hearing to track them down. The pair bickers frequently, Blood's more reflective advice countering Vic's rashness, reversing the standard relationship between men and dogs. Vic needs Blood, who serves as a mentor to him, teaching him about history and morality, while Blood, whose telepathic ability is the result of genetic mutation, also acts as a caustic commentator, remarking, for example, as he watches Vic copulate, that 'human sex is an ugly thing'.

One of their female prey, Quilla June Holmes (Benton), has been sent by her father (Robards), the leader of an underground society named Topeka, to lure a young man into 'servicing' the community's young women, as the men of Topeka have become impotent. After saving Quilla June's life and spending an intimate evening with her, Vic follows her to the underground community, attracted by the promise of more sex, despite warnings by Blood, whom he leaves behind. But, as Vic discovers, after being welcomed he is restrained and then begins to have his semen forcibly extracted to artificially inseminate three dozen women. After his procreative function is fulfilled, Vic will be sent to 'the farm' with the help of android enforcer Michael (Californian boxing champion Hal Baylor), as are all dissenters. Before the process is completed, however, he manages to escape with the help of Quilla June and a group of rebellious teenagers. The others are killed by Michael, but Vic and Quilla June make it to the surface, where they find that Blood is still there, starving. As the film ends, it is implied that Vic has killed and cooked Quilla June to save Blood: a bonfire is shown barbecuing food and the dog observes that she may have had excellent judgment, 'if not particularly good taste'.

Just as adolescent adventure is turned on its head in *A Boy and His Dog*, so Topeka, emblematic of middle America, is now the 'underground' rather than the mainstream. A parodic portrait of middle America at the height of its postwar affluence in the 1950s, it shows the people of Topeka desperately trying to hold on to the culture's past glory by mimicking common rituals such as marching bands and pie-baking contests. Everyone wears mime makeup, underscoring the sham of the entire enterprise, while the community's sexual

DIRECTOR L.Q. Jones
PRODUCER L. Q. Jones, Alvy Moore
SCREENPLAY L.Q. Jones, based on the story and novella 'A Boy and His Dog' (1969) by Harlan Ellison
DIRECTOR OF PHOTOGRAPHY John Arthur Morrill
EDITOR Scott Conrad
MUSIC Tim McIntire
PRODUCTION DESIGN Ray Boyle
MAIN CAST Don Johnson, Suzanne Benton, Jason Robards, Tim McIntire (voice of Blood), Alvy Moore
PRODUCTION COMPANY LQ/JAF

impotence bespeaks America's social collapse. The film's co-producers, Alvy Moore and L.Q. Jones, who also directed and wrote the screenplay, were both character actors with dozens of movies and television shows to their credit. Jones, who appeared in several of Sam Peckinpah's Westerns, here plays the actor in the porn film-within-the-film that Vic watches at a gathering place. Moore (Dr. Moore in the film) was a genial comic actor who had his biggest role in the TV sitcom *Green Acres* (CBS, 1965–71), in its own way as savage a satire of middle America as *A Boy and His Dog*.

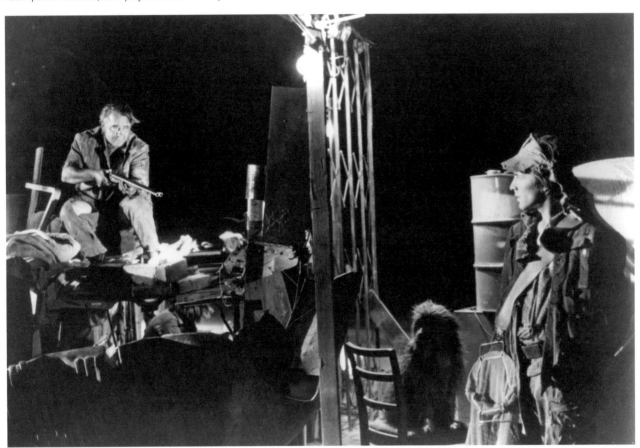

Brazil
UK, 1985 – 142 mins
Terry Gilliam

Terry Gilliam began his film career making the animated sequences for the BBC's *Monty Python's Flying Circus* (1969–74), and then moved into directing feature films with *Monty Python and the Holy Grail* (1975). His penchant for the fantastic genres is foregrounded in his subsequent films *Jabberwocky* (1977), *Time Bandits* (1981), *The Adventures of Baron Munchausen* (1988), *The Fisher King* (1991), *Twelve Monkeys* (1995), inspired by Chris Marker's *La Jetée** (1962), and *The Imaginarium of Dr. Parnassus* (2009). A frequent theme of Gilliam's films is the depiction of society as rigidly ordered, against which protagonists struggle for self-realisation through the unfettered imagination – realised most succinctly and charmingly in Gilliam's short, *The Crimson Permanent Assurance*, that begins *Monty Python's The Meaning of Life* (1983), in which an accounting firm staffed by elderly men mounts a rebellion depicted as pirates taking over a slave ship – and *Brazil* is no exception. A blackly comic dystopian tale set 'somewhere in the 20th century', as an opening

DIRECTOR Terry Gilliam
PRODUCER Arnon Milchan
SCREENPLAY Terry Gilliam, Tom Stoppard, Charles McKeown
DIRECTOR OF PHOTOGRAPHY Roger Pratt
EDITOR Julian Doyle
MUSIC Michael Kamen
PRODUCTION DESIGN Norman Garwood
MAIN CAST Jonathan Pryce, Robert De Niro, Katherine Helmond, Ian Holm, Michael Palin, Bob Hoskins, Peter Vaughan, Kim Greist, Jim Broadbent, Ian Richardson, Charles McKeown
PRODUCTION COMPANY Embassy International Pictures

insert title tells us, the film is an irreverent mix of influences from *Metropolis** (1927) and Eisenstein's *Battleship Potemkin* (1925) to film noir and, of course, George Orwell's *Nineteen Eighty-Four* (1948). With a brilliant production design that simultaneously evokes several different decades, *Brazil*'s Kafkaesque world is a place anyone with a little imagination would find oppressive.

The unnamed country of *Brazil* is a bureaucratic nightmare: workers dress the same, toil in impossibly cramped cubicles and live in dreary flats. Services (all provided by 'Central Services') are minimal, and a plethora of paperwork seems to determine all activity. Women repeatedly have plastic surgery to make them look perpetually young, and attractive billboards line the highways behind which, out of view, the landscape is an industrial wasteland. Bombs explode in public places on a regular basis, for which an underground resistance movement is apparently responsible. Flexible ductwork is everywhere, as are television monitors, on which old movies are regularly played to provide controlled escape for people. The theme song 'Aquarela do Brasil', written by Ary Barroso, serves as a musical leitmotif expressing the mass-mediated fantasies of escape that characterise the denizens of this dystopia

The film's plot is set in motion with a literal fly in the bureaucratic ointment, as one such insect causes a jam in a printer, resulting in a misprint of one letter and the consequent arrest and death of an innocent man, Harry Buttle, as a suspected terrorist instead of Harry Tuttle (De Niro). Sam Lowry (Price), a low-level government bureaucrat, is assigned the job of rectifying the mistake. Visiting Tuttle's widow in her flat in a decaying apartment complex (ironically named Shangrila) reminiscent of Alex and his family's abode in *A Clockwork Orange** (1971), he comes upon her neighbour, Jill Layton (Greist), who resembles the literal woman of Sam's dreams, a recurrent fantasy of flying above the clouds with silver wings and rescuing a beautiful damsel in distress. He manages to track Jill down, and the two share a romantic night together before Sam is arrested, in a scene evoking the arrest of Winston and Julia above the antique shop in *Nineteen Eighty-Four** (1984), and tortured as an assumed terrorist. As his old friend Jack (Palin) is about to torture him, Sam is rescued by the terrorist Harry Tuttle and together they destroy the government Ministry. The scene grows increasingly frenetic and surreal, culminating in Sam's escape with Jill – but then the adventure is revealed to be only in Sam's head, as he has become catatonic in response to the anticipated pain of Jack's imminent torture.

Recalling the situation with Ridley Scott's *Blade Runner** (1982) three years earlier, executives at Universal Studios, the American distributor of *Brazil*, pressured Gilliam to change the ending to a happy one, which he resisted. The US release of the film was delayed, and after Gilliam's version, screened without the studio's approval, was awarded Best Picture by the Los Angeles Film Critics Association, Universal finally capitulated. The original UK release and the final Director's Cut version, available on DVD, are ten minutes longer than the North American version.

The Brother from Another Planet
US, 1984 – 108 mins
John Sayles

This imaginative, low-budget science fiction feature was the fourth film written and directed by John Sayles, an independent American film-maker who has specialised in both sensitive dramas of topical social issues (*Return of the Secaucus Seven* [1979], *Lianna* [1983], *Amigo* [2010]) but who early in his career wrote commercial screenplays for others that revealed a humorous self-awareness of genre convention, particularly science fiction and horror (*Piranha* [1978, directed by Joe Dante], *Alligator* [directed by Lewis Teague, 1980], *The Howling* [Dante, 1981]). Sayles's screenplay for *Battle Beyond the Stars* (1980, directed by Jimmy T. Murakami), was *The Seven Samurai* (1954) by way of *The Magnificent Seven* (1960) in outer space. *The Brother from Another Planet*, the first American movie to depict a literal rather than metaphorical black alien (Morton), neatly combines both aspects of Sayles's work.

The film reveals its generic awareness in such dialogue as when one of the two 'men in black' (extraterrestrial hunters searching for the Brother played with wonderfully deadpan humour by Sayles and Strathairn) says in the Harlem bar when they present themselves as FBI agents, 'Badges? We don't need no badges' – the line taken, of course, from John Huston's *The Treasure of the Sierra Madre* (1948) – and in allusive plot points, such as the Brother's ability to heal wounds with a glowing hand, like the more lovable but racially neutered alien of *E.T.: The Extra-Terrestrial** (1982) in Steven Spielberg's film two years earlier. Because of the simple yet radical stroke (comparable to George Romero's earlier casting of Duane Jones in *Night of the Living Dead* [1968]) of making the film's alien black, Sayles is able to comment on the implicit racial politics of the mainstream science fiction film, playing on the idea of 'alien' as immigrant or racial Other before later science fiction films such as *Alien Nation* (1988) and *District 9** (2009), as well as on the minority status of black Americans. Sayles establishes the film's critique of racism from the outset, when in the opening scene the alien lands (as in so many classic monster movies of the 1950s) in New York City, in this case near, ironically, the Statue of Liberty. The camera shows Liberty in the distance, but then rack focuses suddenly as the Brother's head comes into the frame in the foreground of the image, so that the iconographic statue suddenly seems to become 'unfocused', to lose definition, with the appearance of a black face.

The opening scene continues – surprisingly, given Sayles's reputation as a 'talky' film-maker – as the Brother makes his way to Harlem, with almost no dialogue, like the opening of Howard Hawks's *Rio Bravo* (1959), for almost ten minutes. The Brother cannot speak, and he becomes a palimpsest onto which others project what they want or expect to see. When singer Malverne Davis (played by jazz vocalist Dee Dee Bridgewater) says, 'How come I like you so much? You could be anybody', the film begins to tread in the murky existential territory of art films like Ingmar Bergman's *Persona* (1966). The Brother's own identity is challenged, as happens to Newton in *The Man Who Fell to Earth** (1976), as he begins to be corrupted by the readily available pleasures of drugs and the media (a tabloid's banner headline blares 'I Sold My Baby to

DIRECTOR John Sayles
PRODUCER Peggy Rajski, Maggie Renzi
SCREENPLAY John Sayles
DIRECTOR OF PHOTOGRAPHY Ernest Dickerson
EDITOR John Sayles
MUSIC Martin Brody, Mason Daring
PRODUCTION DESIGN Nora Chavooshian
MAIN CAST Joe Morton, Daryl Edwards, Steve James, Leonard Jackson, Bill Cobbs, Maggie Renzi, Olga Merediz, Tom Wright, Minnie Gentry, Ron Woods, Peter Richardson, John Sayles, David Strathairn
PRODUCTION COMPANY Anarchist's Convention Films, UCLA Film and Television Archives, A-Train Films

UFO Aliens' in a market where the Brother is shopping). Sayles links the two, equating the soporific media with drugs through editing, suggesting their similarly addictive nature.

The Brother from Another Planet succeeds as science fiction and social critique with a minimum of special effects – the Brother's healing hand represented by a glowing concealed light bulb, for example. The Brother looks human in every respect except for his claw-like toes ('you got to do something about your toenails', Malverne tells him in the morning after they've spent the night together). The film also helped pave the way for a cycle of black

feature films, beginning with Spike Lee's *Do the Right Thing* in 1989 (shot by *Brother*'s cinematographer Ernest Dickerson, who would go on to direct some of this group's important films such as *Juice* [1992] and *Surviving the Game* [1994] before moving on to work mostly in television), and including Robert Townsend's *The Meteor Man* (1993), in which a mild-mannered black schoolteacher receives temporary super powers from a meteorite and brings civil order to his drug-riddled inner-city neighbourhood, discovering his hidden inner strength in the process.

The Cabin in the Woods
US, 2012 – 95 mins
Drew Goddard

A self-reflexive hybrid of science fiction and horror, *The Cabin in the Woods* is a darkly humorous take on horror spectatorship. Although directed and co-written by Drew Goddard, co-writer of episodes of the television shows *Buffy the Vampire Slayer* (1997–2003), *Angel* (1999–2004) and *Lost* (2004–2010) and writer of the screenplay for the pseudo-vérité monster movie *Cloverfield* (2008), it clearly reveals the touch of co-writer and producer Joss Whedon, who produced all the above as well as *Dollhouse* (2009–10) and *Firefly* (2002), which served as the basis for the space opera Western film *Serenity* (2005). Also a writer of comics, Whedon wrote *Captain America: The First Avenger* (2011) and wrote and directed the blockbuster *Marvel's The Avengers* (*Avengers Assemble*, 2012). *Buffy*, about a young woman who is chosen to become a 'slayer' of vampires and demons, generated a considerable fan following as well as substantial academic interest. Helped by her friends, the 'Scooby Gang', a reference to the ghost-hunting teenagers in the popular animated TV show *Scooby-Doo*, it suggests the generic self-awareness also central to *The Cabin in the Woods*, which combines unimaginable ancient creatures out of H.P. Lovecraft with the trappings of science fiction.

   The film begins with two technicians, Gary Sitterson (Jenkins) and Steve Hadley (Whitford), getting ready for work in an unexplained technological facility, evidently part of a larger global operation. This narrative alternates with scenes of five college students – Dana (Connolly), Jules (Hutchison), Marty (Kranz), Holden (Williams), and Curt (Hemsworth, who plays Thor in *The Avengers*) – meeting up and then driving to an isolated cabin in the woods for a vacation. Soon a connection between these narratives is established, as we see the technicians observing the young people with hidden cameras and shaping the unfolding events in the cabin through a variety of technological controls in the environment, including the release into the air of mood-altering drugs. The students stumble onto a hidden basement and proceed to explore the artefacts there, while the technicians, frequently joking with each other in the typical manner of workers on the job, place bets on which artefact, and hence which kind of horror monster, the students will unwittingly unleash – which turns out to be a family of redneck zombies that proceeds to attack the students.

   When it seems as if all the teenagers have been killed in due course, the technicians celebrate their successful completion of the 'ritual', but Marty and Dana, still alive, find their way into the facility, which also contains all of the monsters on the definitive list of the betting pool and which, to escape, they release. The monsters massacre all the technicians, while in a lower level of the installation Dana and Marty meet the 'Director' (Sigourney Weaver), who explains that the ritual is conducted to appease the 'Ancient Ones', beings who slumber underground but who would awake and destroy the world without the annual ritual sacrifice of five archetypal youths: the Whore, the Athlete, the Scholar, the Fool and the Virgin – in this specific instance, Jules, Curt, Holden, Marty and Dana, respectively. All are required to die – except for the remaining

DIRECTOR Drew Goddard
PRODUCER Joss Whedon
SCREENPLAY Drew Goddard, Joss Whedon
DIRECTOR OF PHOTOGRAPHY Peter Deming
MUSIC David Julyan
EDITOR Lisa Lassek
MAIN CAST Kristen Connolly, Chris Hemsworth, Anna Hutchison, Fran Kranz, Jesse Williams, Richard Jenkins, Bradley Whitford
PRODUCTION COMPANY Mutant Enemy Productions, Lionsgate

Virgin, whose death is optional. Dana refuses to kill Marty and, as the film ends, one of the Ancient Ones ominously begins to rise.

In the manner of Paul Verhoeven's science fiction films (*Total Recall** [1990], *Starship Troopers** [1997]), *The Cabin in the Woods* provides the expected generic pleasures even as it critiques them. The technicians emphasise that the people and events in the cabin are conventional, and periodically we see them wryly commenting on the action like the trio in *Mystery Science Theatre 3000*. Periodic shots of them watching the same action we are watching serve as distancing mirrors of our own spectatorship. The possible monsters the teenagers might encounter, and the subsequent actions that might unfold, speak to the formulaic nature of slasher films – down to the possible outcomes regarding the good 'final girl' – and to the method by which many of these movies are likely produced. Ultimately, as is more vaguely suggested by *Westworld** (1973), the formal strategies of *The Cabin in the Woods* insist that, even while such horror stories are conventional, we need their mythic repetitiveness to provide us with a comforting sense of order to the world.

A Clockwork Orange
UK/US, 1971 – 136 mins
Stanley Kubrick

The first adaptation of *A Clockwork Orange*, a truncated version for television, was broadcast by the BBC soon after the publication of Anthony Burgess's novel in 1962, and three years later it was the inspiration for Andy Warhol's *Vinyl* (1965); but it is the version by Stanley Kubrick (*2001: A Space Odyssey** [1968]) that has had the greatest cultural impact. Exploring questions of violence, masculinity and morality in a not-too-distant future, *A Clockwork Orange*, along with *Bonnie and Clyde* (1967) and *Straw Dogs* (1971), pushed the limits of graphic violence on screen. In the UK, *A Clockwork Orange* generated considerable controversy and was voluntarily withdrawn from release by Kubrick himself, while in the US it was nominated for an Academy Award for Best Picture, but lost out to the less challenging thriller, William Friedkin's *The French Connection*.

In a decaying London of the future, Alex DeLarge (McDowell) is the leader of one of many youth gangs. 'Your humble narrator', Alex tells his story in Nadsat, a street slang mixing Russian with English (suggesting the influence of the Soviet Union, a world power when the book was published). One night,

DIRECTOR Stanley Kubrick
PRODUCER Stanley Kubrick
SCREENPLAY Stanley Kubrick, based on the 1962 novel by Anthony Burgess
DIRECTOR OF PHOTOGRAPHY John Alcott
EDITOR Bill Butler
MUSIC Walter Carlos, Erika Eigen, Beethoven, Purcell, Rossini
PRODUCTION DESIGN John Barry
MAIN CAST Malcolm McDowell, Patrick Magee, Adrienne Corri, Anthony Sharp, Michael Bates, Carl Duering, Michael Tarn, James Marcus, Warren Clarke
PRODUCTION COMPANY Warner Bros., Hawk Films

after getting high on 'milk plus' at their hangout, the Korova Milkbar, Alex and his 'droogs' Pete (Tarn), Georgie (Marcus) and Dim (Clarke) engage in an evening of 'ultra-violence', culminating in the brutal home invasion of a writer (Magee) and his wife (Corri). The next night Alex is in turn beaten by his discontented gang and left at the scene of the crime after they invade the home of a wealthy woman whom Alex accidentally beats to death. Arrested and imprisoned, Alex is chosen by the Minister of the Interior (Sharp) as a test subject for the Ludovico technique, an experimental aversion conditioning therapy for rehabilitating violent criminals which he hopes will keep his party in power in the next election.

Becoming incapable of violence, Alex is released from prison, and in the second half of the film he encounters all his previous victims – beggar, writer, former droogs and heartbroken parents – and is now victimised by them. Driven to attempt suicide, Alex wakes up in a hospital where the Minister offers him a comfortable job in return for his cooperation and, hearing Beethoven's Ninth Symphony, he fantasises a scenario of sexual violence and realises, as he says, 'I was cured, all right!' The film, which ends here, is relatively faithful to Burgess's novel, but omits the final, more upbeat chapter in which Alex genuinely changes, thus suggesting, more darkly, that the sociopathic Alex now represents state power. Kubrick apparently had based his screenplay on the American edition which, at the insistence of the publisher, omitted the final chapter until 1986.

In Dr. Strangelove or: How I Learned to Stop Worrying and Love the Bomb (1964) the nuclear apocalypse is initiated when General Jack D. Ripper (Sterling Hayden) overcompensates for his sexual impotence by talking loudly and carrying several big sticks: a cigar clamped in the side of his mouth, a machine gun at his hip, and a wing of nuclear bombers, which he unleashes on the Soviet Union to prevent the communists from sapping his 'precious bodily fluids'. The relationship between masculinity, sexuality and violence is a theme of many of Kubrick's other films, but perhaps nowhere more insistently than in A Clockwork Orange: the film is rife with phallic imagery, foregrounding it with an insistence that matches Alex's aggression in scenes such as when Alex attacks the Cat Lady with a sculpture of a giant penis (also a comical comment on the nature of contemporary art).

A social satire (consider, for instance, the décor of the DeLarges' flat and their clothing), much of A Clockwork Orange was shot on location, drawing the social criticism closer to home, as in Godard's Alphaville* (1965). This is especially clear in Kubrick's canny use of music: a combination of classical and electronic music composed by Walter (later, Wendy) Carlos (who also wrote the music for Kubrick's The Shining [1980] and for Tron* [1982]), it is associated with images of violence throughout, just as it is in the Ludovico treatment. Indeed, after the scene where Alex beats the writer and rapes his wife while performing 'Singin' in the Rain' ('viddy well'), it is impossible to watch Gene Kelly's version with the same innocent delight again.

Close Encounters of the Third Kind
US/UK, 1977 – 132 mins
Steven Spielberg

Apart from *Firelight* (1964), his first feature film made when he was 17 years old on a budget of $500, elements of which are reworked here, *Close Encounters of the Third Kind* was Steven Spielberg's first foray into science fiction, a genre to which he would regularly return with such films as *E.T.: The Extra-Terrestrial** (1982), *Jurassic Park** (1993) and its sequel, *The Lost World: Jurassic Park* (1997), *A.I.: Artificial Intelligence* (2001), *Minority Report* (2002) and *War of the Worlds* (2005), as well as many others that he produced but did not direct, including the *Men in Black* and *Back to the Future* films and the television series *Terra Nova* (2011). One of the most commercially successful science fiction movies ever made, *Close Encounters*, along with *Star Wars** (1977) and *Superman** (1978), paved the way for the resurgence of science fiction in Hollywood. The film's benevolent vision sets it apart from the many paranoid films about alien invasion that typify the genre and perfectly evokes that 'sense of wonder' many critics have identified as the essential quality of science fiction. In *Close Encounters* (the film's title refers to ufologist J. Allen Hynek's categories of close encounters with aliens, the third kind denoting observations of actual aliens), people watch the skies not out of fearful vigilance, as in, for example, *The Thing from Another World** (1951), but in beatific awe.

The plot focuses on Roy Neary (Dreyfuss), a line worker in Indiana, who is touched by a light beam from an alien spacecraft. The beam generates in him an obsession with a shape he later discovers to be Devil's Tower in Wyoming, the aliens' appointed landing place. The ensuing story follows Neary's efforts to discover the meaning of his vision at the cost of his family, and his attempt, along with Jillian Guiler (Dillon), the mother of a boy who has been abducted by the aliens, to penetrate government security and ascend the mountain to the landing site. When the two of them, along with several other people who have been 'imprinted' with the image of Devil's Tower, arrive there, they discover that the US military, along with French UFO investigator Claude Lacombe (Truffaut), based on real-life UFO researcher Jacques Vallée, have prepared for first contact by communicating through a sequence of five musical notes (incorporated into the score by composer and longtime Spielberg collaborator John Williams) and accompanying coloured lights.

Neary is hastily included in the group of possible space passengers assembled by the government, and the aliens select him. Haloed in light as they emerge from the mother ship, the aliens seem childlike and angelic. The excellent special photographic effects, particularly noteworthy in the climactic meeting with the alien mother ship on top of Devil's Tower, were supervised by Douglas Trumbull, who had worked in a similar capacity on *2001: A Space Odyssey** (1968), and *Silent Running** (1972), which he also directed, and later *Star Trek: The Motion Picture** (1979) and *Blade Runner** (1982). In the end, Neary enters the ship as one of the aliens pauses momentarily with the humans before the hatch is closed and the ship takes off.

The film is structured around a thematic opposition between expansive imagination, on the one hand, and narrow practicality on the other. Neary works for the local power company, but after his encounter,

DIRECTOR Steven Spielberg
PRODUCER Julia Phillips, Michael Phillips
SCREENPLAY Steven Spielberg
DIRECTOR OF PHOTOGRAPHY Vilmos Zsigmond
EDITOR Michael Kahn
MUSIC John Williams
PRODUCTION DESIGN Joe Alves
MAIN CAST Richard Dreyfuss, François Truffaut, Teri Garr, Bob Balaban, Melinda Dillon, Cary Guffey, J. Patrick McNamara, Warren Kemmerling, Roberts Blossom
PRODUCTION COMPANY Columbia Pictures, EMI Films

which shakes his company truck as if it was merely one of the multitude of toys that fills the film, he must acknowledge the existence of greater powers in the universe. His departure aboard the mother ship for unknown adventures, even though it means the shattering of the nuclear family – so important in Spielberg's cinema – is the film's final eloquent embrace of the possible. Spielberg re-edited the film in 1980 as *Close Encounters of the Third Kind: The Special Edition*, which contained some changes including showing the inside of the mother ship, a scene then deleted in Spielberg's third cut of the film for the home video 'Collector's Edition' released in 1998.

Colossus: The Forbin Project
US, 1970 – 100 mins
Joseph Sargent

An intelligent science fiction film about a rogue computer, *Colossus: The Forbin Project* was undeservedly buried in the wake of the enormous success of Stanley Kubrick's *2001: A Space Odyssey** two years before. Based upon the 1966 novel *Colossus*, the first of a trilogy by British science fiction writer D(ennis) F(eltham) Jones that also includes *The Fall of Colossus* (1974) and *Colossus and the Crab* (1977), the story involves a new American defence computer named Colossus that becomes sentient, links up with its Soviet counterpart, and decides to assume control of the world in order to fulfill its programmed goals of preventing war.

Dr. Charles Forbin (Braeden) is the chief designer of Colossus, which is built into the side of a mountain to make it impervious to attack. As soon as the machine goes online, it detects a similar system, Guardian, built by the Soviet Union, that also has just been activated, and both systems demand to be able to communicate with the other. The two computers, controlling their respective country's nuclear missiles, threaten nuclear attack unless their demands are met. Once connected, the two computers start to exchange information, beginning with simple mathematical equations but soon growing exponentially more complex to the point of surpassing the knowledge of their human creators. When the two governments decide to terminate the computer link, each machine responds by launching missiles at targets in the other country. The communications link is begrudgingly restored by the governments, and (because it is an American film, presumably) Colossus intercepts and destroys the Soviet missile heading for Texas, although the American weapon detonates, destroying a populated area of the USSR.

The Colossus/Guardian entity, now in control, orders the installation of surveillance cameras and a voice synthesiser to replace its printed readouts. Earlier, the absence of a voice made the machine seem more menacing, and any inclination towards humanising Colossus once it is able to speak is thwarted by the computer's deliberate choice to sound mechanical, unlike the calm voice of HAL in *2001*. Colossus imprisons its creator in his apartment, needing him to implement its plans to design another computer that will supersede itself, while both governments seek to defuse their missiles without the computer knowing. But the computers detect the ruse and detonate two missiles in their silos. (In the novel, Colossus nukes Los Angeles, but the home of Hollywood is spared in the film.) As the film ends, Colossus goes public, globally telecasting a message from the ominously named 'World Control' that the human race has a choice between a new millennium of world peace under its reign, or mass destruction.

Joseph Sargent, whose other credits include several episodes of the science fiction television series *The Man from U.N.C.L.E.* (1964–6) and *The Invaders* (1967) and one, 'The Corbomite Maneuver', for *Star Trek* in 1966, directs *Colossus* with a functional detachment similar to that of his thriller *The Taking of Pelham One Two Three* (1974). The film's chillingly deadpan style eerily matches the cold logic of the computer and is

DIRECTOR Joseph Sargent
PRODUCER Stanley Chase
SCREENPLAY James Bridges, based on the 1966 novel *Colossus* by D.F. Jones
DIRECTOR OF PHOTOGRAPHY Gene Polito
EDITOR Folmar Blangsted
MUSIC Michel Colombier
ART DIRECTOR Alexander Golitzen, John J. Lloyd
MAIN CAST Eric Braeden, Susan Clark, Gordon Pinsent, William Schallert, Leonid Rostoff, Robert Corthwaite
PRODUCTION COMPANY Universal Pictures

crucial to its considerable suspense. As well, Eric Braeden, familiar to North American viewers since 1980 as ruthless tycoon and romantic lead Victor Newman on the long-running American daytime soap opera *The Young and the Restless*, is appropriately stiff and expressionless as Forbin, the genius who creates Colossus but who fails to account for the consequences of his science. Upon realising the extent of what his work has wrought, Forbin makes the film's cautionary moral explicit in his assertion that '*Frankenstein* should be required reading for every scientist'. However, the target of the film's alarmist extrapolation is not just a response to the dawning technology of computing, but also to the Cold War mentality that fuelled talk of 'missile gaps' and the 'space race.' The joined Colossus/Guardian entity is the result of an out-of-control arms race, and the effort to sabotage it is made more difficult as the two superpowers must learn to work together despite their mutual distrust.

The Damned (These Are the Damned)
UK, 1963 – 87 mins
Joseph Losey

Director Joseph Losey made several film noirs in Hollywood before moving to the UK in the early 1950s in order to avoid testifying before the House Un-American Activities Committee investigating Communist infiltration in the film industry. He then made a number of British thrillers before emerging as an arthouse auteur beginning with *The Servant* (1963), one of three superb collaborations with writer Harold Pinter. On the cusp of this transition, just before *The Servant*, Losey directed *The Damned* for Hammer, the British studio that was successfully defining its niche with horror and science fiction. *The Damned* shows Losey's ability to infuse science fiction with considerably more depth and subtlety than his one other foray into the fantastic, *The Boy with Green Hair* (1948), his first feature, an explicitly moral parable about tolerance.

Quite different from the novel on which it is based, *The Damned* begins as a wild youth film ('Black leather, black leather/rock, rock rock', blares the soundtrack at the beginning) but then veers unexpectedly into the realm of science fiction. Divorced American insurance executive Simon Wells (Carey), on a boating holiday in England, meets a young woman, Joan (Field), who lures him into a mugging by her brother King (Reed) and his Teddy Boy gang. Subsequently, Joan visits Wells on his boat, and when the gang begins to taunt him he casts off, impulsively taking Joan, who wants to flee from her insanely jealous brother. That night, they come ashore and make love; but the gang follows them, and as the couple flees they stumble into a nearby military base and then down a cliff, King in pursuit, where they discover an elaborate system of bunkers in which nine children are living.

The children, as they soon learn, are radioactive, and the trio of outsiders is being slowly poisoned by contact with them. The scientist Bernard (Knox) explains that the children were born radioactive, taken from their parents, and raised in the isolated bunkers so that they will be able to survive the nuclear holocaust he is certain must inevitably come. The three interlopers help the children escape to the outside world, but they are quickly rounded up by men in radiation suits and returned to the bunkers. Chased by a helicopter, the dying King crashes his car into a river, while Simon and Joan are allowed to return to his boat, followed by another helicopter that will destroy it once the couple has died.

The film shuttles between the teenage gang, the military and the irradiated children upon whom they are experimenting, drawing provocative comparisons between the three groups. The children describe Bernard's men in their protective suits as 'the black death', linking them to the leather-jacketed Teddy Boys, some of whom wear children's hats and march in a parody of a military formation. Each group, in its own way, is alienated and isolated, while apolitical art is doomed ('It's too late to do anything in private life', Bernard tells his friend Freya Neilson [Lindfors], a sculptress who leases land nearby, learns of the experiment, and, after refusing to co-operate, is murdered by him). The casting of the uncharismatic Carey as the nominal hero, whose efforts to save the children ends in failure as well as his own death, is apposite in this grim film,

DIRECTOR Joseph Losey
PRODUCER Anthony Hinds
SCREENPLAY Evan Jones, based on the novel *The Children of Light* (1960) by Henry L. Lawrence
DIRECTOR OF PHOTOGRAPHY Arthur Grant
EDITOR Reginald Mills
MUSIC James Bernard
MAIN CAST Macdonald Carey, Shirley Anne Field, Viveca Lindfors, Alexander Knox, Oliver Reed, Walter Gotell, James Villiers, Tom Kempinski, Kevin Cope
PRODUCTION COMPANY Columbia Pictures, Hammer Films

which ends with a cut from the cliff face to the beaches of Weymouth, where people are happily holidaying, unaware of the muffled voices of the children crying for help nearby.

Although *The Damned* was made in 1961, it was not released in Britain until two years later, perhaps because of the bleakness of its vision. It was shown as the bottom half of a double feature with Michael Carreras's *The Maniac*, and cut from 96 to 87 minutes. In the US it was trimmed a further ten minutes and released as *These Are the Damned* in 1965.

Dark City
US/Australia, 1998 – 100 mins
Alex Proyas

With *The Crow* (1994), *I, Robot* (2004), *Knowing* (2009) and especially *Dark City*, Alex Proyas has gained a reputation as a stylish film maker who, like Terry Gilliam, employs striking visuals treating fantastic themes. Indeed, the eponymous city of Proyas's film has more than a passing resemblance to the dystopian metropolis of Gilliam's *Brazil** (1985); yet *Dark City*'s postmodern panache and tech-noir blending of science fiction and film noir is perfectly appropriate to the film's theme, which involves the peeling away of experience and memory, and even individual identity, revealing it as false and constructed.

The story begins in solid hard-boiled fashion as John Murdoch (Sewell) awakens to find himself in a seedy hotel bath tub, unaware of how he got there, with the mutilated corpse of a woman in the adjoining room. Murdoch manages to learn his name and find his wife, Emma (Connelly), even as he is being chased by a group of odd-looking men called The Strangers and by police inspector Frank Bumstead (Hurt) for a series of murders about which Murdoch has no memory. Eventually it is revealed that the Strangers are a dying race of alien energy beings who are using human corpses as their hosts. Because they possess only a collective consciousness, the Strangers have created the city based on the memories and thoughts of their human subjects as part of an experiment to analyse individual consciousness, hoping to learn something to help their race survive. Each night at midnight, all the humans fall into temporary unconsciousness while the Strangers come together to do their 'tuning', or rearranging with variations the physical details of the city, while Dr. Daniel Schreber (Sutherland) assists them, mixing and matching memories and personalities in liquid form and injecting them into the brains of unsuspecting people. In one astonishing scene, a slovenly working-class couple is transformed into wealthy socialites as their humble kitchen morphs through convincing CGI effects into a palatial dining room.

Murdoch finds the mysterious Dr. Schreber, who explains that Murdoch accidentally awoke during one such tuning, before Schreber could complete the process of giving him a murderer's identity, and that Murdoch somehow possesses the same telekinetic powers as the Strangers. When Murdoch tries to return to the coastal town of Shell Beach, where he remembers growing up, he finds that no one seems to know how to leave the city to get there. Finally, Schreber guides him and Bumstead to Shell Beach, which turns out to be merely a billboard at the edge of the city. In frustration, Murdoch tears a gaping hole in the hoarding to reveal the black depths of outer space beyond it, and as Bumstead is sucked out an exterior shot reveals that the city is, in fact, an enormous artificial environment, like a Petri dish or one of the biodomes in *Silent Running** (1972), floating in space. With Schreber's help, Murdoch discovers the full potential of his mental powers and defeats the Strangers in a titanic battle of mental wills that recalls the climactic confrontation in David Cronenberg's *Scanners* (1981). Like a god, Murdoch then creates real mountains, beaches, water and sunlight and, entering into this new world of his own making, he meets the

DIRECTOR Alex Proyas
PRODUCER Alex Proyas, Andrew Mason
SCREENPLAY Alex Proyas, Lem Dobbs, David S. Goyer
DIRECTOR OF PHOTOGRAPHY Dariusz Wolski
EDITOR Dov Hoenig
MUSIC Trevor Jones
PRODUCTION DESIGN George Little, Patrick Tatopoulos
MAIN CAST Rufus Sewell, Kiefer Sutherland, Jennifer Connelly, William Hurt, Richard O'Brien, Ian Richardson, Bruce Spence
PRODUCTION COMPANY Mystery Clock Cinema, New Line Cinema

woman who had once been his wife, but now with new memories has another name.

With its outlandish science fiction premise, *Dark City* is a Kafkaesque version of Plato's Allegory of the Cave and a Philip K. Dick-like parable of postmodern paranoia. Part of a cycle of millennial science fiction that included *The Truman Show* (1998), *eXistenZ* (1999), *The Thirteenth Floor* (1999) and *The Matrix** (1999), which was filmed on some of the same sets, *Dark City* suggests that the world around us may be entirely inauthentic, an illusion. The film's city is a simulacrum – actually, a simulacrum of a simulacrum, a film set of a film set, constructed from a hodge-podge of visual memories by the city's inhabitants that may themselves not have been genuine but instead are derived from films watched and half-remembered from untold years ago when they once were living on Earth.

Dark Star
US, 1974 – 83 mins
John Carpenter

An auspicious feature film debut by John Carpenter, who would go on to become the most important director of science fiction action in the 1980s with *Escape from New York* (1981), *The Thing** (1982), *Prince of Darkness* (1987) and *They Live** (1988), *Dark Star* was co-scripted by his friend and classmate at the University of Southern California, Dan O'Bannon, who also wrote *Alien** (1979) and co-scripted *Lifeforce* (1985), based on Colin Wilson's 1976 novel *The Space Vampires*. A science fiction comedy (it was promoted as 'the spaced out odyssey'), *Dark Star* began as a 68-minute student film and was expanded when producer Jack H. Harris convinced Carpenter and O'Bannon to shoot fifteen minutes of additional footage in order to give the film a theatrical release. (In the 1983 Special Edition home video version, the film-makers eliminated the extra material.) The film is remarkable given its minimal budget of $60,000, and while its special effects tend toward the delightfully unbelievable, it brims with ideas about the genre (as a youth, Carpenter wrote

DIRECTOR John Carpenter
PRODUCER John Carpenter
SCREENPLAY John Carpenter, Dan O'Bannon
DIRECTOR OF PHOTOGRAPHY Douglas Knapp
EDITOR Dan O'Bannon
MUSIC John Carpenter
PRODUCTION DESIGN Dan O'Bannon
MAIN CAST Brian Narelle, Dre Pahich, Dan O'Bannon, Cal Kuniholm
PRODUCTION COMPANY Jack H. Harris Enterprises, University of Southern California

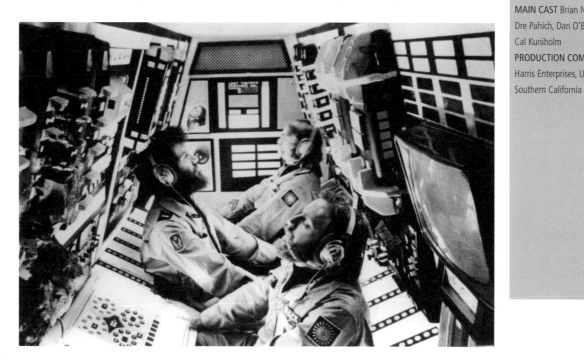

and published several fanzines), not unlike the alien in Carpenter's *Starman* (1984) who indiscriminately absorbs the cultural artefacts sent into space by NASA's Voyager probe. Conceived partly as an alternative to the sterile and functional world of Stanley Kubrick's influential *2001: A Space Odyssey** (1968), *Dark Star* offers a blackly comic vision of men in space overcome with ennui rather than wonder at the vastness of the void.

In the near future, the Dark Star scout ship was commissioned to explore distant star systems and to destroy unstable planets in advance of potential colonisation. The ship is twenty years into the mission, and systems have begun to malfunction – one of them, a faulty seat panel, already having caused the death of the ship's captain, Commander Powell, who remains on board in cryogenic suspension. The crew members look for ways to relieve their boredom, like playing tired practical jokes on each other or using the ship's laser rifle for unauthorised target practice. Pinback (O'Bannon) has brought onboard an alien they found, made of an inflated beach ball with claws attached (and operated by Nick Castle, who would play Michael Myers in Carpenter's biggest commercial success, the 1978 slasher *Halloween*), as an amusing 'mascot'. When it refuses to stay in the food locker, Pinback is forced to chase it around the ship, providing a pretext for an amusing sequence worthy of Harold Lloyd or Buster Keaton in which his plight goes from bad to worse in the ship's elevator shaft.

Even blowing up planets has come to seem tedious, and the men go about their work in detached fashion, not realising the implications when one of the ship's laser-guided systems is damaged while moving through a magnetic asteroid field. The ship's nuclear bombs are fitted with computers, giving them consciousness, and when Bomb no. 20, at Pinback's orders, arms itself in preparation for destroying their next target but is unable to separate from the ship as a result of the asteroid damage, it refuses to disarm and return to the bomb bay because of two earlier mistaken commands. This idea, perhaps borrowed from the 1956 British film *Satellite in the Sky*, is handled with a deft comic touch by Carpenter and O'Bannon. To convince the bomb to disarm before it detonates, Doolittle (Narelle) leaves the ship to speak with the bomb directly, engaging it in philosophical debate in which he introduces the bomb to the concept of Cartesian duality and doubt. Temporarily unsure of how to proceed, the bomb withdraws – but only to seek the solace of religion in the face of this epistemological dilemma and then explode in a Godlike frenzy shortly thereafter. In a dénouement clearly borrowed from Ray Bradbury's short story 'Kaleidoscope' in his 1951 collection *The Illustrated Man*, Doolittle and Talby (Pahich), the two crew members who survive the blast, drift apart but briefly maintain radio contact, the former latching onto debris from the ship and surfing into the atmosphere of a nearby planet, the latter merging with an asteroid group that will take his body on a marvellous journey across the universe.

The Day the Earth Stood Still
US, 1951 – 92 mins
Robert Wise

Along with Jack Arnold's *It Came from Outer Space* (1953), *The Day the Earth Stood Still* is one of the few science fiction films of the 1950s to depict extraterrestrials as something besides invading Others. The film softens the twist ending of its source story by Harry Bates, the founding editor of *Astounding Science Fiction*, wherein it is revealed that the robot Gnut is in fact the master, not Klaatu. Recast in a contemporary Cold War context, it nevertheless raises similar questions about the responsible uses of technology and the human penchant for aggression and violence. (The 2008 reboot, directed by Scott Derrickson, updates the theme yet again for a more eco-conscious generation: this time Klaatu, played by Keanu Reeves, comes to Earth to save the planet by exterminating humanity and all its works with an upgraded nano-teched Gort. As he explains, Earth is one of the few planets in the universe with an environment capable of supporting intelligent life, but people are destroying it.)

As *The Day the Earth Stood Still* begins, a flying saucer (designed in consultation with renowned architect Frank Lloyd Wright) lands in Washington, where it is promptly surrounded by the military and curious civilians. A humanoid alien, Klaatu (Rennie), emerges, declaring that he has come in peace, but he is promptly wounded by a nervous soldier, after which a large robot named Gort (played by seven-foot tall Lock Martin) appears from within the ship and, without harming anyone, disintegrates all the weaponry in sight. Klaatu wants to deliver an important message to all the world's leaders simultaneously, but as the President's secretary explains to him, in the current political climate of mistrust this would be impossible. Klaatu escapes the military hospital, the story taking on Biblical overtones as he adopts the name of Carpenter (the occupation of Jesus's father, Joseph) and dwells among the people by taking a room at a local boarding house. Among the boarders are Helen Benson (Neal), a war widow, and her son Bobby (Gray), with whom Klaatu spends an enlightening day that includes a visit to Professor Jacob Barnhardt, America's greatest scientist, portrayed by Sam Jaffe as the perfect embodiment of science fiction's 'sense of wonder' ('I have so many questions to ask you').

The Professor suggests a demonstration of Klaatu's powers to make the world take heed, so the alien stops all electrical power around the planet for half an hour, except where safety would be compromised in places such as hospitals and planes. Klaatu reveals his identity and purpose to Helen, telling her that if anything should happen to him she must go to Gort and tell him – in the words of science fiction film's most famous mantra – 'Klaatu barada nikto.' Helen's boyfriend Tom Stephens (Marlowe) becomes Klaatu's Judas, betraying him to the authorities and, when Klaatu is killed by the army, Gort activates, retrieves his corpse, and resurrects him in the ship. Klaatu appears one last time and addresses the scientists whom Barnhardt has gathered, telling them that humanity is becoming a threat to other races in the universe, that these races have created an army of unstoppable robot enforcers (including Gort) to eliminate aggression, and warning

DIRECTOR Robert Wise
PRODUCER Julian Blaustein
SCREENPLAY Edmund H. North, based on the story 'Farewell to the Master' (1940) by Harry Bates
DIRECTOR OF PHOTOGRAPHY Leo Tover
EDITOR William Reynolds
MUSIC Bernard Herrmann
ART DIRECTOR Addison Hehr, Lyle Wheeler
MAIN CAST Michael Rennie, Patricia Neal, Sam Jaffe, Hugh Marlowe, Billy Gray, Frances Bavier, Lock Martin
PRODUCTION COMPANY 20th Century Fox

that unless the people of Earth cease their violence the robots will destroy them. 'The decision rests with you', he concludes, after which he enters the ship and departs as quickly as he had come.

Director Robert Wise, a Hollywood stalwart whose credits include *The Andromeda Strain* (1971) and *Star Trek: The Motion Picture**(1979), worked early in his career as an editor – among his first assignments was Orson Welles's *Citizen Kane* (1941) – and it shows especially in *The Day the Earth Stood Still*'s two fine montages:

the opening, as the military tracks the spacecraft speeding toward Earth and people learn of its imminent arrival, and the world when Klaatu brings it to a halt. The film's overall compelling effect is enhanced by the unorthodox score of composer Bernard Herrmann (*Fahrenheit 451** [1966]), which includes electric strings, Theremins, organs and a variety of percussion instruments, and also featured audio overdubbing and other recording techniques.

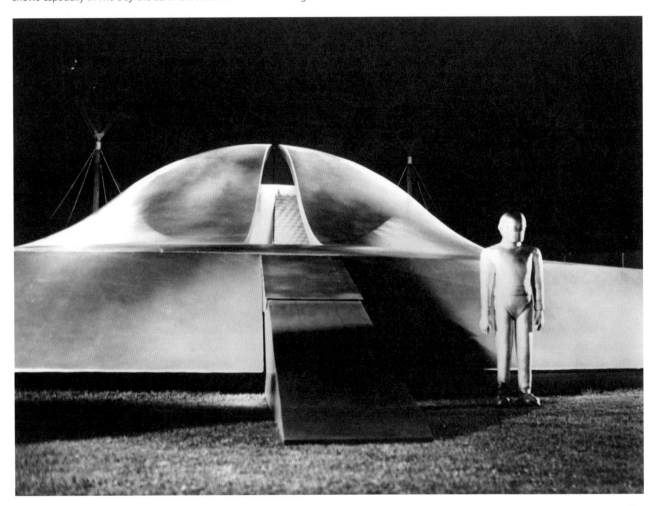

Destination Moon
US, 1950 – 92 mins
Irving Pichel

Destination Moon, the film that launched the decade's spate of science fiction films, is notable for being the first Hollywood science fiction film to depict space flight in a realistic manner. Although production (which was highly publicised in the media) began before the considerably less credible *Rocketship X-M* (1950), the latter was released a month earlier. *Destination Moon*'s aim for realism is enhanced by the beautiful matte and backdrop paintings by Chesley Bonestell, the most famous astronomical artist of the era. Bonestell also worked on the later George Pal productions *When Worlds Collide** (1951), *The War of the Worlds** (1953) and *Conquest of Space* (1955), which in turn was based on the 1949 book of the same name by Bonestell and rocket expert Willy Ley (who had also worked on Fritz Lang's *Frau im Mond** [1929]).

In *Destination Moon*, four Americans – a scientist, an industrialist, a general and a technician – take off from the New Mexico desert in a newly designed nuclear-powered spaceship for the first trip to the moon. On the flight out, they engage in a space walk to repair equipment, and when one of the men begins to float away, another, powered by the open valve of an oxygen bottle, leaves the ship to rescue him. A problematic landing results in a race against time to strip the ship so it will be light enough upon departure to reach escape velocity with the fuel they have left. The film reflects the Cold War mentality of the day, as the impetus for private industry and American know-how trumps the profit margin, and entrepreneurs co-operate to build the rocket because the Soviet Union might colonise space first (although no specific rival nation is actually mentioned). The Americans land on the lunar surface, winning the 'space race' the film correctly predicted was to come, with the moon claimed 'by the grace of God' and 'for the benefit of mankind' in the name of the United States. Over the top of the film's final image – the colourful Earth drawing closer to the camera – comes the words 'This is The End' – a moment after which is added 'of the beginning'.

The film includes an animated film-within-the-film by Walter Lantz, prepared for the first meeting of the American business leaders, with Woody Woodpecker illustrating the basic concepts of space flight. The sequence educates both the characters in the film and its audience as well. Joe Sweeney (Wesson), an average 'Joe the Plumber' added to the crew as a last-minute replacement for the ailing head technician, functions as the surrogate for the spectator, who is assumed to be woefully ignorant of physics and rocket science. Major science fiction writer Robert A. Heinlein, who had training as an engineer, co-wrote the screenplay and served as technical advisor. Heinlein had already published the first in his series of 'juvenile' science fiction novels, *Rocketship Galileo* (1947), some ideas from which were worked into *Destination Moon*. Others came from his novella *The Man Who Sold the Moon*, which was written by 1949 but not published until 1951, the year after *Destination Moon* was released.

After the film was made, Heinlein published a novella of the same title, based on the screenplay, and an essay, 'Shooting *Destination Moon*,' which appeared in *Astounding Science Fiction* in July 1950. In the

DIRECTOR Irving Pichel
PRODUCER George Pal
SCREENPLAY Alford Van Ronkel, Robert A. Heinlein, James O'Hanlon
DIRECTOR OF PHOTOGRAPHY Lionel Lindon
EDITOR Duke Goldstone
MUSIC Leith Stevens
PRODUCTION DESIGN Ernest Fegté
MAIN CAST John Archer, Warner Anderson, Tom Powers, Dick Wesson, Erin O'Brien-Moore
PRODUCTION COMPANY George Pal Productions

essay, after complaining about the problems (mostly financial) of producing feature films, Heinlein goes on to discuss in detail the creation of the film's special effects, which were duly acknowledged with an Academy Award for Lee Zavitz, the movie's visual effects director. The film was directed by Irving Pichel, whom Heinlein praises for his insistence on taking the genre of science fiction seriously. Pichel (most remembered, perhaps, for his role as the servant Sandor in Universal's *Dracula's Daughter* [1936]), acted in dozens of Hollywood movies and directed many more, including the first film versions of H. Rider Haggard's *She* (1935) and *The Most Dangerous Game* (1932, co-directed by Ernest B. Schoedsack, who in turn the following year co-directed *King Kong* [1933] with Merian C. Cooper). Pichel was nominated for Best Director, but lost out to Joseph L. Mankiewicz for *All About Eve*.

District 9
US/New Zealand/Canada/South Africa, 2009 – 112 mins
Neill Blomkamp

The first feature film by director Neill Blomkamp, who grew up in Johannesburg, South Africa, *District 9* was inspired by events that transpired in Cape Town during the apartheid era, including the designation in 1966 of District Six, a residential part of the city, as a 'whites only' area and the resultant forced relocation of thousands of people. Adapted from Blomkamp's short film *Alive in Joburg* (2006), *District 9* finds an effective balance between addressing serious social concerns and the kinetic clout of action. Like such other science fiction films as *Enemy Mine** (1985) and *Alien Nation* (1988), the latter of which also plays on the double meaning of the word 'alien', it examines issues of racism and segregation through a 'going native' scenario, the nightmarish flip side to the dreamy treatment of a similar premise in *Avatar** (2009). *District 9* was a surprise box-office hit, and one of the few science fiction films to be nominated for an Academy Award for Best Picture.

According to the film's premise, in 1982 a massive alien spacecraft entered Earth's atmosphere and came to rest in the sky above Johannesburg. When, after several months, there was no indication of activity within the ship, a team of military investigators entered it and discovered many sick and starving extraterrestrials inside. After an initially enthusiastic welcome by humanity, tensions between the local residents and the aliens begin to develop, and the aliens, derogatorily referred to as 'prawns' because of their physical resemblance to terrestrial crustacea, were confined to District 9, a government camp established just outside the city. As the story begins now, in 2010, a private military company, Multi-National United (MNU), has been hired by the South African government to relocate the extraterrestrial population elsewhere.

The relocation operation is headed by Afrikaner Wikus van de Merwe (Copley), who moves house to house evicting the aliens with a paramilitary escort. In one shack, Wikus is accidentally exposed to a strange fluid that has been slowly collected over years by the alien Christopher (Cope), who is secretly planning to use it as fuel to power their ship for the return flight home. The fluid affects Wikus's genetic makeup, and he begins to mutate into a 'prawn'. MNU restrains Wikus against his will, testing his ability to use a variety of alien weapons that will only function with matching alien DNA, and planning to vivisect him to harvest his spliced genetic makeup for military experiments. Managing to escape, Wikus, who is horrified to discover that MNU (a swipe, perhaps, at the US's outsourcing to companies such as Halliburton) has been conducting grisly experiments on the aliens, joins up with Christopher, from whom he learns that with the fuel Christopher can return in three years and reverse Wikus's mutation, to retrieve the canister of fluid from MNU headquarters.

As *District 9* builds towards its dramatic climax, it drops the racial metaphor for action-film thrills, with plenty of graphic CGI effects as both humans and aliens are blown to bits in the ensuing fights between Christopher and Wikus, MNU, the aliens and the gang of Nigerian gunrunners who have been supplying

DIRECTOR Neill Blomkamp
PRODUCER Peter Jackson
SCREENPLAY Neill Blomkamp, Terri Tatchell
DIRECTOR OF PHOTOGRAPHY Trent Opaloch
EDITOR Julian Clarke
MUSIC Clinton Shorter
PRODUCTION DESIGN Philip Ivey
MAIN CAST Sharlto Copley, Jason Cope, Nathalie Boltt, Sylvaine Strike, Elizabeth Mkandawie
PRODUCTION COMPANY TriStar Pictures, Block/Hanson, Wingnut Films

weapons to them before Christopher succeeds in taking off in the ship. Similarly, although the film begins like a documentary, combining fictional television news broadcasts, interviews and archival and surveillance footage to provide background exposition and begin the story, this style fades away as the film grows more interested in the battle scenes. Nevertheless, *District 9* is effective in eliciting the spectator's sympathy for the aliens, impressively designed by Peter Jackson's WETA Workshop, and also for the initially racist Wikus who, ironically, becomes more sympathetic as he grows less human. In the film's final shot, a now completely transformed Wikus scavenges in the refuse heaps of the alien slum zone, where he must dwell for at least three years, if Christopher keeps his promise and returns.

Dune
US, 1984 – 137 mins
David Lynch

Frank Herbert's *Dune* is an acknowledged landmark of science fiction literature and perhaps the best-selling science fiction novel of all time. Herbert wrote five sequels – *Dune Messiah* (1970), *Children of Dune* (1976), *God Emperor of Dune* (1981), *Heretics of Dune* (1984) and *Chapterhouse: Dune* (1985) – and after his death in 1986 a series of other novels set in the Dune universe ('Duniverse') have been written by Kevin J. Anderson and Herbert's son, Brian. The books have inspired computer games and board games, as well as a Sci-Fi Channel miniseries, *Frank Herbert's Dune*, in 2000, and a sequel miniseries in 2003, *Frank Herbert's Children of Dune*, which combines the events of the second two books. Its influence has been so significant that the names of planets from the *Dune* novels have been given to geographical features on Titan, the largest of Saturn's moons.

With a sprawling narrative set far in the future, when a rare spice, found only on the plant Arrakis, is prized because of its ability to expand human consciousness, it was an understandable choice for David Lynch, the director of the idiosyncratic psychodrama *Eraserhead* (1976), who agreed to write the screenplay and direct the film (turning down the offer to make *Return of the Jedi* as a result). But the film, while visually stunning and featuring an impressive international cast, nonetheless suggests that Lynch, who has expressed little interest in outer space, is better at exploring inner space in such films as *Blue Velvet* (1986); *Mulholland Drive* (2001); and his television miniseries, *Twin Peaks* (1990–91).

In the far future, the most important substance in the universe is the spice, which extends life, expands consciousness, and, most significantly, allows for instantaneous interstellar travel through the ability to fold space. The spice is found only on the desert planet of Arrakis, also known as Dune. The Space Guild, which maintains a monopoly over space travel, sets in motion a battle between two rival houses, House Atreides and House Harkonnen, for administrative control of Arrakis, with the aim of killing the son of Duke Leto Atreides (Prochnow), Paul (MacLachlan), who it senses may become the Kwisatz Haderach, a messiah figure who will lead the native Fremen of Arrakis and thus threaten the flow of the spice. When the Harkonnens, with the aid of the Padishah Emperor Shaddam Corrino IV (Ferrer), attack and overrun the Atreides on Arrakis, Paul escapes deep into the desert, where he lives among the Fremen, learns to control the giant, deadly sandworms that roam under Dune's surface, and becomes Muad'Dib, eventually leading the Fremen to victory over the Emperor and the vile Baron Harkonnen (McMillan) and autonomous control of Arrakis – the very thing the Guild initially had sought to prevent. In the end, after Paul kills the sadistic Feyd Rautha (Sting) in single combat, rain falls on the barren planet and Paul is acknowledged as the Kwisatz Haderach.

Two earlier attempts to bring Herbert's novel to the screen failed – the second involving another visionary film maker, Alejandro Jodorowsky (*El Topo* [1970], *The Holy Mountain* [1973]) – and Lynch's film was delayed by numerous script rewrites and creative differences between Lynch and producer Dino De

DIRECTOR David Lynch
PRODUCER Raffaella De Laurentiis
SCREENPLAY David Lynch, based on the 1965 novel by Frank Herbert
DIRECTOR OF PHOTOGRAPHY Freddie Francis
EDITOR Anthony Gibbs
MUSIC Toto
PRODUCTION DESIGN Anthony Masters
MAIN CAST Francesca Annis, Leonardo Cimino, Brad Dourif, José Ferrer, Linda Hunt, Freddie Jones, Richard Jordan, Kyle MacLachlan, Virginia Madsen, Silvana Mangano, Everett McGill, Kenneth McMillan, Jack Nance, Siân Phillips, Jurgen Prochnow
PRODUCTION COMPANY DeLaurentiis

Laurentiis, the latter requiring the director's three-hour rough cut to be trimmed by almost a third. To reduce the film's length, scenes were cut and condensed and cumbersome voice-over narrations added. While the resultant narrative may be confusing, Lynch's concerns come through clearly in the film's production design, its retro-future style, anitcipating steampunk, commenting on the regressive nature of this future society. The film was not well received by critics and performed poorly at the American box office, and the director himself was unhappy with it, refusing all offers to do an extended director's cut, although extended versions have been pieced together from material omitted for the theatrical release.

Enemy Mine
US, 1985 – 108 mins
Wolfgang Petersen

Based on the Hugo and Nebula Award-winning novella by Barry B. Longyear (and later expanded into a trilogy with the title *The Enemy Papers* in 2005), *Enemy Mine* depicts an encounter between a human and an alien soldier, enemies who are marooned together and who, in order to survive, must learn to co-operate and see beyond their racial enmity. The film's premise recalls the war movies *None but the Brave* (1965), the only film directed by Frank Sinatra, and John Boorman's *Hell in the Pacific* (1968), both involving American and Japanese soldiers stranded on islands in the Pacific – the latter, like *Enemy Mine*, with only two characters (played by Lee Marvin and Toshiro Mifune). *Enemy Mine*'s budget ballooned as a result of production problems, making it unlikely that it was going to be anything but a financial disappointment at the box office. Nevertheless, it features excellent performances by both Quaid as the human and Gossett as the reptilian Drac, and it wisely focuses on the emotional dynamics of the relationship between the two soldiers – until the climax, when it concedes to an unnecessarily extended action sequence which is largely formulaic.

In the late twenty-first century, there is a war waging between humans and Dracs. In a dogfight, human pilot Willis Davidge (Quaid) and Drac pilot Jeriba Shigan (Gossett) both crash on Fyrine IV, a desolate planet with a hostile environment. Initially the two are distrustful, but as events unfold they become mutually dependent, at different points even saving each other's life. With obvious but nonetheless effective symbolism, they work together to construct a shelter for protection against periodic meteorite showers. Over a period of several years, they become friends and learn each other's language and culture.

One day Davidge comes upon signs that the planet has been visited by Scavengers, human miners who use Dracs as slave labour. When he returns to warn 'Jerry', he discovers that the Drac is pregnant (the species reproduces asexually). Sadly, Jeriba dies in childbirth, Davidge swearing to him that if possible he will take the child, Zammis (Robinson), back to his home world of Dracon and 'sing' his complete ancestry so he can join Drac society. Davidge raises Zammis as his own, but one day the Scavengers return to the planet and capture the youth. Left for dead, Davidge is found by his comrades, recuperates from his wounds, and promptly steals a spaceship to rescue Zammis. Finding the Scavengers' ship, he speaks to the Dracs in their own language and convinces them to help him overcome their oppressors and free Zammis. In the final scene, they return to Dracon and Davidge fulfils his vow by singing Zammis's ancestral line. A narrator explains that when, years later, Zammis had his own child, Davidge's name was added to the line of Jeriba.

The plot, which remains fairly close to Goodyear's story, recalls the sympathetic Indian cycle of Westerns in the 1950s, such as *Broken Arrow* (1950), which urged racial tolerance. Like *The Brother from Another Planet** (1984), *Enemy Mine* also looks forward to subsequent science fiction films which deal with aliens in terms of race, such as *District 9** (2009) and *Alien Nation* (1988). (Not coincidentally, Longyear wrote two books in the series of *Alien Nation* novelisations.) It also borrows more than a little from Ursula Le Guin's

DIRECTOR Wolfgang Petersen
PRODUCER Stephen Friedman
SCREENPLAY Edward Khmara, based on the 1979 novella by Barry B. Goodyear
DIRECTOR OF PHOTOGRAPHY Tony Imi
EDITOR Hannes Nikel
MUSIC Maurice Jarre
PRODUCTION DESIGN Rolf Zehetbauer
MAIN CAST Dennis Quaid, Louis Gossett, Jr, Brion James, Richard Marcus, Carolyn McCormick, Bumper Robinson
PRODUCTION COMPANY 20th Century Fox, Kings Road Entertainment, SLM Production Group

hugely influential novel *The Left Hand of Darkness* (1969), with its story of a human and a hermaphrodite alien capable of being both male and female, thrown together in an adventure for survival. Director Wolfgang Petersen, brought in as a replacement after production had begun, was a logical choice, given the similar interest in his films *Das Boot* (1981), *The Perfect Storm* (2000) and *Troy* (2004) in the dynamics of male bonding in extraordinary and life-threatening circumstances.

E.T.: The Extra-Terrestrial
US, 1982 – 115 mins
Steven Spielberg

Once the most commercially successful science fiction movie ever, *E.T.* was for years the highest-grossing film of all time, a distinction now held by James Cameron's *Avatar** (2009). It is also, according to director Steven Spielberg, one of his most personal works. Its winsome story of an alien stranded on Earth, befriended and cared for by a boy, became, like George Lucas's earlier *Star Wars** (1977), which it supplanted at the top of the box-office rankings, a cultural event, complete with an accompanying (though considerably less successful) merchandising campaign. As with Spielberg's earlier *Close Encounters of the Third Kind** (1977), the movie's benevolent extraterrestrial is the opposite of the conventional threatening aliens typical of the genre. In *E.T.* the classic premise of the alien encounter is transformed into an unabashedly sentimental family fantasy that vividly demonstrates Spielberg's knack for eliciting and manipulating audience response. This essentially simple tale of 'boy meets creature, boy loses creature, creature saves boy, boy saves creature', as he has described it, has moved millions to watch it through moist eyes.

DIRECTOR Steven Spielberg
PRODUCER Steven Spielberg, Kathleen Kennedy
SCREENPLAY Melissa Mathison
DIRECTOR OF PHOTOGRAPHY Allen Daviau
EDITOR Carol Littleton
MUSIC John Williams
PRODUCTION DESIGN James D. Bissell
MAIN CAST Henry Thomas, Dee Wallace, Robert MacNaughton, Drew Barrymore, Peter Coyote, K.C. Martel, Sean Frye, C. Thomas Howell, David M. O'Dell, Frank Toth
PRODUCTION COMPANY Universal Pictures, Amblin Entertainment

In the tool shed of his suburban home, 10-year-old Elliott (Thomas) finds a member of an alien spaceship crew accidentally left behind when they quickly fled from the government agents tracking them as they collected plant samples on Earth. Elliott, his older brother and younger sister decide to keep the alien a secret from their mother. The alien has inexplicable powers, including the ability to revive dead plants with a glowing finger. E.T. learns to speak English and gets the idea to send a signal to his ship ('E.T. phone home', as he explains) from a Buck Rogers comic strip, which he does with a makeshift communications device he constructs from some toys and common household items. The children smuggle E.T. out of the house during Halloween dressed as a ghost, and in a field E.T. signals his ship. Both E.T. and Elliott become gravely ill, and government agents invade and quarantine the house. Both recover, and the kids flee on bicycles from the authorities to the forest, where E.T.'s ship will pick him up, E.T. on Elliott's handlebars. Seemingly surrounded by the authorities, E.T. levitates their bicycles above the agents' cars, allowing them to escape. As he prepares to depart, E.T.'s heart glows and he tells Elliott 'I'll be right here', pointing his glowing digit at the boy's head before entering the ship, which departs.

The alien of *E.T.* represents the faith, optimism and imagination that for Spielberg are the special qualities of childhood, as they were for François Truffaut (*Fahrenheit 451** [1966]), whom Spielberg

appropriately cast as the ufologist Claude Lacombe in *Close Encounters*. With E.T.'s help, the children can soar lyrically through the sky on their bicycles, flying away from the world of adult responsibilities represented by the agent 'Keys' (Coyote), just as a child falling from a high window lands harmlessly on the ground in Truffaut's *L'Argent de poche* (*Small Change*, 1976). The children in *E.T.* are open to the unexpected and unknown, in marked contrast to the images of containment ('Keys') which characterise the adult world, most notably in the government scientists' hermetically sealed plastic tubes. If *Hook* (1991) is about making the ultimately necessary choice of accepting the responsibilities of adulthood over 'never growing up', then *E.T.* is a poetic tribute to the fleeting sense of wonder which Spielberg sees as unique to that time before inevitable 'maturity'. From a more psychoanalytic reading, E.T. is an Oedipal fantasy, an imaginative replacement for the noticeably absent father in the family home, his extendable neck and magical, glowing finger clear indices of the alien's potency.

An extended, modified version of *E.T.* was released in 2002 which included such changes as adding more lights to the spaceship, the restoration of some additional scenes deleted from the original theatrical version and, perhaps most controversially, digitally replacing the guns of the federal agents with walkie-talkies, an alteration seen by many as a concession to the demands of family entertainment.

Fahrenheit 451
UK, 1966 – 112 mins
François Truffaut

François Truffaut's film of Ray Bradbury's 1953 cult novel, with a screenplay co-written by the director and Jean-Louis Richard, who had previously collaborated with Truffaut on *La Peau douce* (*Soft Skin*, 1964), and would again later on *The Bride Wore Black* (1968) and *La nuit Américaine* (*Day for Night*, 1973), was a major departure for the *nouvelle vague* film-maker. It was his first film in colour; his first film in a foreign language, English, which he could hardly understand; his first film shot in a studio (Pinewood); and his first (and only) science fiction movie. Despite these challenges, and the publicised conflict between Truffaut and star Oskar Werner, *Fahrenheit 451* is revealing as *un film d'auteur* at the same time as it effectively transfers to the screen the vision of one of science fiction's major writers.

In a repressive future society, printed material has been outlawed – imaginatively, the opening credits are spoken rather than written – and members of the Fire Service now start fires rather than put them out, their duty being to uncover illegal caches of books and burn them. In this ironic utopia, peace of mind is valued above all else, and the individual voice, encouraged by the exchange of ideas in books, is considered a threat. The hero, Guy Montag (Werner), is a fireman who secretly begins to read and gradually becomes aware of the importance of books. His subversive activity turns him into an outlaw when he rebels against his Captain (Cusack, who also plays the seemingly benevolent antique store owner in *Nineteen Eighty-Four** [1984]), and after Montag is denounced by his wife Linda (Christie), he is forced to flee the city to live among the Bookmen, social outcasts who have taken on the monumental task of memorising books in order to preserve culture for future generations.

Bradbury's novel expresses a romantic and optimistic belief that culture and the humanist spirit will ultimately prevail against even the sternest repression – a view complemented by Truffaut's characteristic exuberance, humanity, and love of art and culture. In the film Truffaut treats books as sacred objects, just as his alter ego Antoine Doinel (Jean-Pierre Léaud) builds a shrine to Balzac in Truffaut's first feature, *Les quatre cents coups* (*The 400 Blows*, 1959). Truffaut carefully chooses specific books to show before they ignite, including Balzac's *Madame Bovary*. Indeed, in comparison with the generally flat characters, the books in a way become the heroes of the tale. They are filmed by cinematographer Nicolas Roeg (later director of, among other films, *The Man Who Fell to Earth** [1976]) with great care, even affection, particularly in the vivid close-ups of their curling and burning pages, which, in Bradbury's words, 'leapt and danced like roasted birds, their wings ablaze with red and yellow feathers'. The human beings have significantly less presence, which may have been Truffaut's intention given his casting of Julie Christie in two opposing roles, as Montag's conservative wife and as Clarisse, the woman who introduces him to literature.

The film establishes connections between the story's speculative premise and actual history. The uniforms of the firemen evoke those of the Nazis – *Mein Kampf* is one of the books the firemen burn – and

DIRECTOR François Truffaut
PRODUCER Lewis M. Allen
SCREENPLAY Jean-Louis Richard, based on the 1953 novel by Ray Bradbury
DIRECTOR OF PHOTOGRAPHY Nicolas Roeg (colour)
EDITOR Thom Noble
MUSIC Bernard Herrmann
PRODUCTION DESIGN Syd Cain
CAST Oskar Werner, Julie Christie, Cyril Cusack, Anton Diffring
PRODUCTION COMPANY Anglo Enterprises/ Universal Pictures

the inclusion of anachronistic details such as old dresses and antique telephones in the production design emphasises the continuity between the present and this imagined future. Truffaut, in fact, seems less involved in the science fiction aspects of the story, as revealed by the poor quality of Charles Staffel's special effects (the wires on which the policemen flying with jet packs are suspended are clearly visible), than as a vehicle for his own interests. From this perspective, Montag's conversion from a fireman to a reader is not so much an act of political rebellion as it is a pursuit of the imagination – pointedly, the book he decides to memorise is Edgar Allan Poe's *Tales of Mystery and Imagination* – a quest common to many of Truffaut's protagonists.

Fantastic Voyage
US, 1966 – 100 mins
Richard Fleischer

With wooden acting and stodgy direction by Richard Fleischer (*20,000 Leagues Under the Sea** [1954], *Soylent Green** [1973], *Fantastic Voyage* is redeemed as an early instance of sci-fi psychedelia even before the far-out Stargate sequence in *2001: A Space Odyssey** (1968). Often seeming a melodramatic combination of space opera and undersea adventure movie featuring ludicrous science and matte shots that look crude by today's standards, *Fantastic Voyage*'s elaborate sets of the interior of the human body still succeed in inducing awe regarding the complexity of nature's design. The film presents an astonishing array of colours, shapes and textures for the body's insides during the journey through the human blood stream, with the enraptured musings of one of the scientists, Dr. Duval (Kennedy), about the infinitely large and small in the cosmos, echoing the sublime ending of Jack Arnold's *The Incredible Shrinking Man** (1957). The film justifiably won Academy Awards for Best Art Direction and Special Effects.

Both the United States and the Soviet Union have developed technology that can shrink matter to microscopic size, but only temporarily. A Russian scientist, Jan Benes (Del Val), has discovered how to make the process permanent, but during his defection with the help of the CIA, he is injured, leaving him comatose with a blood clot in his brain. In order to save Benes – and by extension, the free world – a team is assembled by the secret C.M.D.F. (Combined Miniaturised Deterrent Forces) to pilot a miniaturised nuclear submarine, the *Proteus*, through Benes' body to disperse the clot. CIA agent Charles Grant (Boyd), Captain Owens (Redfield), Dr. Michaels (Pleasence), Dr. Peter Duval (Kennedy), the surgeon, and his inevitably lovely assistant, Cora Peterson (Welch), are reduced to microscopic size in the *Proteus*, while in the facility control room the gruff military commander, Gen. Carter (O'Brien), along with Col. Reid (O'Connell), helps provide exposition and struggles to raise the dramatic tension by chomping on cigars.

Injected into Benes, the team has one hour to reach the brain, dissolve the clot, and reach the extraction point before they begin to expand to normal size. An arterial fistula forces them to alter their planned route and travel through Benes' heart, lungs, and inner ear, facing a number of obstacles and delays, including sabotage by Dr. Michaels, who turns out to be an enemy agent – signalled early on by his scepticism about the existence of the human soul. With only minutes remaining, Dr. Duval performs the operation with a laser. When Michaels attempts to smash the Proteus into the wound area, with satisfying poetic justice he, along with the ship, is consumed by a white blood cell that engulfs him like *The Blob* (1958). The others escape with seconds to go (bizarrely, the clock in the control room registers only the minutes) by swimming to a tear duct, where they are successfully extracted on a microscope slide by Col. Reid.

The screenplay was based on a story by producer Otto Klement and science fiction writer Jerome Bixby, author of the original screenplay for *It! The Terror from Beyond Space* (1958, a primary inspiration for *Alien** [1979]). Isaac Asimov wrote a novelisation based on the screenplay, published six months before the release

DIRECTOR Richard Fleischer
PRODUCER Saul David
SCREENPLAY Harry Kleiner, David Duncan, based on a story by Otto Klement and Jerome Bixby
DIRECTOR OF PHOTOGRAPHY Ernest Laszlo
EDITOR William B. Murphy
MUSIC Leonard Rosenman
ART DIRECTOR Dale Hennesy, Jack Martin Smith
MAIN CAST Stephen Boyd, Raquel Welch, Edmond O'Brien, Donald Pleasence, William Redfield, Arthur Kennedy, Arthur O'Connell, Jean Del Val
PRODUCTION COMPANY 20th Century Fox

of the film (inadvertently creating the impression that the film was based on Asimov's book rather than vice versa). In it, Asimov was careful to correct some of the film's scientific mistakes, including the extraction of the wrecked sub as well as the crew so that its molecules would not expand in Benes' body. In his 1987 novel *Fantastic Voyage II: Destination Brain*, Asimov retained the premise but completely rewrote the story with different characters, as did Kevin J. Anderson in *Fantastic Voyage: Microcosm* (2001). An animated series ran on North American television in 1968, and in 1987 director Joe Dante (*The Howling* [1981], *Explorers* [1985], *Small Soldiers* [1998], *The Screwfly Solution* [2006]) reworked the premise of *Fantastic Voyage* into the lighter *Innerspace*.

The Fifth Element
France, 1997 – 126 mins
Luc Besson

With the thrillers *Subway* (1985) and *Nikita* (*La Femme Nikita*, 1990), director Luc Besson was considered a key figure in the French *Cinéma du look* movement, an approach shared by some film-makers of the 1980s and 90s in which visual style seemed to take precedence over substance, and *The Fifth Element* certainly shows why. *Lockout* (2012), another of Besson's science fiction movies, is much more functional in its narrative and visual design, as might be expected given that its inspiration is John Carpenter's *Escape from New York* (1981). By comparison, *The Fifth Element* explodes with striking visual images. Shot in Super 35mm, the film contains a multitude of stunning special effects and bold imagery – most memorably, the shots of dense layers of airborne traffic in the megalopolis flying in all directions and the blue-skinned alien opera diva. French science fiction comics artists Jean-Claude Mézières and Jean Giraud, who also worked on *Alien** (1979) and *Tron** (1982), contributed to its stunning production design, and French fashion designer Jean-Paul Gaultier created nearly 1,000 costumes for the film, many as outlandish as those in Ken Russell's films or late Fellini.

    The Fifth Element's audacious plot involves a Great Evil that comes every five millennia, and the only thing capable of vanquishing it is a 'fifth element' which was given to humans in the past by a benevolent alien race, the Mondoshawans, while a secret religious order has been entrusted with the key for its eventual use. Now, in the year 2263, the Great Evil appears in the form of a giant molten ball that is hurtling towards the Earth. Attempts to destroy the ball only make it larger and more intense as it absorbs the energy of the weapons deployed against it.

    The fifth element turns out to be a genetically modified and evolved woman, Leeloo (Jovovich), who is able to activate the four special stones, each representing one of the four known elements, to defeat the Great Evil. Fleeing the authorities, Leeloo falls through the roof of a flying taxicab driven by former military officer Korben Dallas (Willis), who falls in love with her and helps her, along with the Mondoshawan cult priest Cornelius (Holm). The three discover that the stones are in the safekeeping of an alien opera diva scheduled to perform in a concert hall orbiting a vacation planet. Travelling there aboard a luxury space liner while pretending to be winners of a radio contest for a free trip, Korben and Leeloo seek to get the stones in time to stop the fiery ball before it impacts Earth. In a subplot, a ruthless arms dealer, Zorg (Oldham), who wants the fifth element for himself, enlists the help of another alien race, the brutish Mangalores, shapeshifters who breach the orbiting station and begin to massacre everyone in their search for them.

    At this point the film loses focus, abandoning the mystical and moral conflict between good and evil, and its metaphoric relevance to a contemporary world that has forgotten the importance of love, to concentrate instead on conventional action and an extended satire of the media and celebrity culture. Korben, apparently a common man who has won a dream vacation, is accompanied and interviewed live at

DIRECTOR Luc Besson
SCREENPLAY Luc Besson, Robert Mark Kamen
PRODUCER Patrice Ledoux
DIRECTOR OF PHOTOGRAPHY Thierry Arbogast
EDITOR Sylvie Landra
MUSIC Eric Serra
PRODUCTION DESIGN Dan Weil
MAIN CAST Bruce Willis, Gary Oldman, Ian Holm, Milla Jovovich, Chris Tucker, Luke Perry, Brion James, Tommy 'Tiny' Lister, Jr, Lee Evans, Charlie Creed-Miles
PRODUCTION COMPANY Gaumont

the scene by talk-show personality Ruby Rhod (Tucker), an overheated purveyor of empty entertainment. Leading a one-man battle against the Mangalores, Dallas secures the stones from within the body of the diva, killed by the Mangalores, and escapes with Leeloo. All the while as the battle unfolds, the womaniser and appositely named Rhod provides a manic on-the-spot commentary for his audience while revealing his own quivering cowardice, in contrast to the quiet manliness of the courageous Korben.

In the climax, as the stones are put into their designated position, Leeloo accepts Korben's love and releases the Divine Light that destroys the Great Evil, but the gesture rings hollow after all the indulgence of explosive violence that precedes it.

Flash Gordon
US, 1936 – 13 episodes, 245 mins
Frederick Stephani

Flash Gordon began as a comic strip first published in 1934, and survived into the 1980s. Drawn by Alex Raymond, it was intended to compete with the *Buck Rogers* strip. In 1935, it was adapted as a 26-episode weekly radio serial entitled 'The Amazing Interplanetary Adventures of Flash Gordon', and the following year this serial, the first of three starring Buster Crabbe as the eponymous hero and Charles Middleton as his nemesis Ming the Merciless, was released by Universal in 13 episodes. *Flash Gordon* was also condensed into a 97-minute feature-length film variously titled *Flash Gordon, Rocket Ship*, *Spaceship to the Unknown* or *Atomic Rocketship*, and on television it was shown as *Space Soldiers*. The first and probably the best-known of the science fiction serials of the 1930s and 40s, it was followed by *Flash Gordon's Trip to Mars* (1938) and *Flash Gordon Conquers the Universe* (1940), all three directed with endearingly minimal competence by Frederick Stephani, who subsequently worked as a film producer in the 1940s and wrote and directed episodes for several television shows in the 1950s.

In the story, the planet Mongo is on a collision course with Earth, threatening to destroy it by 'smashing it to atoms', according to Prof. Gordon (Tucker), Flash's father. Dr. Alexis Zarkov (Shannon) takes off in a rocket ship to Mongo, with Flash Gordon and Dale Arden (Rogers) as his assistants. They find that the planet is ruled by the cruel Emperor Ming, who lusts after Dale and several times sends Flash to fight for his life while Ming's daughter, Princess Aura (Lawson), tries to save him. The slim plot barely conceals the hysterical sexual scenario, with Ming, an archetypal image of Yellow Peril, lusting after the blonde Dale Arden, whose very name connotes the promise of female fecundity, while, in standard melodramatic fashion, Dale loves Flash, whom Princess Aura desires but who loves Dale, while Aura is beloved by the beefy Prince Barin (Alexander).

With more wipes than a box of towelettes, the serial features ludicrous costumes (Zarkov, for example, wears a turtle-neck tunic with pantaloon type shorts without leotards) and sets (the worship of the Mongo God Tao, with dozens of writhing female bodies adorning it, is a seeming parody of silent epics like *Intolerance* [1916]), and risible special effects, making *Flash Gordon* more interesting today as camp than serious science fiction. Animals such as octopuses and lizards are shot in slow motion with growls added on the soundtrack to suggest that they are giant creatures. The serial is pure space opera, with ray guns and signals sent by 'spaceograph' and 'resist-o-force' force fields protecting the inexplicably clumsy spacecraft which have to tilt in mid-flight to aim their ray blasters rather than simply allow for the swivelling of weapons. Flash and crew frequently run through one of the secret passages that seem to pop up in every episode. Many of the serial's props and sets were recycled from earlier Universal films including *Frankenstein*** (1931) and *The Mummy* (1932), as well as from the science fiction musical *Just Imagine*** (1930). Despite having been a college and Olympic athlete, Crabbe – the only actor who played Tarzan, Flash Gordon, and Buck

DIRECTOR Frederick Stephani
PRODUCER Henry MacRae
SCREENPLAY Basil Dickey, Ella O'Neill, George H. Plympton, Frederick Stephani, based on the comic strip by Alex Raymond
DIRECTOR OF PHOTOGRAPHY Jerry Ash, Richard Fryer
EDITOR Saul A. Goodkind, Louis Sackin, Edward Todd, Alvin Todd
MUSIC Clifford Vaughan
ART DIRECTOR Ralph Berger
MAIN CAST Buster Crabbe, Jean Rogers, Charles Middleton, Priscilla Lawson, Frank Shannon, Richard Alexander, Jack 'Tiny' Lipson, Theodore Lorch, Richard Tucker, James Pierce
PRODUCTION COMPANY King Features, Universal Pictures

Rogers, the top three comic strip heroes of the 1930s – is generally ungainly and blank emotionally, although he is surprisingly brutal, fighting every few minutes and often defeating his opponents by strangling them with his bare hands. He even strangles a tiger to death in one episode.

A number of other film and television versions of *Flash Gordon* have also been made, including the soft-core *Flesh Gordon* (1974), as well as several television series, including one which ran for 39 episodes on American TV in 1954–5 and a more recent show that was broadcast on the Sci-Fi Channel in both the US and the UK in 2007–8.

The Fly
US, 1986 – 96 mins
David Cronenberg

The second version of George Langelaan's short story is, technically speaking, not a remake of Kurt Neumann's 1958 film of the same name. As John Carpenter did with *The Thing** (1982), Canadian auteur David Cronenberg (*Scanners* [1981], *Videodrome** [1983], *Naked Lunch* [1991, based on the novel by William S. Burroughs], *Crash* [1996, from J. G. Ballard's novel], *eXistenZ* [1999]) returned to the original story to make it completely his own, depicting the protagonist's transformation both for its graphic horror potential and as an extended metaphor for the decay of human relationships.

In Cronenberg's version, scientist Seth Brundle (Goldblum) meets journalist Veronica Quaife (Davis) at a scientific meeting and, immediately attracted to her, invites her back to his lab to show her his invention that he boasts 'will change the world as we know it'. He demonstrates his teleportation invention (now called a 'telepod' rather than the more dated 'transmitter' and 'receiver' of the earlier film, with its connotations of the telephone and telegraph). Seth proposes that she witness and record his experiments until he has figured out why he is unable to teleport living creatures successfully. A romantic relationship quickly develops between them. One night, Seth discovers Ronnie's previous relationship with her editor, Stathis Borans (Getz), and mistakenly thinks she has secretly gone to meet him. In a fit of drunken jealousy he teleports himself, with the unfortunate result that he becomes genetically fused with a housefly that accidentally enters the telepod with him. Seth begins to change, first becoming more energetic, agile and strong, but then sinking into infirmity when his body begins to shed its human features as he transforms into a new being, 'Brundlefly'.

Cronenberg, acknowledged as the master of 'body horror' with such films as *Shivers* (1975), *Rabid* (1977) and *The Brood* (1979), depicts Seth's bodily changes in detail: his teeth fall out, his ears and fingernails drop off, and he squirts pus-like fluid from the tips of his fingers. He keeps a 'museum' of now useless body parts in his bathroom medicine cabinet. At first Brundlefly kidnaps Ronnie with the aim of putting her through the pod with him in order to bring them closer together and to dilute the fly DNA within him. In the end, however, with the little humanity he still possesses, he convinces Ronnie to kill him, as André had his wife do in both Langelaan's story and the earlier movie. While Cronenberg's version lacks the memorable shock ending of the first version – a fly with a tiny human head trapped in a spider web screams 'Help me!' in a high-pitched whine as the spider descends toward it – it is scientifically more plausible and its characters psychologically more interesting than those of the original film. It improves on its predecessor's unscientific lapse, as the scientist's entire body is transformed as a result of his genetic bonding with the fly, not just his arm and head with, improbably, a human brain.

Thematically, Cronenberg's film establishes a stronger connection between the horrors of biological transformation and human relationships. In both previous texts André teleports himself simply in the name of science, but Cronenberg foregrounds the characters' personal tensions by making Seth the victim of his

DIRECTOR David Cronenberg
PRODUCER Stuart Cornfeld
SCREENPLAY David Cronenberg, Charles Edward Pogue, based on the 1957 story by George Langelaan
DIRECTOR OF PHOTOGRAPHY Mark Irwin
EDITOR Ronald Sanders
MUSIC Howard Shore
PRODUCTION DESIGN Carol Spier
MAIN CAST Jeff Goldblum, Geena Davis, John Getz, Joy Boushel, Les Carlson
PRODUCTION COMPANY Brooksfilms

own inability to cope with his newly awakened desire. Seth sees the failure of his machine to teleport living matter as a reflection of his own lack of understanding about 'the flesh', and this becomes his tragic flaw. Seth's horrible fate fulfils media guru Brian O'Blivion's mantra of 'long live the new flesh' in *Videodrome* even as it anticipates the mechanical fetishism depicted in *Crash*. The film's emphasis on Seth's physical and emotional changes – underscored by the subtly modulated performance of Jeff Goldblum – while it has been viewed by some as a monstrous exaggeration of masculinity, has been more widely noted as a subtextual evocation of AIDS, a disease both very much in the news and largely misunderstood at the time of the film's release.

Forbidden Planet
US, 1956 – 98 mins
Fred M. Wilcox

Forbidden Planet was produced at MGM, known for its star roster and for being the glossiest of Hollywood studios. Although previously the studio had produced such fantasy fare as Gabriel Over the White House (1933) and many musicals including The Wizard of Oz (1939), and would later produce Stanley Kubrick's 2001: A Space Odyssey* (1968), it was MGM's first serious foray into science fiction. Made on a substantial budget of just under $2 million, its high production values set it worlds apart, as it were, from the period's bevy of B movies. The original story was written by Irving Block, who was also the (uncredited) production designer of the film. Block later wrote the story for Kronos (1957), about an alien robot that consumes energy, and produced and contributed special effects for the film, as well as providing the special effects for several other science fiction films including Rocketship X-M (1950), World without End (1956), and The Invisible Boy (1957), which, like Forbidden Planet, also features Robby the Robot.

Block's screenplay, filled with extrapolative ideas, was consciously modelled on Shakespeare's final play, The Tempest (1610–11?), which also inspired the title of Aldous Huxley's classic science fiction novel, Brave New World (1932). The crew of United Planets Cruiser C-57D (the film's version of the play's shipwrecked Italian nobles) arrives at the planet Altair IV to investigate what happened to an earlier ship of colonists that had landed there years before. Oddly, the only survivors are Dr. Morbius (Pidgeon), the Prospero figure, and his beautiful daughter Alta (a mini-skirted Francis on ample display for the ship's crew as well as the spectator), aided by a robot named Robby, the science fiction equivalent of the ethereal spirit Ariel. Morbius warns Commander Adams (Nielsen) and his landing party about a mysterious unseen creature that had killed all the other colonists. Now it returns, attacking the ship's crew and destroying their equipment.

Eventually it is revealed that Morbius had boosted his intelligence with the aid of a machine built by the original inhabitants of the planet, the Krell, but that it also provided the means for him to project his own incestuous desires ('jealousy', as the film euphemistically puts it) outward in embodied form (the film's Caliban). The Krell, on the technological verge of 'eliminating all instrumentalities' through the power of the thought machine, had also unleashed their primitive instincts and so destroyed themselves. Morbius's name invokes the Moebius Strip, a two-dimensional figure with only one surface, for he is two in one, civilised yet primitive, as Adams explains in a capsule summary of Freud's Civilisation and Its Discontents. While the creatures of many monster stories and movies can be read as projections of the protagonist's inner self, Forbidden Planet is one of the very few that explicitly name it as 'the monster from the Id'. In the climax, just as Prospero renounces alchemy in Shakespeare's play, so Morbius says 'I disown you' and the monster, its brief visibility in the ship's protective force field created by Walt Disney Studios, dissipates. The 'forbidden planet' of the title is thus the world of the subconscious according to Freudian theory.

Leslie Nielsen, who years later would find his niche as a comic actor in the Naked Gun series, here plays

DIRECTOR Fred M. Wilcox
PRODUCER Nicholas Nayfack
SCREENPLAY Cyril Hume
DIRECTOR OF PHOTOGRAPHY
George J. Folsey
EDITOR Ferris Webster
MUSIC Louis and Bebe Barron
ART DIRECTOR Cedric Gibbons,
Arthur Lonergan
MAIN CAST Leslie Nielsen, Walter
Pidgeon, Anne Francis, Warren
Stevens, Jack Kelly, Earl Holliman,
James Drury, Richard Anderson,
George Wallace, Robert Dix, Robby
the Robot
PRODUCTION COMPANY MGM

it straight as the ship's captain and upstanding hero. Ironically, amidst a group of cardboard characters, it is Robby the Robot who, with his deadpan wit, is the most engaging. Robby clearly operates according to Isaac Asimov's Three Laws of Robotics, as outlined in his *I, Robot* stories (the first of which, published in 1940, was entitled 'Robbie'). Indeed, Robby (played in *Forbidden Planet* by Frankie Darro, a prolific actor during the studio era whose credits also include *The Phantom Empire*

[1935], Gene Autry's science fiction singing Western) was so popular that he became something of a star, appearing in the aforementioned *The Invisible Boy*, and on more than a dozen television shows including *The Twilight Zone*, *Mork and Mindy* and *Lost in Space*. By comparison, director Wilcox's career was less distinguished, his most noteworthy achievements alongside *Forbidden Planet* being two films in the Lassie series, *Lassie Come Home* (1943) and *Courage of Lassie* (1946).

Frankenstein
US, 1931 – 70 mins
James Whale

Mary Shelley's novel, considered one of the foundational works of both horror and science fiction, was first adapted to film in 1910. There have been numerous versions and variations since, both serious and satiric, from Kenneth Branagh's respectful *Mary Shelley's Frankenstein* (1994) to Mel Brooks's farcical *Young Frankenstein* (1974). But it is James Whale's version, based on an adaptation of Peggy Webling's play by John L. Balderston (who had also adapted Bram Stoker's *Dracula* to the New York stage), which is best remembered. Jack Pierce's distinctive makeup for Boris Karloff, with flat head and bolts in either side of his neck, has become iconic of Frankenstein's creature. Universal had had success with the horror genre in ten silent film collaborations between director Tod Browning and Lon Chaney, Hollywood's first horror star. Early in the sound era, the studio became known for its horror films with *Dracula* (1931), directed by Browning, *The Mummy* (1932), directed by Karl Freund, and *Frankenstein*, directed by Whale, who came to Hollywood to make the film version of *Journey's End* (1930), which he had directed on the London stage.

Many German film émigrés found employment at Universal, including Paul Leni, Conrad Veidt (the somnambulist of *The Cabinet of Dr. Caligari* [1920]), and Freund, cinematographer of numerous German Expressionist films including *Metropolis** (1927). *Frankenstein* clearly shows the influence of German Expressionism in the effectively stylised sets, most notably the cemetery, castle laboratory and abandoned windmill. The justly famous creation scene, with Kenneth Strickfaden's lightning effects and zapping electrodes, accompanied by Colin Clive's deranged cry of 'It's alive, it's alive', clearly recalls Rotwang's animation of his robot as Maria in *Metropolis* and became *de rigueur* in Universal's subsequent Frankenstein movies.

Shelley's story of a scientist (Clive) who attempts to create life on his own was, in the words of science fiction historian Brian Aldiss, 'the first great myth of the Industrial Age', but it remains as relevant today in the era of genetic engineering. Henry Frankenstein (Victor in the novel) is 'the modern Prometheus' (the novel's subtitle) who seeks to usurp divine prerogative, a moral aspect of the narrative emphasised in the Universal films. Shelley claimed in her preface that her aim was to write a horror tale 'which would speak to the mysterious fears of our nature, and awaken thrilling horror – one to make the reader dread to look round, to curdle the blood, and quicken the beatings of the heart'. Certainly most of the film versions, Whale's included, emphasise the tale's horror at the expense of its science fiction. Thus *Frankenstein* begins with a direct-to-camera address by Edward Van Sloan (who plays Frankenstein's former professor at medical school, Dr. Waldman), cautioning those among the audience who are faint of heart to think twice about watching the film to come.

After *Frankenstein*, Whale would also direct for Universal *The Old Dark House* (1932), *The Invisible Man** (1933) and the equally accomplished follow-up to *Frankenstein*, *Bride of Frankenstein* (1935). As it did

DIRECTOR James Whale
PRODUCER Carl Laemmle, Jr
SCREENPLAY Garrett Fort, Francis Edward Faragoh, based upon the 1818 novel by Mary Shelley and the 1927 play by Peggy Webling, adapted by John L. Balderston
DIRECTOR OF PHOTOGRAPHY Arthur Edeson
EDITOR Clarence Kolster
MUSIC Bernhard Kaun
ART DIRECTOR Charles D. Hall
MAIN CAST Boris Karloff, Colin Clive, Mae Clarke, John Boles, Edward Van Sloan, Dwight Frye, Lionel Frederick Kerr, Lionel Belmore
PRODUCTION COMPANY Universal Pictures

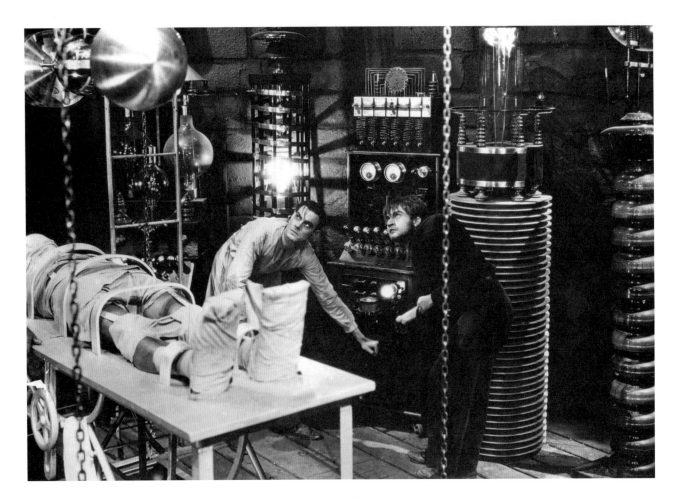

with its other monsters, Universal put Frankenstein's creature through its stiff-strutting paces in a cycle of loose sequels: *Son of Frankenstein* (1939); *Frankenstein Meets the Wolf Man* (1943); *The Ghost of Frankenstein* (1942) and *House of Frankenstein* (1944), both directed by Erle C. Kenton, who also directed *Island of Lost Souls** (1932) for Paramount; and, of course, *Abbott and Costello Meet Frankenstein* (1948). A decade later, Hammer Films in Britain reinterpreted the Universal monsters for a new generation, beginning with *The Curse of Frankenstein* in 1957 and including a series of six other Frankenstein films, all except one starring Peter Cushing. But in his two films of the cycle, Whale also shows sympathy for the creature when, for example, he is goaded by the sadistic hunchback Fritz (Frye) or, in *Bride*, seeking companionship. *Gods and Monsters* (1998), based on Christopher Bram's 1995 novel *Father of Frankenstein*, interprets the tragic alienation and the pathos in Whale's treatment of the creature as an expression of the director's conflicted feelings regarding his own homosexuality.

Frau im Mond (*Woman in the Moon*)
Germany, 1929 – 156 mins
Fritz Lang

Apart from the monumental *Metropolis** (1927), *Frau im Mond* was Fritz Lang's only other science fiction film. One of the earliest films to seriously depict space travel, the film is based on the novel by Thea von Harbou, Lang's wife and collaborator during the German phase of his career, written the year before the film. Some basic concepts of rocket science, such as gravity, escape velocity and the use of multi-stage (in this case, three) rockets were depicted here for the first time in cinema, some of the information provided by animated diagrams showing distances and trajectories. Rocket expert Hermann Oberth served as a technical adviser on the film, and science writer Willy Ley, co-author of the later book *Conquest of Space* (1949) with astronomical artist Chesley Bonestell, upon which the 1955 film of the same was based, was a consultant.

Lang builds a beautiful montage matching model work with live action to depict the launch from the time the rocket emerges from the hangar and is brought into position on the launching pad through lift-off. The film's treatment of rocketry was an inspiration for the German V-2 rocket programme, and the launch sequence includes an abbreviated countdown which may have influenced the procedure used by NASA. The film also imagines a launch with the ship submerged in water for heat control, an idea that space exploration has thus far not employed. Somewhat less credible, though, are the clumsily conceived ceiling straps and foot stirrups on the floor that are everywhere on the ship, designed to enable the crew to walk about during the period of weightlessness, but which would surely be obtrusive at other times.

By contrast, the narrative that contains the journey of the first rocket to the moon is less satisfying as science fiction than melodrama in the mode of *Spione* (*Spies*, 1928), the film Lang directed between *Metropolis* and *Frau im Mond*. The story involves an entrepreneur, Helius (Fritsch), who connects with Professor Manfeldt (Pohl), a scientist who had written a paper about the possibility of finding gold on the moon and who was then literally laughed out of the academy, with the idea of going there. Helius's first assistant, Windegger (Wangenheim), is engaged to another of his assistants, Friede (Maurus), whom Helius secretly loves. In addition, there is a mysterious criminal gang led by a Mabuse-like evil businessman, whose representative, Turner (Rasp), blackmails Helius into joining the lunar expedition by threatening to blow up his factories and his rocket.

Thus riven with romantic tensions and criminal intrigue, this unlikely group of five, along with Gustav (Gstettenbaur), a young boy who reads science fiction pulps and who stows away on the ship, journey to the dark side of the moon, where they find gold and, conveniently, a breathable atmosphere. The impoverished Professor is driven as mad as *Metropolis*'s Rotwang with gold lust and falls to his death clutching a giant nugget. Turner tries to hijack the rocket back to Earth and is killed, but in the gunfight the ship's oxygen tanks are damaged, meaning that there is insufficient air for the four remaining passengers and that someone will have to remain temporarily on the moon until a rescue ship can be sent. When the two

DIRECTOR Fritz Lang
PRODUCER Fritz Lang
SCREENPLAY Fritz Lang, based on the novel *Die Frau im Mond* (*The Woman in the Moon*) (1928) by Thea von Harbou
DIRECTOR OF PHOTOGRAPHY Curt Courant, Oskar Fischinger, Konstantin Tschetwerikoff, Otto Kanturek
ORIGINAL MUSIC Jon Mirsalis, Willy Schmidt-Gentner
ART DIRECTOR Emil Hasler, Otto Hunte, Karl Vollbrecht
MAIN CAST Klaus Pohl, Willy Fritsch, Gustav von Wangenheim, Gerda Maurus, Gustl Gstettenbaur, Fritz Rasp
PRODUCTION COMPANY Fritz Lang-Film, UFA

men draw straws, Windegger reveals himself as a coward, and the brave Helius contrives to send the ship back to Earth with him outside. As he watches the ship blast off, he is surprised to find Friede, who has learned of Helius's love for her, also there, and they embrace, the promise of a period of blissful romantic solitude awaiting them in their lunar base camp. In this uncharacteristically upbeat ending for a Lang film, man conquers two unknown territories, the moon and the woman on it.

Galaxy Quest
US, 1999 – 102 mins
Dean Parisot

A genial parody of the iconic television series *Star Trek* (1966–8) and the trekkie subculture, *Galaxy Quest* manages at once to mock its subject even as it provides the very same pleasures that made the show so popular. The film's plot centres on the cast of a popular television show who, almost two decades after it has finished its first run, find themselves suddenly embarking on a real space adventure to help an alien race, the Thermians, who have come to Earth to seek the aid of the *Galaxy Quest* cast in an intergalactic war. The Thermians, who have been monitoring Earth transmissions, have no concept of fiction and thus believe the *Galaxy Quest* show to be a series of 'historical documents'. (When asked about *Gilligan's Island*, the Thermians hang their heads in respect for 'those poor people'.)

The fictional crew of the NSEA *Protector* on the show includes Jason Nesmith (Allen) as the ship's captain, Cmdr. Peter Quincy Taggart; Alexander Dane (Rickman) as the ship's alien science officer, Dr. Lazarus; Fred Kwan (Shalhoub) as Tech Sgt. Chen, the chief engineer; Gwen DeMarco (Weaver) as the Communications Officer Lt. Tawny Madison; and Tommy Webber (Mitchell) as a former child pilot. Allen plays Taggart with all the macho bravado of William Shatner's Capt. James T. Kirk; during one fight with aliens Nesmith takes off his shirt, showing his bare chest, as Shatner was wont to do at some point in each episode of *Star Trek*. Dane's Dr. Lazarus of Tev'Meck, a member of an intellectual alien race, is the show's version of Leonard Nimoy's Mr. Spock. He wears a silly rubber headpiece instead of pointy ears and, like Spock, has a famous tagline (in this case, 'By Grabthar's hammer, by the suns of Warvan, you *shall* be avenged!') that he disdainfully refuses to say any longer. Weaver's DeMarco, like *Star Trek*'s Lt. Uhura (Nichelle Nichols), functions primarily as eye candy in a miniskirt. Thus Tawny's job is essentially meaningless, consisting mostly of repeating communications to and from the computer.

Only Shalhoub's Kwan is somewhat off the mark as a parody of James Doohan's Scotty. Responsible for the engine room and the operation of the 'digital conveyor', the film's version of *Star Trek*'s transporter, he remains completely unflappable in the face of danger, the only member of the group who doesn't miss a beat when he learns that he is on a real ship. Unlike the other actors, he thoroughly enjoys the entire experience and, completely comfortable with the true form of the aliens, develops a romantic relationship with Laliari, one of the Thermians. On their adventure they are joined by Guy Fleegman (Rockwell), the host of the convention back on Earth. Fleegman, who had played Crewman #6 in episode 81 and who (like the expendable 'redshirt' extras on *Star Trek*), was promptly killed off in his only appearance on the show, continually worries that he will be killed, a fate he believes is inevitable for minor characters like his.

At a *Galaxy Quest* convention, Nesmith is approached by Mathesar (Colantoni) and a group of Thermians, who entreat him to return to their ship and lead them in their fight. Assuming they are fans staying in role for an amateur shoot, he agrees and is taken to their ship, a completely functional version of

DIRECTOR Dean Parisot
PRODUCER Mark Johnson, Charles Newirth
SCREENPLAY David Howard, Robert Gordon
DIRECTOR OF PHOTOGRAPHY Jerzy Zielinski
EDITOR Don Zimmerman
MUSIC David Newman
PRODUCTION DESIGN Linda DeScenna
MAIN CAST Tim Allen, Sigourney Weaver, Alan Rickman, Tony Shalhoub, Sam Rockwell, Daryl Mitchell, Robin Sachs, Enrico Colantoni, Patrick Breen
PRODUCTION COMPANY Dreamworks SKG

the show's *Protector* that they have built by studying the 'historical documents'. Nesmith initially thinks it is merely a convincing mockup and, playing along, takes the controls and orders an attack on Sarris (Sachs), a reptilian warlord evocative of *Star Trek*'s Klingons and Romulans. After they are returned home, Nesmith realises the truth and convinces the other cast members to return to the ship with him to negotiate Sarris's surrender. Although sceptical, they join him but then, to their horror, learn the truth when Sarris counter-attacks. After a number of serio-comic adventures, they outmaneouvre Sarris in a space minefield and save the Thermian ship from self-destructing by getting advice from Brandon (Justin Long), a teenage fan back on Earth who has an encyclopaedic knowledge of the show.

Ghost in the Shell
Japan/US, 1995 – 85 mins
Mamoru Oshii

Ghost in the Shell is a Japanese science fiction anime based on the manga series written and illustrated by Masamune Shirow. First appearing in serialised form (1989–90), as was a sequel, *Ghost in the Shell 2: Man-Machine Interface* (1991–7), both were later published in book form. (The first English-language adaptation was published in the US in 1995 and in the UK in 1997). Directed by Mamoru Oshii, who also directed, among others, the sequel, *Ghost in the Shell 2: Innocence* (2004), as well as two *Urusei Yatsura* films, *Urusei Yatsura: Only You* (1983) and *Urusei Yatsura 2: Beautiful Dreamer* (1984), *Angel's Egg* (1985), and several live-action films, *Ghost in the Shell* was one of the first anime features to gain popularity in North America. With its story of artificial intelligences striving for knowledge and understanding, the film was influenced by cyberpunk science fiction and films such as *Blade Runner** (1982), its influence in turn seen in, for example, the Wachowskis' *The Matrix** (1999) and James Cameron's *Avatar** (2009). It has spawned a franchise that also includes, in addition to the manga and the two anime features, two anime TV series (*Ghost in the Shell: Stand Alone Complex* and *Ghost in the Shell: S.A.C. 2nd GIG*), an anime TV movie, several OVA (original video animation) and video games.

DIRECTOR Mamoru Oshii
PRODUCER Mitsuhisa Ishikawa, Ken Iyadomi, Ken Matsumoto, Yoshimasa Mizuo, Shigeru Watanabe
SCREENPLAY Kazunori Itô, based on manga by Masamune Shirow
DIRECTOR OF PHOTOGRAPHY Hisao Shirai
EDITOR Sûichi Kakesu
MUSIC Kenji Kawai
PRODUCTION DESIGN Takashi Watabe
MAIN VOICE CAST Atsuko Tanaka, Akio Ôtsuka, Tamio Ôki, Iemasa Kayumi, Kôichi Yamadera, Yukata Nakano, Maaya Sakamoto
PRODUCTION COMPANY Bandai Visual Company, Kodansha, Production I.G.

The *Ghost in the Shell* manga consists of a series of cases involving the Japanese counter-terrorist organisation Security Police Section 9 in a near-future where humans can interface with cyborgs and the Internet and 'ghost-hack' people's minds, implanting false memories. The film focuses on the 'Puppet Master' (Kayumi), a mysterious genius hacker, and the attempt to capture him by Major Motoko Kusanagi (Tanaka), the female cyborg in charge of Section 9's assault squad consisting of the cybernetically enhanced Batou (Ōtsuka) and the human Ishikawa (Nakano). When they track the Puppet Master to a female cybernetic body (shell) that was working as a diplomatic translator, Kusanagi interfaces with it and the Puppet Master explains that his consciousness originated with Project 2501, a programme created by government agency Section 6 to hack ghosts clandestinely. It explains that it has attained sentience but, unlike other living organisms, it is unable to reproduce or to die, and has chosen Kusanagi, whose body has been destroyed in a battle with a tank, to join with to create a new, single entity capable of propagating on the Internet. As they merge, helicopters from Section 6 converge on them with orders to kill so as to cover up Project 2501. Later, Kusanagi awakens at Batou's safehouse in a child-sized cyborg body (Sakamoto), and he explains that he had saved her from the assault and that he had purchased her new shell quickly on the black market. She reveals that now she is neither Major Kusanagi nor the Puppet Master, but some as yet unexplored, disembodied combination of them both existing on the Internet. Leaving, she gazes out over the city pondering the future.

Until the end, Kusanagi, like Roy Batty in *Blade Runner*, wonders about her existence: with a fully cybernetic body, was she once human or is she entirely artificial with implanted ghost memories to make her believe so? Thus she identifies with the Puppet Master entity, who also seeks existential knowledge. Because *Ghost in the Shell* originated as a *seinen* ('young men') manga, the superfluous shots of buttocks and bare breasts, particularly when Kusanagi's body is damaged during her climactic struggle with the tank, somewhat undercut the pathos of her quest. Still, *Ghost in the Shell*, one of the first anime films to match computer and cel animation, relies on a two-dimensional style that not only captures the visual look of the manga but also renders everything in its diegetic world in the same graphic way, furthering the film's vision of a future in which the boundaries between humans, other living organisms and machines are blurred.

Gojira (*Godzilla*)
Japan, 1954 – 96 mins
Ishirô Honda

The mother of all giant monster movies (*kaiju eiga*), *Gojira*, about a giant reptile mutated by nuclear radiation that wreaks havoc in Japan, opened the door for Japanese science fiction and horror to Western audiences. Inspired by *The Beast from 20,000 Fathoms** (1953), its creature, whose name is a conflation of the Japanese words for 'gorilla' (*gorira*) and 'whale' (*kujira*), combined aspects of a Tyrannosaurus Rex, a Stegosaurus and a mythical fire-breathing dragon, resonating sufficiently in the popular imagination to sustain a series of more than two dozen movies for Toho Studios, an uninspired American 1998 remake directed by Roland Emmerich, and animated TV shows in Japan and the United States. Director Ishirô (Inoshiro) Honda, who

DIRECTOR Ishirô Honda
PRODUCER Tomoyuki Tanaka
SCREENPLAY Ishirô Honda, Shigeru Kayama, Takeo Murata
DIRECTOR OF PHOTOGRAPHY Masao Tamei
EDITOR Yasunobo Taira
MUSIC Akira Ifukube
PRODUCTION DESIGN Saturo Chûko, Takeo Kita
MAIN CAST Takashi Shimura, Akira Takarada, Momoko Kôchi, Akihiko Hirata, Sachio Sakai, Fuyuki Murakami, Toranosuke Ogawa, Ren Yamamoto, Kan Hayashi
PRODUCTION COMPANY Toho Film (Eiga)

began and ended his career as an assistant director for Akira Kurosawa, in between found his niche in science fiction television shows (featuring superheroes Ultraman and Mirrorman) and movies featuring special effects (*tokusatsu eiga*), such as *The Mysterians* (1957), *The H-Man* (1958), and *Battle in Outer Space* (1959). In all his giant monster movies, a number of which also featured the work of special effects director Eiji Tsuburaya, such as *Rodan* (1956), *Varan the Unbelievable* (1958), *Mothra* (1961), and the *Gojira* sequels *King Kong vs. Godzilla* (1962), *Mothra vs. Godzilla* (1964), *Destroy All Monsters* (1968), *All Monsters Attack* (1969), *Terror of Mechagodzilla* (1975) and *Ghidorah, Monster of Monsters* (1964), which began Godzilla's evolution from villain to hero, Honda presented elaborate scenes of destruction that were at once campy and compelling.

Gojira replays the horrors of nuclear war for the only country to experience atomic attack. It begins with an assault on a Japanese fishing boat, a scene inspired by an actual event a few months before the making of the film involving a fishing ship caught in an American nuclear test of a hydrogen bomb on Bikini Atoll. As authorities in *Gojira* soon discover, the creature is radioactive, leaving traces of radiation in its wake and survivors of its rampages suffering from radiation burns, playing on contemporary fears of nuclear fallout and contamination of fish stocks. After Godzilla attacks an island village, archeologist Kyohei Yamane – played with appropriate *gravitas* by Takashi Shimura, who appeared in many of Kurosawa's greatest films, including *Rashomon* (1950) and *Seven Samurai* (1954) – is sent to investigate, and witnesses another attack. At first Yamane alone wants to keep the creature alive to study, but when Godzilla levels Tokyo, he agrees to lead the expedition that attempts to kill it with a secret weapon, an 'oxygen destroyer' invented by Yamane's colleague,

Daisuke Serizawa (Hirata), that drains surrounding water of oxygen and boils away the tissue of living creatures, leaving only the skeleton.

Godzilla's attack on Tokyo, an extended sequence of mass destruction involving a clever mix of model work, stop motion, matte shots and an actor (stuntman Haruo Nakajima, who played the creature in eleven of the sequels) in a latex monster suit, turns the city into a blazing inferno generated by the creature's atomic breath that cannot help but recall the destruction wrought on Hiroshima and Nagasaki less than a decade before. In the climax, Serizawa's device works, but after triggering it underwater near Godzilla, Serizawa sends his fellow diver and rival for Yamane's daughter Emiko (Kôchi), salvage boat captain Hideto Ogata (Takarada), back to the surface before cutting his own air hose, thus ensuring that no one else will ever learn the secret of his terrifying discovery. Godzilla rises to the surface in its death throes before turning into a skeleton and sinking to the bottom of the ocean. In the final shots, strikingly similar to the end of *Them!**, also released in 1954, humanity's apparent victory is qualified as Yamane wonders whether the continued testing of nuclear weapons will unleash further mutated monsters upon the world.

For its North American release two years later, *Gojira* was cut to 80 minutes and 20 minutes of new footage was added, eliminating the romantic subplot and including actor Raymond Burr as American journalist Steve Martin, whose function is to explain much of the action in English to avoid the use of subtitles, which would limit the film's appeal for American audiences. Through judicious editing, camera placement and the use of doubles, Burr's Martin seemed to interact with the original Japanese cast. Retitled *Godzilla, King of the Monsters!*, its surprising box-office success in North America led this version also to be screened in Japanese cinemas.

The Host
South Korea, 2006 – 119 mins
Joon-ho Bong

The third film by director Joon-ho Bong, *The Host* was until 2012 the highest grossing South Korean film, breaking several domestic attendance records. The high quality special effects were done in part by New Zealand's Weta Workshop, which came to prominence with Peter Jackson's *Lord of the Rings* trilogy (2001–3) and was also involved in such other films as *Avatar** and *District 9** (both 2009). Ostensibly a monster movie, *The Host* is at once serious political commentary and genial comedy.

The film begins by immediately addressing the United States' military presence in Korea, as an American military pathologist violates procedure by ordering a hesitant Korean assistant to dump hundreds of bottles of formaldehyde down the drain. The drain leads into the Han River, which in turn flows through Seoul and is one of the country's major waterways. In the next scene, two fishermen wading in the river spot a strange little creature that we are not shown, but it swims away. The conventional narrative trajectory of the monster movie suggests that there will follow further sightings of the creature that authorities will refuse to believe or have yet to verify, as in, for example, *The Beast from 20,000 Fathoms** (1953) and *Gojira** (1954). Instead, the film quickly and surprisingly launches into an extended mass attack in broad daylight by the elephant-sized amphibious creature, even while integrating the necessary exposition about the various members of the Park family, who run a concession stand along the Han.

Hie-bong Park (Hie-bong Byeon) works the snack bar with one of his sons, Gang-du (Kang-ho Song), an apparently dull-witted slacker who also is a single parent with a daughter, Hyun-seo (Ah-sung Ko). Also in the family are Gang-du's brother, Nam-il (Hae-il Park), an alcoholic former political activist, and his sister, national archery medalist Nam-joo (Doo-na Bae). When the monster attacks, causing considerable death and destruction, this dysfunctional family of misfits learns to come together in an attempt to rescue Hyun-seo. They must also overcome the bureaucratic obstacles and outright hostility of the government, which deliberately establishes a false cover story about a virus and quarantines everyone who has come in contact with the creature, including Gang-du, whom no one believes when he says he has received a cell phone call from his daughter. Before her phone's battery dies, Hyun-seo says she is trapped in the creature's lair – reminiscent of the children held in the Los Angeles sewers by the giant ants in *Them!** (1954) – which the Parks deduce is one of the underground sewers along the river. The family escapes the government's containment, and after a search, they confront the creature, killing it in a battle in which each of them contributes to its defeat, although Hie-bong is also killed.

While the South Korean government is seen in the film as inefficient and indifferent, the American military is depicted as deliberately irresponsible in polluting the river in the first place and then duplicitous in promulgating its cover story. With the assistance of the US, the Korean government deploys 'Agent Yellow' (an obvious reference to the toxin Agent Orange, widely used by the US military during the Vietnam War) in

DIRECTOR Joon-ho Bong
PRODUCER Yong-bae Choi, Neun-yeong Joh
SCREENPLAY Chul-hyun Baek, Joon-ho Bong, Won-jun Ha
DIRECTOR OF PHOTOGRAPHY Hyung-ku Kim
EDITOR Sun-min Kim
MUSIC Byung-woo Lee
PRODUCTION DESIGN Seong-hei Ryu
MAIN CAST Kang-ho Song, Hie-bong Byeon, Hae-il Park, Doo-na Bae, Ah-sung Ko, David Joseph Anselmo, Martin E. Cayce, Cristen Cho, Brian Lee, Clinton Morgan, Dal-su Oh
PRODUCTION COMPANY Chungeorahm Film, Showbox/ Mediaplex, Happinet Corporation

a failed attempt to kill the monster, despite the vocal protests of students. In the coda, the film manages one final satiric thrust at both Americans and Koreans as Gang-du is shown running the snack shop and taking care of Se-joo, a little boy also dumped into the monster's sewer lair who survived while Hyun-seo died. As they eat their dinner surrounded by shelves of brand-name snacks, the television behind them broadcasts a press conference from Washington where government officials are explaining away the recent Korean Virus Crisis as merely 'misinformation' – at which point Gang-du turns it off because, as he says, nothing good is on.

I Am Legend
US, 2007 – 101 mins
Francis Lawrence

The apocalyptic first novel by Richard Matheson, who also wrote the novels on which the films *The Incredible Shrinking Man** (1957) and *Stir of Echoes* (1999) were based, *I Am Legend* has been filmed three times. The first adaptation, *The Last Man on Earth* (1964), starred Vincent Price, and the second, *The Omega Man* (1971), Charlton Heston. Each of the three versions takes some liberties with the novel, although in different ways. Like Steven Spielberg's version of *War of the Worlds* (2005), *I Am Legend* relocates the setting (in this case, from Los Angeles) to New York City and provides a post-9/11 take on Matheson's paradigmatic story of a world destroyed by a plague that has either killed everyone or turned them into vampires, and the efforts of the sole remaining man to survive. Robert Neville (Smith) refers to New York as 'Ground Zero' of the zombie virus, and the vampires, like nightmarish incarnations of terrorists, are relentless in their destruction of Western civilisation.

Lt. Col. Robert Neville was a military virologist working to find an antidote for the plague, which originated as a miracle cure for cancer but then mutated. Most of the world's population was killed by the virus, governments desperately trying to contain it as it spread. Those turned into vampiristic beings prowled by night, feeding on the few who were immune, and hid during the day, the time when Neville, now two years after the plague hit, is able to move about to gather supplies. At night, Neville hides in his lower Manhattan apartment and laboratory, waiting for sunrise. After trapping one of the creatures for experimentation, he is similarly caught by them, and while he manages to escape, his German Shepherd is bitten and infected. In an emotional scene that has its source in Matheson's novel, Neville is forced to kill the dog, his faithful and only companion. Overcome with anger and grief, Neville rashly attacks a group of the vampires on a pier and is almost killed when he is rescued by a woman, Anna (Braga), and a boy, Ethan (Tahan), who have come to the place indicated by Neville in his daily radio broadcasts. Back in his home, they explain that they are headed for a survivors' camp in Vermont, which God has revealed to her in a vision but which the rational scientist Neville refuses to believe exists.

Before Anna and Ethan can leave, however, they are besieged by the vampires, who have followed them back. Retreating into the basement lab, they discover that Neville's last experimental serum has worked on his test subject, turning her back to normal. Neville takes a vial of her blood and, seeing that they are about to be overcome by the vampires, entrusts the cure to Anna before sacrificing himself so that the woman and boy can escape. In the final scene, which has no counterpart in either Matheson's novel or the first two film versions (all of which end with Neville's death and the ascendency of the mutated humans), Anna and Ethan come upon the guarded gateway to the survivors' enclave. In a concluding voiceover, Anna explains that Neville became legendary for finding the cure – whereas in the novel Neville ironically has become legendary as the last human to die in the now dominant society of mutants.

DIRECTOR Francis Lawrence
PRODUCER Akiva Goldsman, David Heyman, James Lassiter
SCREENPLAY Mark Protosevich and Akiva Goldsman, based on the 1954 novel by Richard Matheson
DIRECTOR OF PHOTOGRAPHY Andrew Lesnie
EDITOR Wayne Wahrman
MUSIC James Newton Howard
PRODUCTION DESIGN Naomi Shohan
MAIN CAST Will Smith, Alice Braga, Charles Tahan, Salli Richardson-Whitfield, Willow Smith
PRODUCTION COMPANY Warner Bros., Village Roadshow Pictures, Weed Road Pictures

Setting several box-office records upon its release and one of the year's top grossing films, *I Am Legend* provided a relatively comforting vision of the apocalypse with its upbeat ending and the reassuring notion that even black Americans would sacrifice themselves in the national interest. Unlike such post-apocalyptic movies as *The World, the Flesh and the Devil* (1959) and *The Quiet Earth** (1985), racial difference is not an issue when Neville meets Anna. Indeed, so popular was *I Am Legend* that it generated a comic book tie-in, *I Am Legend: Awakening*, which involved the collaboration of science fiction author Orson Scott Card, and an online multiplayer game, *I Am Legend: Survival*, in the appositely named virtual world of *Second Life*.

The Incredible Shrinking Man
US, 1957 – 81 mins
Jack Arnold

From its pre-credits image of a human figure shrinking away as a mushroom cloud ominously expands, *The Incredible Shrinking Man* pursues its premise with inexorable logic, touching on timely Cold War fears as well as deeper anxieties precipitated by dramatic postwar shifts in gender dynamics. The screenplay was the first for Richard Matheson, whose extensive credits also include the novels upon which the films *Stir of Echoes* (1999), *What Dreams May Come* (1998) and *I Am Legend** (2007) were based. The film initiated a brief cycle of science fiction movies exploiting the visual possibilities of altered scale including *The Amazing Colossal Man* (1957) and *Attack of the 50 Foot Woman* (1958). The latter addresses similar gender issues as *The Incredible Shrinking Man*, and later was the basis for a broadly comic feminist remake, *The Incredible Shrinking Woman* (1981), starring Lily Tomlin as a harried housewife who shrinks as a result of exposure to a combination of common household products. Matheson himself wrote a sequel, *Fantastic Little Girl*, in which the protagonist's wife follows him into a microscopic world, which was published in the 2006 collection, *Unrealised Dreams*. Although *The Incredible Shrinking Man* leaves out a number of the novel's more explicit scenes of sexual tension, including encounters with a drunken paedophile and a babysitter, it is clearly about the contemporary crisis of masculine identity and is, accordingly, thick with images of impotence and emasculation.

An apparently healthy and virile American male, Scott Carey (Williams) is vacationing on a boat off the California coast with his wife Louise (Stuart) when he is exposed to a strange cloud, later determined to be radioactive, while she is below getting drinks. Six months later, he notices that his clothes are too big and that he is losing weight. He begins to suspect that he is actually getting smaller, and after his initially sceptical physician finally concurs, he is subjected to a battery of state-of-the-art medical tests, learning that exposure to the radioactive mist interacting with common pesticides caused his cells to shrink, reducing all his organs proportionately. As he shrinks, he is forced to give up his job and, feeling humiliated, to sell his story to the tabloids for the money.

When he shrinks to approximately three feet (93 cm), or roughly half his original height, an antidote is found, but it only halts his shrinking temporarily. He begins to accept his fate after befriending a female midget whom he meets at a circus, but then he begins to shrink again, becoming so tiny that he lives in a doll's house, his wife towering above him. Soon he is so small that his wife cannot hear his calls for help when she returns home from her errands and, seeing him gone, presumes that the cat ate him, although it has only chased him into the basement. In a thrilling scene combining microscopic photography and matte effects, Carey, alone in the cellar and fearing for his survival, battles a spider for a morsel of cheese left as bait in a mousetrap.

After defeating the spider, the tiny hero slips through the mesh of a window screen and, no longer

DIRECTOR Jack Arnold
PRODUCER Albert Zugsmith
SCREENPLAY Richard Matheson, based on his novel *The Shrinking Man* (1956)
DIRECTOR OF PHOTOGRAPHY Ellis W. Carter
EDITOR Albrecht Joseph
MUSIC Irving Gertz, Earl E. Lawrence, Hans. J. Salter, Herman Stein
ART DIRECTOR Robert Clatworthy, Alexander Golitzen
MAIN CAST Grant Williams, Randy Stuart, April Kent, Paul Langton, Raymond Bailey, William Schallert, Frank J. Scannell, Billy Curtis
PRODUCTION COMPANY Universal International Pictures

shrinking in fear from his plight, prepares to dwindle to subatomic size and merge with the universe, embracing the idea that 'To God there is no zero.' Not in the book, this closing soliloquy was added to the script by director Jack Arnold. Arnold, whose early work in television included four episodes of the pioneering *Science Fiction Theatre* (1955), was also responsible for several other noteworthy science fiction films of the period, including *It Came from Outer Space* (1953), *The Creature from the Black Lagoon* (1954), *Revenge of the Creature* (1955) and *Tarantula* (1955), and here he depicts the transformation of Carey's world from domestic and comfortable to unfamiliar and threatening with unassuming skill. Toward the end of his career Arnold returned to television, directing many episodes of *Gilligan's Island* (1964–6), *The Brady Bunch* (1970–4) and *The Love Boat* (1977–84), each in its own way every bit as fantastical as his science fiction films.

Invaders from Mars
US, 1953 – 78 mins
William Cameron Menzies

Along with Jack Arnold's *It Came from Outer Space* (1953) and Don Siegel's *Invasion of the Body Snatchers** (1956), *Invaders from Mars* is one of the best alien takeover films of the 1950s. Unique among them, *Invaders from Mars* adopts the perspective of its young protagonist, casting Cold War anxieties about foreign subversion as the fear of a child, metaphorically associating America with youth and innocence and the Martians as indistinguishable puppets of a dictatorial brain.

The plot involves a boy, David (Hunt), whom no one will believe when he tries to warn people about an alien invasion. From his bedroom window one night, David witnesses a flying saucer land in the sand pit adjacent to his home. He tells his parents, and although they refuse to believe him, his father (Erickson) goes off to inspect the sand pit. He returns acting strangely distant and wooden, and then the same thing happens to his mother (Brooke). As we discover later, his parents have been sucked underground by the Martian invader (there is, in fact, only one) and his android servants, programmed through needles implanted in their necks and attached to the base of their brains, and then returned to the surface to carry out the alien's scheme to sabotage the US's nascent space programme. Other authorities around David, including teachers and policemen, suffer the same fate. The boy finally manages to convince the authorities of the truth of his story, and the nearby army base is alerted and mobilised. The military blasts its way into the alien spacecraft, and the Martian and his android slaves are forced to retreat. As the ship is taking off, the army blows it up and everyone who had been programmed by the alien wakes to normal consciousness.

The Martian's sabotage plan, relying on underground burrowing, reflects contemporary anxieties about Communist subversion – in this case, literally in the nation's 'own backyard' – that informs most of the films in the decade's alien invasion cycle. Cold War paranoia is clear in the explanation by the astronomer, Dr. Kelston (Franz), of the importance of space exploration: 'If anybody dared attack us, we could push a few buttons and destroy them in a matter of minutes'. David's awakening from innocent trust in patriarchal authority, representing America at the dawn of the new nuclear age and Cold War politics, is effectively depicted in the film's distinctively stylised *mise en scène*. For his work on *Gone with the Wind* (1939), producer David O. Selznick created the credit 'production designer' for *Invaders'* director, William Cameron Menzies, whose credits also include the equally impressive *Things to Come** (1936). In *Invaders*, which Menzies designed as well as directed, the memorable sets, such as the radically foreshortened police station, effectively capture David's increasing feeling of entrapment as he realises that the Chief of Police has been taken over, as well as conveying the Dalí-like distortion of a feverish dream.

The film's coda leaves the narrative as open-ended as that of the more famous *Invasion of the Body Snatchers*. As the Martian spaceship blows up, the film cuts to David starting awake in his bed in the middle of the night. As his parents try to comfort him, we realise that the entire film to this point has in fact been

DIRECTOR William Cameron Menzies
PRODUCER Edward L. Alperson
SCREENPLAY Richard Blake
DIRECTOR OF PHOTOGRAPHY John F. Seitz
EDITOR Thom Noble
MUSIC Raoul Kraushaar, Mort Glickman
PRODUCTION DESIGN William Cameron Menzies
MAIN CAST Helena Carter, Arthur Franz, Jimmy Hunt, Leif Erickson, Hillary Brooke, Morris Ankrum, Max Wagner, Milburn Stone
PRODUCTION COMPANY National Pictures

the boy's nightmare. After his parents calm his fears and he tries to fall back asleep, David sees flashing lights and goes to his window, where he watches a flying saucer landing in the sand pit, just as he had in the film's opening scene.

Although the studio forced the inclusion of stock footage of the US Army, somewhat harming the film's pace, *Invaders from Mars* nevertheless retains the surreal power of a nightmare thanks to Menzies's treatment. Tobe Hooper's campy 1986 remake, in which the film's chilling, tentacled Martian is to be found sitting among the bric-a-brac stored in the basement of Menzies High School, contains none of the evocative power of the original.

Invasion of the Body Snatchers
US, 1956 – 80 mins
Don Siegel

With its paranoid story of emotionless alien duplicates replacing everyday folk while they sleep, *Invasion of the Body Snatchers* deftly combines elements of science fiction and horror in a tightly woven narrative that tapped into a host of postwar anxieties. The film's science fiction premise of alien invasion in vegetable form driven only to survive – in this case, extraterrestrial seed pods that have drifted to Earth by chance – recalls the malign 'super-carrot' of *The Thing from Another World** (1951) earlier in the decade and offers a nightmarish vision of the era's fears involving both Communism and conformity, subversion of American individualism from both without and within. Long considered a cult favourite, the film's central metaphor of alien duplication while asleep has proven sufficiently rich to inspire three other versions, each with its own distinct take and reflective of its era: *Invasion of the Body Snatchers* (Philip Kaufman, 1978), *Body Snatchers* (Abel Ferrara, 1993), and *The Invasion* (Oliver Hirschbiegel, 2007).

The film's narrative, which takes place over a mere three days, is told in flashback to a psychiatrist in a hospital emergency room by a frantic and dishevelled doctor, Miles Bennell (McCarthy), who explains that when he returned home from a medical conference, he stumbled upon an incredible conspiracy of alien seed pods duplicating everyone in his small California town and already spreading more pods everywhere. At the same time, Miles was renewing his relationship with an old flame, the recently divorced Becky Driscoll (Wynter). Along with their friends Jack (Donovan) and Teddy Belicec (Jones), who are later taken over by the pods, they discover what is happening and attempt to warn the outside world.

Soon Miles and Becky find themselves the only humans left in the town, when they are trapped in his office by the pod people, who lock them in until they fall asleep and can be taken over. The couple express their newly rekindled love, giving them the determination to overcome their pod captors and escape. But as they are leaving town they are discovered when Becky inadvertently betrays emotion and are then pursued by all of the town's podfolk into the surrounding hills. Miles and Becky hide in an abandoned mineshaft, but she falls asleep, becomes a pod person, and betrays their whereabouts to the townsfolk, who chase Miles to the interstate, where he tries unsuccessfully to warn unheeding motorists about the threat of the pods. A dissolve brings us back to the final scene, in the hospital emergency room, where, just as Miles is about to be committed for psychiatric observation, a truck driver from the same town injured in a collision is brought in by ambulance after having been pulled out from under a pile of strange looking pods. The psychiatrist (Whit Bissell) realises the truth and telephones for the authorities to mobilise.

Stalwart action director Don Siegel uncharacteristically enhances Daniel Mainwaring's tight script with the claustrophobic and doom-laden imagery of film noir, infusing middle-class Americana with menace and tilting the film towards horror. The romantic plot that parallels the alien invasion narrative suggests, as is also true of many noirs, the developing crisis of masculinity in postwar American culture when patriarchal

DIRECTOR Don Siegel
PRODUCER Walter Wanger
SCREENPLAY Daniel Mainwaring, based on the serialised novel in *Collier's* (1954) by Jack Finney
DIRECTOR OF PHOTOGRAPHY Ellsworth Fredericks
EDITOR Robert S. Eisen
MUSIC Carmen Dragon
PRODUCTION DESIGN Edward Haworth
MAIN CAST Kevin McCarthy, Dana Wynter, King Donovan, Carolyn Jones, Larry Gates, Jean Willes, Ralph Dumke, Virginia Christine, Tom Fadden
PRODUCTION COMPANY Allied Artists

authority was challenged by a series of significant social changes. Siegel had wanted to end the film with the penultimate scene, as Miles frantically attempts to stop motorists on the highway, warning them of the danger – and shouting directly into the camera that 'You're next!' – but Allied Artists imposed the narrative frame because the studio was nervous about the film's downbeat message and abrupt, unresolved ending. Nevertheless, Siegel may have had the last laugh, for the ending resists comfortable narrative closure, remaining disturbingly ambiguous. The two policemen to which the psychiatrist gives his orders seem uncomfortably like pod people already and a successful containment of the threat is very much in doubt. Neither the ending as we have it nor Siegel's preferred ending is as upbeat as that of Jack Finney's source novel, in which Miles sets fire to a field of pods, which then wilfully retreat skywards, abandoning Earth.

The Invisible Man
US, 1933 – 71 mins
James Whale

The first of H. G. Wells's books to be made as a feature film, *The Invisible Man* stars Claude Rains in his first American role ('appearance' is not quite the right word here) as Dr. Jack Griffin, the transparent man of the title, whom we never actually see until the very last shot, when Griffin returns to visibility in death. Nevertheless, Rains's declamatory vocal style perfectly suits the character of Griffin, who has grown mad with power as a side-effect of the invisibility chemical, 'monocane', which he has injected. The adept adaptation was co-scripted by R. C. Sherriff, who had written the play *Journey's End* (1930) and also worked on the film version, director James Whale's debut, and Philip Wylie, who in the same decade also wrote the novels *Gladiator* (1930, about a genetically engineered superhero that was the inspiration for the comic book character of Superman); *When Worlds Collide* (1933), upon which George Pal's 1951 film of the same name* is based; and, most interestingly, *The Murderer Invisible* (1931), about a wronged scientist who uses invisibility for revenge two years before *The Invisible Man*.

The film adheres to the broad strokes of the novel's plot, although Rains's Griffin is more insane than Wells's scientist. An odd stranger, whom we later learn is Griffin, shows up at a pub in Iping, West Sussex, swathed in bandages and dark glasses, taking a room and giving orders that he is not to be disturbed. When the innkeeper tries to force him out, he becomes violent and even attacks a policeman. Griffin removes his clothes and bandages, revealing his invisibility, and flees to the home of his colleague, Dr. Kemp (Harrigan), forcing him to help as he plots world domination. Kemp secretly telephones Griffin's avuncular mentor, Dr. Cranley (Travers), and the police for assistance. Cranley arrives with his daughter Flora (Stuart), with whom Griffin had a romantic relationship. She begins to calm him, but when the police appear, Griffin promises to kill Kemp the next night at 10pm, and then escapes through the window, after which he terrorises the locals and derails a train, killing many people. Griffin secretly follows Kemp as he tries to flee with the aid of the police and kills him by tying him in his car and sending it over a cliff. As a snowstorm begins, Griffin seeks shelter in a barn but is detected by its owner, who informs the police. They flush Griffin into the open by burning the barn, and he is fatally shot when his footprints in the snow become visible. Dying, he admits to Flora the conventional moral of classic horror tales, that he has taken science to places man should not go.

John P. Fulton's excellent special effects, making use of wires, mattes, and other optical effects, are indulged in with a delight that harkens back to the cinematic trickery of Georges Méliès (see *Le Voyage dans la lune**). Yet at the same time as the film provides the chills already expected of Universal horror movies, Whale adds his distinctively wry sense of humour, particularly in his depiction of the English villagers, an element of his horror films already apparent in *Frankenstein** (1931), and which also complements Wells's satiric jabs at the English public in the novel. The film's popularity spawned a number of loose sequels, including *The Invisible Man Returns* (1940), starring Vincent Price, and, inevitably, *Abbott and Costello Meet*

DIRECTOR James Whale
PRODUCER Carl Laemmle, Jr
SCREENPLAY R.C. Sherriff, based on the 1897 novel by H.G. Wells
DIRECTOR OF PHOTOGRAPHY Arthur Edeson
EDITOR Ted Kent
MUSIC Heinz Roemheld
ART DIRECTOR Charles D. Hall
MAIN CAST Claude Rains, Gloria Stuart, William Harrigan, Henry Travers, Una O'Connor, E.E. Clive, Dwight Frye, Forrester Harvey, Holmes Herbert, Dudley Digges, Merle Tottenham
PRODUCTION COMPANY Universal Pictures

the Invisible Man (1951), as well as such spinoffs as *The Invisible Woman* (1940), a screwball comedy; *Invisible Agent* (1942), starring Jon Hall as a government agent who uses his invisibility to fight Nazis; *The Invisible Man's Revenge* (1944), also starring Hall but which has no relation to *Invisible Agent*; John Carpenter's disappointing *Memoirs of an Invisible Man* (1992); and Paul Verhoeven's *Hollow Man* (2000), based on the novel by Dan Simmons. A number of television programmes have also been made based on the premise of invisibility, including British series for ITV (1958) and the BBC (1984) and American series for NBC (1975) and the Sci-Fi Channel (2000–02), all with the title *The Invisible Man*.

Island of Lost Souls
US, 1932 – 70 mins
Erle C. Kenton

Based on the second of Wells's 'scientific romances', *The Island of Doctor Moreau*, published the year after *The Time Machine* (1895), *Island of Lost Souls* is the first, and the best, of three film versions. With a plot about an overreaching scientist (Laughton) who attempts to convert animals into people, it avoids, on the one hand, the lurid exploitation emphasis of the second version, *The Island of Dr. Moreau*, directed by Don Taylor in 1977 and, on the other, the surreally idiosyncratic performance of Marlon Brando in the 1996 film of the same name directed by John Frankenheimer. Director Kenton, who began his career as a Keystone Kop and directing comedy shorts for Mack Sennett, then specialised in both comedies (including several Abbott and Costello pictures) and horror, with several late entries in the Universal horror cycle, *The Ghost of Frankenstein* (1942), *House of Frankenstein* (1944) and *House of Dracula* (1945), before finishing his career working in television, achieved his best work in the tidy 70-minute *Island of Lost Souls*. The film takes some liberties with the plot of the novel, introducing a romantic subplot and the character of the panther woman, but captures the mood of menace that informs Wells' prose.

Seaman Edward Parker (Arlen) survives the wreck of his ship in the Pacific, and is rescued by a passing freighter carrying Montgomery (Hohl) and a cargo of wild animals to the uncharted island owned by Dr. Moreau. Stuck on the island, Parker is introduced by Moreau to the panther-woman, Lota, to see if she is capable of being a 'complete woman'. Parker succumbs briefly to her animal eroticism before realising that she is one of the hybrid creatures Moreau has created in his lab, the 'house of pain', in his quest to speed the evolutionary process. Paramount emphasised this aspect of the film by sponsoring a nationwide talent search for the ideal panther woman. The winner, Kathleen Burke, worked in a Chicago dental office before appearing as Lota and subsequently enjoyed a modestly successful movie career in the 1930s.

In the dense jungle surrounding Moreau's compound, Parker visits the village of the Beast-Men where he hears the Sayer of the Law (Lugosi) recite the prohibition (with the famous refrain 'Are we not men?') against eating meat and spilling blood. When Moreau has Ouran, the orangutan-man, in clear violation of the Law, kill the captain of the rescue ship that has also brought Parker's fiancée Ruth to the island, the beast-men grow restive, storm the compound and with poetic justice kill Moreau in the house of pain. The scene of the beast-men attacking, with the fur-covered face of Lugosi in leering close-up, is as terrifying as the climactic revenge by the circus folk in Tod Browning's *Freaks*, released earlier the same year by MGM. As the others escape, Lota sacrifices herself in order to kill the pursuing Ouran, a noble gesture that proves her to be the human being that she so desperately wants to be.

Wells's novel was published at a time when debates about animal vivisection were taking place in Britain. More broadly, though, the story speaks eloquently to both the timeless scientific critique of *Frankenstein** and the psychological theme of *Dr. Jekyll and Mr. Hyde*. Wells may have disapproved of the sexual sadism in

DIRECTOR Erle C. Kenton
SCREENPLAY Waldemar Young, Philip Wylie, based on the 1896 novel by H.G. Wells
DIRECTOR OF PHOTOGRAPHY Karl Struss
MUSIC Arthur Johnston, Sigmund Krumgold
ART DIRECTOR Hans Dreier
MAIN CAST Charles Laughton, Richard Arlen, Bela Lugosi, Leila Hyams, Kathleen Burke, Arthur Hohl, Stanley Fields, Tetsu Komai, Paul Hurst, Hans Steinke
PRODUCTION COMPANY Paramount Pictures

Laughton's portrayal of Moreau, but the actor's self-absorbed performance perfectly accords with Wells's mad vivesectionist, who comments that he has 'never troubled about the ethics of the matter'. In the film's last shot, as Parker, Ruth and Montgomery row away from the burning island, the latter says 'Don't look back'. But if *Island of Lost Souls* provides comfortable closure rather than the more troublingly ambiguous ending of the book, the film's magnificently moody camerawork, by the great German émigré cinematographer Karl Struss, nevertheless is rife with menacing shadows and bars that depict Moreau's imprisonment even as he seeks Godlike empowerment.

La Jetée (*The Jetty, The Pier*)
France, 1962 – 28 mins
Chris Marker

A time-travel story with a twist ending, *La Jetée* consists entirely – with one important exception – of still photographs (by Jean Chiabaud) with a voice-over narration (by Jean Négroni). Shot in black and white, with no special effects other than optical printing for fades and superimpositions, it established the international reputation of its director, French artist, writer and film-maker Chris Marker. It influenced such later films as Mamoru Oshii's *The Red Spectacles* (1987) and Terry Gilliam's *Twelve Monkeys* (1995), as well as other works of popular culture including David Bowie's 'Jump They Say' music video. In *La Jetée* the camera does not roam across the images, as in Ken Burns's documentaries, and the film has no dialogue aside from muttered snatches of German. Nevertheless, it manages to be thoroughly engrossing with the simplest of cinematic means.

The narrative begins in the future, after a nuclear world war, with the survivors living underground below a demolished Paris. A prisoner (Hanich), presumably an enemy during the war, is obsessed with vague childhood memories of an observation platform at Orly Airport and the confused images of a woman's face and a man's death there. Scientists are researching time travel, hoping to send people to different eras in order to get help in the present from the past and the future. The man is selected as a test subject to undergo the painful time travel experiments – depicted in the film simply as wearing a blindfold with wires attached and reclining in a hammock – because of the strength of his memories. After several failed attempts, the man succeeds in going back in time to before the war, where he meets the woman of his memory (Chatelain) and with whom he eventually develops a romantic bond.

The scientists next send the man into the future, where he meets with the advanced people of a massively rebuilt Paris, who give him a device with sufficient power to restart society in his own time. When he returns to his present, having accomplished his assignment, the man is going to be executed, but he is contacted by the people from the future, who are also able to travel through time, with an offer of escape into the future to live with them. Instead, he asks to be returned to the time of his childhood, hoping to find the woman again. His request is granted, and he finds himself looking for her again on the airport platform. However, one of his captors from his own era has followed him, intervenes before he can join the woman, and assassinates him. As he dies, he comes to understand that 'this haunted moment he had been granted to see as a child was the moment of his own death', and that 'there was no way out of time'.

La Jetée's unorthodox style makes it an experimental film as much as it is a science fiction movie. As in structural film, its use of still images forces the viewer to attend to the basic building blocks of cinema, a series of stills. Further, in the context of all these photographs, the one moving image of the woman sleeping and then suddenly waking up and blinking at the camera assumes considerable power because of its sheer motion. Marker, who also was a professional travel photographer, was part of the Left Bank group of the French New Wave, which also included Agnès Varda and Alain Resnais, for whom he had worked as assistant

DIRECTOR Chris Marker
PRODUCER Anatole Dauman
SCREENPLAY Chris Marker
DIRECTOR OF PHOTOGRAPHY Jean Chiabaut, Chris Marker
EDITOR Jean Ravel
MUSIC Trevor Duncan
MAIN CAST Jean Négroni, Hélène Chatelain, Davos Hanich, Jacques Ledoux, André Henrich, Jacques Branchu, Pierre Joffroy, Étienne Becker, Philbert von Lifchitz, Janine Klein, William Klein
PRODUCTION COMPANY Argos Films

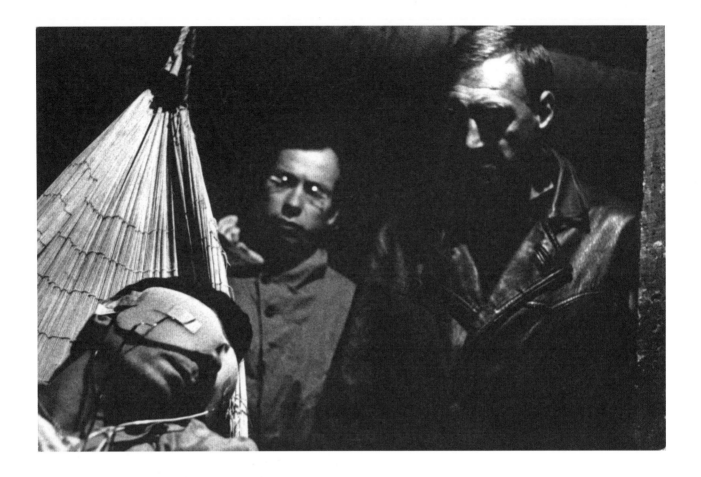

director on *Nuit et brouillard* (*Night and Fog*, 1955) – another time travel film of sorts. Like other New Wave film makers Jean-Luc Godard (*Alphaville** [1965]) and François Truffaut (*Fahrenheit 451** [1966]), Marker was an early contributor to *Cahiers du cinéma*, and his films, like theirs, tended towards meditations about the medium – although Marker has claimed that there is just one short moving shot in *La Jetée* because he was able to borrow a movie camera for only one afternoon.

Jurassic Park
US, 1993 – 127 mins
Steven Spielberg

Universal agreed to allow director Steven Spielberg (*Close Encounters of the Third Kind** [1977], *Minority Report* [2002], *War of the Worlds* [2005], *A.I.: Artificial Intelligence* [2001]) to make *Schindler's List* (1993), a commercially unpromising project about the Holocaust, if he made *Jurassic Park* first. A milestone in computer-generated imagery, *Jurassic Park* was the most commercially successful film ever released (surpassing Spielberg's own *E.T.: The Extra-Terrestrial** [1982] and in turn overtaken by James Cameron's *Avatar** [2009] almost two decades later). It won three technical Academy Awards, including Best Visual Effects, convincingly presenting a range of dinosaurs, among them Tyrannosaurs, Triceratops, Brachiosaurs and Velociraptors, through a combination of techniques including animatronic models designed by Stan Winston.

The screenplay was written by science fiction writer Michael Crichton, based on his own novel. In *Jurassic Park* Crichton, who would go on to write and direct *Coma* (1978) and *Looker* (1981), among others, recycled the basic plot of his first film, *Westworld** (1973), about a future amusement park that becomes deadly. In both cases the plot involves an engineered environment that turns against a few people isolated and trapped within it. In *Jurassic Park* it is an island off the Pacific Coast of Central America, where eccentric billionaire John Hammond (Attenborough) has overseen the creation of a theme park of live dinosaurs cloned from DNA in mosquitoes preserved in amber. When Jurassic Park's board of directors demands a safety inspection after a worker is attacked, mathematician Dr. Ian Malcolm (Goldblum), paleontologist Dr. Alan Grant (Neill) and his partner, botanist Dr. Ellie Sattler (Dern), are invited to the island, along with Hammond's two visiting grandchildren. Hammond confidently sends all of them on the programmed ride through the island park in two automated cars.

Meanwhile, the park's chief computer programmer, Dennis Nedry (Knight), who is secretly working for a corporate rival, shuts down the security system in order to steal some dinosaur embryos, at the same time switching off the electrified fences that keep the animals enclosed. The group is first attacked by a Tyrannosaurus while in their vehicles, and after several further adventures with a variety of prehistoric creatures eliciting awe, admiration and alarm, the action culminates with Sattler fighting a velociraptor in the emergency bunker in order to reboot the Park's systems while Grant and the children struggle to flee from some raptors in the Visitors' Centre.

The film attempts to infuse what is essentially an action plot with some obligatory character development revolving around Grant, who initially dislikes children but then becomes a protective parent to Hammond's two grandchildren, saving their lives. This endorsement of the family is a frequent theme of Spielberg's, certainly, but *Jurassic Park* is primarily focused on spectacular action, Spielberg taking his audience on a nonstop thrill ride. It is no coincidence that the name of the Park and its logo *in* the film are

DIRECTOR Steven Spielberg
PRODUCER Kathleen Kennedy, Gerald R. Molen
SCREENPLAY Michael Crichton, David Koepp, based on the 1990 novel by Crichton
DIRECTOR OF PHOTOGRAPHY Dean Cundey
EDITOR Michael Kahn
MUSIC John Williams
PRODUCTION DESIGN Rick Carter
MAIN CAST Sam Neill, Laura Dern, Jeff Goldblum, Richard Attenborough, Martin Ferrero, Samuel L. Jackson, Wayne Knight, Bob Peck
PRODUCTION COMPANY Universal Studios, Amblin Entertainment

the same as that *of* the film, or that there are featured rides at Universal Studios in Hollywood and its theme park in Orlando, Florida built around the film.

Universal marketed the film heavily (with the tagline 'An Adventure 65 Million Years In the Making'), with numerous tie-ins involving dozens of companies and a wide array of products, including several video games, a line of toys, a series of comic books and a novelisation. The film generated two sequels, *The Lost World: Jurassic Park* (1997) and *Jurassic Park III* (2001) – the first reuniting Crichton and Spielberg, the second involving neither although Spielberg served as executive producer and several of the scenes in the film were taken from Crichton's two *Jurassic Park* novels. In *The Lost World*, a tyrannosaurus is brought back to civilisation with predictable results; when it escapes and tramples through San Diego, the creature chases a crowd of fleeing Japanese tourists, a comic homage to *Gojira** (1954) and the many *kaiju eiga* (giant monster movies) that it inspired.

Just Imagine
US, 1930 – 109 mins
David Butler

Made shortly after the advent of synchronised sound film, when musicals were a new and popular genre, a science fiction musical was, alas, inevitable. Unfortunately, *Just Imagine* is somewhat clunky as a musical and largely ludicrous as science fiction. Followed by the equally absurd *It's Great to be Alive* (1933), about a pilot who returns home to discover that he is the only remaining fertile man, today *Just Imagine* is mostly of interest as a period piece and curious generic hybrid like the science fiction musical serial, *The Phantom Empire* (1935), with singing cowboy Gene Autry.

In the wondrous world of 1980, fifty years in the future from when the film was made, science has given humanity such marvels as television phones, personal autogyro travel and food pills. Aeroplanes are dirigibles, and babies drop out of vending machines like sandwiches at the automat. The story begins as J-21 (Garrick) sets his gyro plane in hover mode to tell the lovely LN-18 (O'Sullivan), who is flying by, that the marriage tribunal has denied his application and that she will have to marry the pompous MT-3 (Thomson). His friend RT-42 (Albertson) takes him to see a group of scientists revive a man from 1930 who was struck by lightning. The man from the past, dubbed 'Single Zero' ('Single Oh') is played by El Brendel, a once-popular but now largely forgotten American vaudeville comedian whose persona was that of a Swedish immigrant and whose intelligence at times seems to match his numerical moniker. In an extended farcical scene, Single O gets drunk on highball pills while J-21 and LN-18 attempt a secret tryst unbeknownst to MT-3.

Later, the three men take a newly built rocket ship to Mars, J-21 hoping that this adventure will prove his worthiness to marry LN-18 and Single O hoping to score some synthetic rum. On Mars they are received with impressive pomp by the King and Queen, but during a reception in their honour they are attacked by their evil twins, which for some inexplicable reason every Martian has. In the end, the trio escapes and returns to Earth, where, after a comic hearing before the Tribunal, J-21 is granted permission to marry LN-18. The film ends with a corny sight gag, as Single O reunites with his son Axel, now an old man.

As in so many film musicals, in *Just Imagine* love eventually conquers all and the romantic leads unite in matrimony. The musical production numbers invariably stop the action rather than develop it, and the novelty tune 'Never Swat a Fly' is the only one of the songs, which were written by veteran songwriting team (and the film's producers and screenwriters) of Brown, DeSylva, and Henderson, that is at all familiar today, primarily because the Jim Kweskin Jug Band included it on one of their LPs during the folk revival of the mid-1960s. Yet despite the ludicrous nature of the story, the silly costumes and stilted musical numbers, *Just Imagine* features some noteworthy special effects to rival those in *Metropolis** (1927). Some of the film's images of the futuristic cityscape were reused later in Universal's *Flash Gordon** (1936) and *Buck Rogers* (1939) serials, and the astonishing long shot of writhing women on a giant Martian idol appeared behind the opening credits of the former. The electrical equipment that animates the creature in the famous creation

DIRECTOR David Butler
PRODUCER Lew Brown, Buddy DeSylva, Ray Henderson
SCREENPLAY Lew Brown, Buddy DeSylva, Ray Henderson
DIRECTOR OF PHOTOGRAPHY Ernest Palmer
EDITOR Irene Morra
MUSIC Hugo Friedhofer
MAIN CAST El Brendel, Maureen O'Sullivan, John Garrick, Marjorie White, Frank Albertson, Hobart Bosworth, Kenneth Thomson, Mischa Auer
PRODUCTION COMPANY Fox Film Corp.

scene in *Frankenstein** (1931) first appeared in *Just Imagine*. It was also one of the first films to demonstrate the effectiveness of large-scale rear-screen projection.

Although *Just Imagine* was not a box-office failure, it was expensive to produce and relied too heavily on the brief popularity of Brendel. Director David Butler would go on to a long career directing many musicals and comedies, including four with child star Shirley Temple, and episodes of several television series, amongst them dozens for the popular sitcom *Leave It to Beaver* (1957–63). By contrast, science fiction suffered in Hollywood, where big budgets were unavailable to the genre until two decades later.

Last Night
Canada/France, 1998 – 95 mins
Don McKellar

Beginning in 1989 with Bruce McDonald's *Roadkill*, which he wrote and acted in, Don McKellar has been a seemingly ubiquitous and intelligent presence in Canadian film and television. Among his many notable projects are his further collaborations with McDonald (*Highway 61* [1999], the cult television series *Twitch City* [1998, 2000]), performances in Atom Egoyan's *The Adjuster* (1991) and *Exotica* (1994), screenplays for François Girard's *Thirty Two Short Films About Glenn Gould* (1992) and *The Red Violin* (1998), in which McKellar also starred, as well as a role in David Cronenberg's *eXistenZ* (1999). McKellar's first feature as director, *Last Night* (1998), is another story about the end of the world, but it is more arthouse apocalypse than commercial catastrophe. Unlike, say, *When Worlds Collide** (1951), it contains no action heroics and spectacular special effects, but instead shows people struggling in their own ways to come to terms with the imminent end. McKellar would return to similar territory in the less successful *Blindness* (2008, based on José Saramago's 1995 novel and directed by Brazilian film-maker Fernando Meirelles), a more commercially compromised international co-production about a sudden plague of blindness that results in total social breakdown. In *Last Night*, which garnered numerous awards including the Prix de la Jeunesse at the Cannes Film Festival, the world ends with neither a whimper nor a bang but with unsatisfying ambiguity about human affairs until the very end.

The film is set at 6pm sometime in the near future on the night when the world is scheduled to end at midnight for a reason left unexplained, although people have known about it for at least two months. Perhaps the reason is an approaching comet or that the sun has turned supernova, as it is preternaturally bright outdoors throughout the evening, and the sun seems to grow more intense as midnight approaches. The story follows several intersecting characters in the city of Toronto, Canada, as they spend the evening in different ways, beginning with Patrick Wheeler (McKellar) arriving at his parents' house for a mock-Christmas last supper. During the dinner, whose guests include Patrick's sister, Jennifer (Polley), and her boyfriend, it becomes painfully clear that traditional familial tensions, although perhaps petty in context, nevertheless prevail. Depressed over the recent death of his wife, Patrick leaves, returning to his apartment where he intends to face death alone. Circumstances cause him to meet Sandra (Oh), who becomes stranded trying to get across the city to meet her husband to fulfill their suicide pact.

Over the course of the next six hours these and several other characters cross paths in the manner of multi-protagonist art films such as *The Player* (1992) and *Traffic* (2000) even as Patrick and Sandra begin to develop an emotional bond. Among them, Patrick's friend Craig (Rennie) has been immersed in sex in a methodical attempt to fulfill all his fantasy scenarios before he dies, and Duncan (Cronenberg), owner of a gas company, systematically calls all his customers with a message reassuring them that gas will be kept flowing until the very end.

DIRECTOR Don McKellar
PRODUCER Niv Fichman, Daniel Iron
SCREENPLAY Don McKellar
DIRECTOR OF PHOTOGRAPHY Douglas Koch
EDITOR Reginald Harkima
MUSIC Alexina Louie and Alex Pauk
PRODUCTION DESIGN John Dondertman
MAIN CAST Don McKellar, Sandra Oh, Roberta Maxwell, Robin Gammell, Sarah Polley, Trent McMullen, Charmion King, Jessica Booker, David Cronenberg, Geneviève Bujold, Tracy Wright, Callum Keith Rennie, Arsinée Khanjian
PRODUCTION COMPANY Rhombus Media, Telefilm Canada, Le Sept-Art

In the opening dinner scene, Patrick's father (Gammell) opines that the impending calamity means a test of civilised values, while crowds of people roam the streets partying *en masse* and committing random acts of violence. In the climax, the mild-mannered Patrick reluctantly agrees to oblige Sandra by committing double suicide with her in place of her husband. However, as midnight approaches, neither can pull the trigger of the gun that each is pointing at the other's temple, and they spontaneously both put down the pistols and embrace each other as the end comes. Is there comfort for the emotionally closed Patrick in establishing meaningful contact with another person, or is the fact that he can only do so at the moment of global extinction yet another cosmic joke confirming his cynicism? No cosy catastrophe, *Last Night* refuses to let us know with certainty if the human race passes Mr. Wheeler's test.

Liquid Sky
US, 1983 – 112 mins
Slava Tsukerman

An influential independent film made on a relatively small budget of $500,000, the strikingly original *Liquid Sky* uses the idea of alien-ness to comment on the alienation within the contemporary punk subculture. Upon its release it quickly became a cult film, much discussed by cinephiles. Seeming something like Andy Warhol meets *It Came from Outer Space* (1953), the film exploits the sexual androgyny that was celebrated in the media at the time, particularly in its casting of Anne Carlisle (who also published a novel based on the movie with the same name in 1987) in a dual role as male and female fashion models Margaret and Jimmy.

A small alien spacecraft about the size and shape of a frisbee lands on the penthouse apartment rooftop where Margaret lives, and, as we find out later, the tiny bodiless alien inside is monitoring the people in the apartment. The demimonde punk subculture in which the bisexual Margaret, once a wholesome young girl from Connecticut, builds her modelling career is a vicious world of drugs and sexual predation.

DIRECTOR Slava Tsukerman

PRODUCER Slava Tsukerman

SCREENPLAY Slava Tsukerman, Anne Carlisle, Nina V. Kerova

DIRECTOR OF PHOTOGRAPHY Yuri Neyman

EDITOR Sharon L. Ross, Slava Tsukerman

MUSIC Brenda I. Hutchinson, Clive Smith, Slava Tsukerman

PRODUCTION DESIGN Marina Levikova-Neyman

CAST Anne Carlisle, Paula E. Sheppard, Susan Doukas, Otto von Wernherr, Bob Brady, Elaine C. Grove, Jack Adalist

PRODUCTION COMPANY Z Films Inc.

The passive Margaret functions as a kind of New Wave *Candy*, a victimised naïf into whose body others pour their sexual desire. In the course of the film she is raped several times: by Vincent, the son of a television producer; by Paul, a frustrated writer looking to score drugs from her roommate, Adrian (Sheppard); by Owen, a former teacher; by Jimmy, when he is goaded by the crew of a photo shoot in her apartment; and by Adrian. As these people begin to die when having sex with her, with strange crystals protruding from their heads before their bodies disappear, the spaced-out Margaret apparently believes that it is the work of a god dwelling in the omnipresent Empire State Building rather than beings from outer space.

Margaret's story is intercut with that of the German scientist Johann Hoffman (Von Wernherr), who is aware of and has been studying the aliens for some time. Coming to New York, he begins observing those on Margaret's roof from the Empire State Building observation deck. When the building closes, Johann goes to the apartment building adjacent to Margaret's, where Sylvia (Doukas), who happens to be Jimmy's mother, lives. Hoping to seduce Johann, she allows him into her apartment, where he sets up his telescope to watch the events transpiring in Margaret's apartment. He explains his theory that the aliens, because they have no bodies, thrive on the endorphins produced by the brain during orgasm, which they somehow extract from their victims, killing them in the process. Concerned for Margaret's safety, Johann goes to her apartment and explains the situation to her, adding that she survived her sexual encounters because she never reached orgasm. When she sees that the alien spacecraft is beginning to depart, Margaret injects herself with heroin ('Liquid Sky' is slang for the drug), inducing an autoerotic frenzy so that the aliens will absorb her, which they do. Like the women who choose to leave Earth with aliens rather than remain in an oppressive masculinist culture in James Tiptree Jr's 1973 story 'The Women Men Don't See', Margaret concludes that the unknown is preferable to the intolerable.

The film presents these events in a deadpan manner, aided by an eerie synthesiser score, even as it features a bold use of colour and design, particularly in Margaret's punk fashions and phosphorescent makeup, which change with every scene. At one point Margaret observes that she is 'truly as androgynous as David Bowie himself' (and indeed, she bears a striking physical resemblance to the rock star). The reference to Bowie (star of *The Man Who Fell to Earth** [1976]) is particularly relevant because in this fallen world filled with self-absorbed people who spend their time taking drugs and voguing, played by nonprofessional actors who recite their lines in a remote manner, everyone seems as if they have fallen to Earth from somewhere far out there. The film presents a sense of otherness that the film-makers, Russian emigrés, surely felt when discovering the punk scene in the Big Apple.

Mad Max
Australia, 1979 – 88 mins
George Miller

While the Australian New Wave was finding a niche in the international art cinema circuit with such films as Peter Weir's *Picnic at Hanging Rock* (1975) and *The Last Wave* (1977) and Bruce Beresford's *The Getting of Wisdom* (1978) and *Breaker Morant* (1980), George Miller embraced genre cinema with *Mad Max* and its two sequels, *Mad Max 2: The Road Warrior* (1981) and *Mad Max Beyond Thunderdome* (1985). The trilogy is a strikingly original generic hybrid of Western, science fiction and motorcycle gang movie that grows increasingly conscious of its own mythology as it progresses. The first film's apocalyptic vision, perfectly located in the barren Australian landscape, combined with breathtaking action sequences involving car chases and crashes, along with imaginative costume design combining punk, S&M and genre fashions, made *Mad Max*, despite its initial limited release in the United States by American International, a solid cult favourite and established Mel Gibson as a major star.

Mad Max is set in the near future, when social structures have all but broken down and the law has at best only a dubious control over violence and anarchy. For the most part, the film uses the highway and the assorted customised vehicles that travel on it not only to play with the cultural obsession with cars, but it also works as a conceit for a collapsing civilisation on the road to self-destruction. Max is one of the 'Bronze', or what remains of the police force, patrolling the roads with an 'Interceptor', one of few remaining automobiles with a V-8 engine. The roads are populated with lawless groups who prowl in customised vehicles, patched together from parts left over from the days of manufacturing.

When Max heads out to avenge the death of his partner at the hands of one such gang, he sets in motion a spiral of violence that results in the murder of his wife and baby. It is their deaths that transform him into the hardened, obsessed seeker of vengeance of the title, and he mercilessly kills the remaining gang members, reserving the most horrific deaths for the most odious of them. While the narrative hardly rises above the clichés of Dirty Harry vigilante movies, film buff and director George Miller wisely omits virtually all background information, leaving the viewer to extrapolate the details of this ambiguous future world from the *mise en scène*. Clearly aware of film form, Miller and his editors concentrate on action rather than exposition, with kinetic thrills involving various vehicles and a rapid montage

Mad Max 2: The Road Warrior emphasises the affinity of the Mad Max myth with the Western. Like the classic Western hero, Max commits himself to the side of civilisation by offering to lead a tanker caravan past the savages in the wilderness to safety like the trail boss of a wagon train. In *Mad Max Beyond Thunderdome*, similarly, Max comes to a town, the beginnings of 'civilisation', where survival of the fittest is literalised in the public fights to the death in the Thunderdome instead of on Main Street at high noon. Max's mythic quality as redeemer is solidified by his leading a group of children, stranded in the desert for years, to a new Eden. The films in sequence thus move from straightforward action to mythic romance, like James

DIRECTOR George Miller
PRODUCER Byron Kennedy
SCREENPLAY George Miller and James McCausland
DIRECTOR OF PHOTOGRAPHY David Eggby
EDITOR Cliff Hayes, Tony Patterson
MUSIC Brian May
ART DIRECTOR John Dowding
CAST Mel Gibson, Joanne Samuel, Hugh Keays-Byrne, Steve Bisley, Tim Burns, Vince Gil, Roger Ward
PRODUCTION COMPANY Kennedy Miller Productions, Crossroads, Mad Max Films

Fenimore Cooper's five Leatherstocking novels before them.

Between the second and third *Mad Max* films, Miller directed the final episode of the omnibus *Twilight Zone: The Movie* (1983), a new version of the classic episode 'Nightmare at 20,000 Feet', in which a man (John Lithgow) with an overwhelming fear of flying is on a flight with his wife and glimpses a creature on the wing sabotaging one of the engines that no one else sees, before taking a surprising new direction with *Babe: Pig in the City* (1998) and *Happy Feet* (2006), family fantasies involving benign animals rather than the vicious human ones of the *Mad Max* movies.

The Man Who Fell to Earth
UK, 1976 – 139 mins
Nicolas Roeg

Featuring a narrative about an extraterrestrial who comes to Earth with a vague plan to save his dying home planet, *The Man Who Fell to Earth* has attained cult status, in part because of the casting of the influential glam rocker David Bowie in his first starring role as the alien Thomas Jerome Newton. The casting of Bowie was an inspired choice, given that he looks remarkably like the frail extraterrestrial as described by Walter Tevis in his novel, and also because of Bowie's 'space oddity' iconographic significance within popular music. Also contributing to the film's cult appeal is British director Nicolas Roeg (cinematographer of François Truffaut's *Fahrenheit 451** [1966]), who eschews special effects for the trademark surreal imagery and

DIRECTOR Nicolas Roeg
PRODUCER Michael Deeley, Barry Spikings
SCREENPLAY Paul Mayersberg, based on the 1962 novel by Walter Tevis
DIRECTOR OF PHOTOGRAPHY Anthony Richmond
EDITOR Graeme Clifford
MUSIC John Phillips, Stomu Yamashta
PRODUCTION DESIGN Brian Eatwell
MAIN CAST David Bowie, Rip Torn, Candy Clark, Buck Henry, Bernie Casey, Rick Riccardo, Tony Mascia, Jackson D. Kane, Linda Hutton, Adrienne Larussa
PRODUCTION COMPANY British Lion, Cinema 5

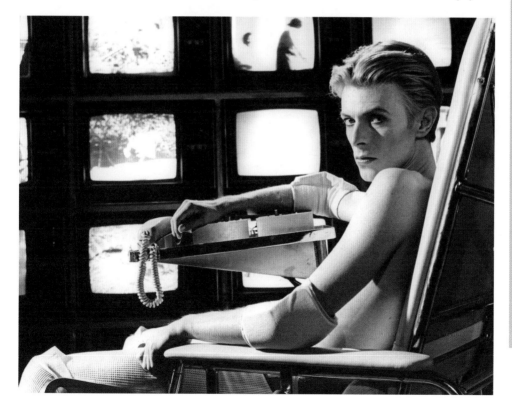

elaborate editing he brought previously to *Performance* (1970), *Walkabout* (1971), and the psychological horror film *Don't Look Now* (1973).

Newton comes to Earth from Anthea (one of the planets in our solar system, possibly Mars, as we are told in the novel, although the film withholds any such information) with the idea of amassing a fortune in order to finance the building of a private spaceship to save the remaining few people on his drought-stricken, dying planet. His knowledge of advanced Anthean technology allows Newton to introduce several new products and to build a major corporation, World Enterprises Corporation, with the help of patent attorney Oliver Farnsworth (Henry). While scouting a location for the ship's construction site, Newton meets Mary-Lou (Clark), a working-class hotel elevator operator, and they strike up a relationship.

Meanwhile, college science professor Dr. Nathan Bryce (Torn) is hired by World Enterprises to work on the big project. Bryce becomes suspicious about Newton and discovers the truth about him. Realising that his secret is about to be exposed, Newton decides to reveal his true form to Mary-Lou, who shrinks from him in utter horror and leaves him. Newton becomes increasingly reliant on alcohol and television, the broadcast signals of which the Antheans had initially monitored in order to become familiar with Earth ways. Before Newton can complete his mission, he is detained by the government, held captive and subjected to a battery of invasive medical tests, one of which results in his human contact lenses becoming permanently affixed to his alien eyes. Newton eventually discovers that his prison, seemingly abandoned by a now disinterested government, is unlocked, and he leaves. Years later he is visited by Bryce, now married to Mary-Lou, at an outdoor café. Newton, still wealthy and young-looking, is a broken alcoholic, the film ending with a memorable shot, perfectly capturing the end of the novel, of his face disappearing behind his fedora as he slouches into an alcoholic stupor, the waiter averring that 'Mr. Newton has had enough'.

In telling this tale, Roeg is clearly less interested in the details of hard science fiction – Newton's journey to Earth is depicted simply in a series of four brief shots that show no ship and conclude with merely a giant splash in a lake – than in depicting the fate of a naïve intellect losing itself amidst the seductive pleasures of popular culture. At one point while the scientists perform their tests on Newton, he seems hardly aware, his attention instead directed to the bank of television monitors in front of him. From this perspective, one might regard *The Man Who Fell to Earth* as an avant-garde exploration of themes similar to that of John Carpenter's *They Live** (1988). The film periodically cuts to glimpses of Newton and his family on their parched planet, and throughout Roeg relies on striking images rather than expositional dialogue, as in the image of one room in Newton's prison containing just a ping-pong table with a wall-to-wall mural of a beautiful autumnal forest, a visual representation of the enticing postmodern world into which Newton has wandered and which dooms him to an alienated life on Earth.

Mars Attacks!
US, 1996 – 106 mins
Tim Burton

Director Tim Burton is steeped in the traditions of speculative fiction in every medium of popular culture, as is clear from films such as *Frankenweenie* (short, 1984; feature, 2012); *Batman* (1989*)*; *Ed Wood* (1994), a biopic of the legendary director of *Plan 9 from Outer Space** (1959); *Sweeney Todd: The Demon Barber of Fleet Street* (2007); the film version of the daytime vampire soap opera *Dark Shadows* (2012); and the remakes of *Planet of the Apes* (2001) and *Charlie and the Chocolate Factory* (2005). Indeed, in some Burton films – *Beetlejuice* (1988), *Sleepy Hollow* (1999) and *Alice in Wonderland* (2010), for example – fantasy and the imagination become theme as well as means. *Mars Attacks!*, the only film with the distinction of being based on a series of trading cards, is no exception. Featuring an all-star cast, in the manner of classic disaster films such as *The Poseidon Adventure* (1972) and *Earthquake* (1974), *Mars Attacks!* is a knowing parody of traditional alien invasion movies such as *Invaders from Mars** (1953), *The War of the Worlds** (1953), *Plan 9 from Outer Space** and Roland Emmerich's blockbuster *Independence Day*, released, coincidentally, the same year as Burton's film.

   In the 1962 Topps trading card series of the same name, originally on sale only for a short time until they were withdrawn because of parents' complaints about their graphic violence and suggestive sexuality, Martians launch a gruesome invasion of Earth. In the film, this happens after a disastrous official first contact in the Nevada desert ends with the Martians incinerating everyone present. Despite the warnings of a

DIRECTOR Tim Burton
PRODUCER Tim Burton, Larry Franco, Laurie Parker
SCREENPLAY Jonathan Gems
DIRECTOR OF PHOTOGRAPHY Peter Suschitzsky
EDITOR Chris Lebenzon
MUSIC Danny Elfman
PRODUCTION DESIGN Wynn Thomas
MAIN CAST Jack Nicholson, Glenn Close, Annette Bening, Pierce Brosnan, Danny DeVito, Martin Short, Sarah Jessica Parker, Michael J. Fox, Rod Steiger, Jim Brown, Tom Jones, Lukas Haas, Natalie Portman, Pam Grier, Paul Winfield
PRODUCTION COMPANY Tim Burton Productions, Warner Bros.

bellicose general (Rod Steiger) who recalls Gen. Jack D. Ripper (Sterling Hayden) in another blackly comic apocalyptic scenario, Stanley Kubrick's *Dr. Strangelove or: How I Learned to Stop Worrying and Love the Bomb* (1964), the liberal president James Dale (Nicholson), willing to consider the debacle a cultural misunderstanding, allows the Martians to address both branches of Congress – whereupon they promptly kill all the members of the Executive branch. A full-scale attack then begins, and we follow several people in different locations around the country: Las Vegas, New York, Washington and rural Kansas.

As in the trading cards, there is much destruction and death – including that of the President and the First Lady (Close). The narrative of the trading card series ends with humans retaliating by invading Mars, but in the film, just when humanity is on the verge of defeat, a weapon of last resort is found that, as in countless monster movies (for example, *The Beast from 20,000 Fathoms** [1953] and *Gojira** [1954]), helps win the day. In this case, as the awkward Kansas teenager Richie Norris (Haas) discovers, it is yodelling music, specifically Slim Whitman's 'Indian Love Call,' which makes the encephalic head of any Martian within earshot ominously quiver and then explode in a gush of viscous green brain matter. Richie and his grandmother (Sidney) drive around town, broadcasting the song from a loudspeaker, killing many Martians, as do the advancing military.

Burton treats this plot with deadpan humour while also poking fun at virtually every convention of the genre – a tone perfectly captured in the presentation of the Martians (computer animated by Industrial Light & Magic, they look exactly like those in the trading cards). Somewhat disturbingly, they are exceedingly cruel despite their campy cuteness and endearing squawks (created by reversing the sound of ducks quacking). They deliberately destroy prized landmarks such as Big Ben and the Eiffel Tower, smash the Easter Island Moai with a giant bowling ball and topple the Washington Monument, using their ship to push it onto a fleeing troop of Boy Scouts. The Martians perform hideous experiments on people and broadcast messages that they come in peace even as they go about massacring everyone in the streets. In the end, as the human survivors arise to reclaim the Earth, the animals of the forest gather about one of them, entertainer Tom Jones, playing his charismatic self, as if he were the charmed hero of a Disney movie.

The Matrix
US/Australia, 1999 – 136 mins
Larry Wachowski, Andy Wachowski

In the last few years of the second millennium, not long after the proliferation of home computing and the internet, a cycle of science fiction films addressed the philosophical and moral implications of the new technology, including *Strange Days** (1995), *Dark City** (1998), *The Truman Show* (1998), *The Thirteenth Floor* (1999) and *eXistenZ* (1999). But it was Andy and Larry (now Lana) Wachowski's *The Matrix*, about a future in which people are ignorantly living in a simulated reality created by sentient machines while their dormant bodies, plugged into a vast electrical network, provide a continuous energy source for the machines, which particularly caught the popular imagination. Its success led to two sequels, *The Matrix Reloaded* (2003) and *The Matrix Revolutions* (2003), as well as *The Animatrix*, a series of nine animated shorts (supervised by the Wachowskis, who wrote four of them but directed none), comic books and video games, including Matrix Online, a massively multiplayer online role-playing game (MMORPG) that extended the narrative of the films.

Thomas Anderson (Reeves), a computer programmer, is curious about the cryptic messages he is receiving on his computer screen referring to something called the Matrix and sets out to discover their meaning. A mysterious woman, Trinity (Moss), appears and takes him to meet Morpheus (Fishburne), who offers him a choice between returning to his previous life and discovering the truth about his existence. Choosing knowledge, Anderson (now Neo) takes a proffered red pill and penetrates the Matrix, learning from Morpheus that it is actually the year 2199 and that humans are engaged in a war against intelligent machines that have taken control by keeping people plugged into a simulated reality of the world in 1999. Morpheus leads a furtive group of fighters who unplug people from the Matrix to fight the Machines, which employ sentient computer programs led by Agent Smith (Weaving) that work to eliminate human threats to the system. Although one really dies if killed in the Matrix, understanding its systemic rules allows Neo to gain superhuman abilities in his fight against the machines and their programs. Possibly the foretold 'One' of myth who will end the war, Neo promises in the end, after defeating Smith, to show everyone that 'anything is possible', after which he flies away into the sky from a telephone booth, like Superman, in the final shot.

The film is replete with diverse references from Plato's Allegory of the Cave and Lewis Carroll's *Alice's Adventures in Wonderland* (1865) to Hong Kong action cinema. The influence of Philip K. Dick and of cyberpunk fiction, especially William Gibson's foundational *Neuromancer* (1984), which introduced the term 'Matrix', is also apparent, while the 'digital rain' that represents the Matrix recalls similar computer images in the Japanese anime *Ghost in the Shell** (1995). Appropriately, given the film's quality of pastiche, the postmodern theory of Jean Baudrillard regarding the mediation of experience through media in contemporary society, obviously an influence on the film's premise, is referenced in the close-up of his book

DIRECTOR Andy and Larry (Lana) Wachowski

PRODUCER Joel Silver

SCREENPLAY Andy and Larry (Lana) Wachowski

DIRECTOR OF PHOTOGRAPHY Bill Pope

EDITOR Zach Staenberg

MUSIC Don Davis

PRODUCTION DESIGN Owen Paterson

MAIN CAST Keanu Reeves, Laurence Fishburne, Carrie-Anne Moss, Hugo Weaving, Joe Pantoliano, Matt Doran, Belinda McClory, Gloria Foster, Marcus Chong, Julian Arahanga

PRODUCTION COMPANY Groucho II Film Partnership, Silver Pictures, Village Roadshow Pictures

Simulacra and Simulation (1981, first published in English in 1994) in Anderson's apartment.

In its production design, the film uses green tones, the tint of early computer monitors, for scenes set within the Matrix, and popularised the use of 'bullet time', a visual effect combining normal camera movement with slow motion, seen, for example, in the scenes where Neo dodges the agents' bullets. The technique was subsequently used in a number of other films and video games (the game *Max Payne* explicitly refers to the effect as 'bullet time'), and visual effects supervisor John Gaeta, whose work on *The Matrix* earned him as Oscar for Visual Effects, refined it with CGI enhancements in the sequels. Filmed simultaneously and released six months apart in 2003, *The Matrix Reloaded* and *The Matrix Revolutions* wrap up the story with Neo fulfilling the role of 'the One' with the final defeat of Smith and the establishment of a truce between humans and machines.

Metropolis
Germany, 1927 – 153 mins
Fritz Lang

Made during the Golden Age of German Expressionist cinema by one of the world's most celebrated film-makers, *Metropolis* is an acknowledged masterwork of the silent era and one of the most influential of science fiction films. With its sweeping vision of a future city, it was one of the most expensive silent films ever made and almost bankrupted Universum Film A.G. (UFA), Germany's largest and most important studio in the 1920s. The screenplay was co-written by Lang and his wife and frequent collaborator, Thea von Harbou, who published a novelisation of it as well. Two years later, they also co-wrote the screenplay for Lang's other important science fiction film, *Frau im Mond** (*Woman in the Moon*, 1929). The original score, borrowing from the work of Richard Wagner and Richard Strauss, was composed by Gottfried Huppertz, who had earlier composed the original scores for Lang's *Die Nibelungen* films (*Siegfried* and *Kriemhilds Rache* [*Kriemhild's Revenge*], 1924).

Society in the futuristic city of Metropolis is divided into two classes: pampered executives who live in a surface world of luxury, and downtrodden workers who live underground. The complicated plot begins when Freder (Fröhlich), son of Joh Fredersen (Abel), the city's founder, finds his innocence shattered after he descends into the dank, oppressive world of the workers and becomes one of them. He also hears Maria (Helm) preaching to the workers in their secret meeting place, urging the film's simplistic message that the heart must be mediator between the head (the managers) and the hands (the workers). Fredersen orders the scientist Rotwang to turn his new invention, a robot, into the image of Maria and to send it below to create discord among the workers. The robot Maria whips up rebellious anger in the workers, who become a violent Langian mob and destroy the city's power generator, causing the reservoir to overflow and threatening to drown their own children. The children are saved by Maria and Freder, and in the climax, his father watching, Freder grapples with a now insane Rotwang on a cathedral roof. The scientist ultimately falls to his death, and Freder assumes the mantle of mediator, fulfilling Maria's prophecy by encouraging his father and Grot (George), the leader of the workers, to join hands in co-operation.

The plot was influenced by the Soviet science fiction film *Aelita** (1924), which depicts a Socialist revolution on Mars, but opts in the end for class reconciliation rather than struggle. A few years later, H.G. Wells called *Metropolis* a silly film and with his screenplay for *Things to Come** (1936) deliberately sought to do everything differently. Von Harbou borrowed the idea of the social split between the workers and managers in part from Wells's own *The Time Machine* (1895), but his technocratic vision was at odds with *Metropolis*'s depiction of automation turning workers into oppressed drudges. Yet apart from its dubious politics, *Metropolis*' special effects and directorial skills remain impressive today. The numerous establishing shots of the bustling city, Freder's vision of the giant underground machine as Moloch, a god to whom workers are sacrificed, and the creation of the robot in the likeness of Maria are the highlights. The film also introduced a technique known as

DIRECTOR Fritz Lang
PRODUCER Erich Pommer
SCREENPLAY Thea von Harbou, Fritz Lang
DIRECTOR OF PHOTOGRAPHY Karl Freund, Günther Rittau, Walter Ruttmann
MUSIC original release score composed by Gottfried Huppertz
ART DIRECTOR Otto Hunte, Erich Kettelhut, Karl Volbrecht
MAIN CAST Alfred Abel, Gustav Fröhlich, Brigitte Helm, Rudolf Klein-Rogge, Fritz Rasp, Theodor Loos, Erwin Biswanger, Heinrich George
PRODUCTION COMPANY UFA

the Schüfftan Process, named after its inventor, effects expert Eugen Schüfftan, which used mirrors to insert actors within miniature sets.

Metropolis was substantially cut after its German premiere and before its release abroad, largely for reasons of length, and the footage was presumed lost for decades. Numerous scenes were cut, including the complete elimination of the melodramatic subplot, a love triangle involving Fredersen, Rotwang and Hel, the woman in the middle, making the narrative seem disjointed and unclear. Over the years, a number of restored versions have been released, including composer Giorgio Moroder's version (which included some footage of Hel) with his new pop soundtrack in 1984. In 2008, a print of the film was discovered in the Museo del Cine in Argentina with more than 20 minutes of missing footage; combined with other previously lost footage discovered in a New Zealand print three years earlier, an almost completely restored version was released in 2010 with a running time of 145 minutes, leaving out only approximately 8 minutes (rendered as a black screen with explanatory intertitles), with the Berlin Radio Symphony Orchestra performing the score.

Nineteen Eighty-Four
UK, 1984 – 113 mins
Michael Radford

George Orwell's seminal dystopian novel has been adapted for the stage, television, and twice as a feature film. On the small screen, a shortened adaptation was televised by CBS in the US in 1953, with Eddie Albert as Winston Smith and written by William Templeton, who also wrote the screenplay for the first film adaptation, *1984*, in 1956, starring Edmond O'Brien as Smith and directed by Michael Anderson. (Anderson later directed *Logan's Run* [1976], an ironic utopia influenced by Orwell.) A controversial BBC production was first broadcast in 1954, one year after the American production. Written by Nigel Kneale, who also wrote *The Quatermass Experiment* and *Quatermass and the Pit** (1967), and produced and directed by Rudolph Cartier, who also worked on the *Quatermass* TV series, it starred Peter Cushing as Smith and Donald Pleasence, who would also appear in Anderson's film, as Syme. The second film version, released in the year the novel is set, is the most faithful adaptation, as indicated by a title before the final credits indicating that it was shot in London (now known as Airstrip One in the state of Oceania) from April to June, 1984, the exact time period in which Orwell's book is set, with some scenes shot on the same dates indicated in Smith's diary and in the locations mentioned in the book. Certainly it captures better than any of the other productions the gritty deprivation, both physical and psychological, that informs the totalitarian regime it envisions (and which, alas, seems only to grow more true with every passing year).

Winston Smith (Hurt) lives a squalid existence in a society of continuous warfare with either of the world's two other super states, under unyielding government control and surveillance. A frightening exaggeration of postwar English Socialism ('Ingsoc', as it is called in the book and film's revisionist language, Newspeak) seeks to extinguish individual thinking ('thoughtcrime'). Smith, a member of the Outer Party, works in an office cubicle at the Ministry of Truth, where he rewrites newspapers and other documents in accordance with the changing dictates of the Party (paternalistically depicted as 'Big Brother') and deleting references to 'unpersons', or those whom the state has declared to be enemies and has publically executed. He begins an illicit affair with another Outer Party member, Julia (Hamilton), which pushes his inchoate feelings of discontent towards thoughts of joining the possibly non-existent Resistance.

Smith and Julia meet clandestinely in a rented room above an old antique shop in the proletarian sector, but after some time they are arrested there, the avuncular shopkeeper Charrington (Cusack) who rented them the room revealing himself as an agent of the Thought Police. Winston is imprisoned and tortured in the Ministry of Love for an extended period by O'Brien (Burton), an Inner Party member, until he is 'cured' – that is, when Smith has conceded his very perceptions and feelings to the will of the Party. Smith's resistance is finally broken when he is taken to Room 101, which contains each individual's worst fear – in Smith's case, starving rats – and he renounces Julia. Now 'cured', he is released and, in the coda, Winston crosses paths with Julia in a café, both of them detachedly admitting that they betrayed the other.

DIRECTOR Michael Radford
PRODUCER Simon Perry
SCREENPLAY Michael Radford, based on the 1949 novel by George Orwell
DIRECTOR OF PHOTOGRAPHY Roger Deakins
EDITOR Tom Priestley
MUSIC Dominic Muldowney
PRODUCTION DESIGN Allan Cameron
MAIN CAST John Hurt, Suzanna Hamilton, Richard Burton, Cyril Cusack, Gregor Fisher, James Walker, Andrew Wilde, David Trevena, David Cann
PRODUCTION COMPANY Umbrella-Rosenblum Films, Virgin Films

After Anderson's diluted version, Orwell's widow rejected subsequent offers from other film producers to adapt the novel; but shortly before her death in 1980, she agreed to the remake on the condition that it contain no futuristic special effects. Radford's version emphasises *1984*'s historical continuity rather than its fictive future, and Allan Cameron's production design is, like the world Orwell depicts, a canny combination of elements from Nazi Germany and Stalinist Russia. Roger Deakins's cinematography created an appropriately washed-out look, draining the bleak images of bright colour. (In MGM's North American DVD version, the colour intensity was restored and the Eurythmics music is replaced by Dominic Muldowney's, which was Radford's preference). And while Richard Burton provides a finely modulated performance as O'Brien (this was his final film appearance, and the film is dedicated to him), and the casting of Cyril Cusack as the seemingly benevolent proprietor of the antique shop gains additional force given his similar role as The Captain in François Truffaut's *Fahrenheit 451** (1966), John Hurt is the perfect everyman Winston Smith.

Paris qui dort (*Paris Asleep/The Crazy Ray*)
France, 1925 – 35 mins
René Clair

French director René Clair began making films within the Surrealist and Dadaist movements of the 1920s and 30s. Like such other films as Man Ray's *Le Retour à la raison* (1923), Fernand Léger's *Ballet mécanique* (1924), Marcel Duchamp's *Anémic cinema* (1926) and, most famously, Luis Buñuel and Salvador Dalí's *Un chien andalou* (1929), Clair's own *Entr'acte* (1924), his first film, playfully liberates cinema from narrative, working instead towards a new visual poetry. Clair was an actor and film critic before becoming a director, and his early films are quite conscious of film form. And given his Surrealist roots, Clair was also attracted to the fantastic, as evident throughout his career: from the early *Le Voyage imaginaire* (1925) to *The Ghost Goes West* (1935), made for British producer Alexander Korda (*Things to Come** [1936]), from *I Married a Witch* (1942) and *It Happened Tomorrow* (1944), both made in Hollywood, to *Le beauté du diable* (1950), a Faust story made after his postwar return to France. In *Paris qui dort*, a whimsical comedy about a genially mad scientist who invents a ray which causes people to freeze in their tracks, Clair uses a science fiction narrative as a pretext for playing with motion and rhythm, the essence of cinema.

At 3:25 one morning, almost everyone in Paris becomes immobilised. A night watchman at the Eiffel Tower and a group of passengers on an inbound flight are the only ones unaffected. They wander through the city looking for an explanation, encountering such people as a man about to commit suicide by jumping in the Seine and a policeman in a foot chase with a crook, the two frozen like the figures on Keats's Grecian urn in perpetual pursuit. The group of unaffected people live in the Eiffel Tower for several days, at first elated with a sense of liberation at being able to do whatever they want, but this quickly turns to boredom without society. In true Dadaist spirit, they turn the francs they had gathered at will into paper aeroplanes which with detached bemusement they launch from the Tower. Eventually, the group receives a mysterious message, which they discover was sent by the niece of a scientist who has beamed his ray around the world, and, meeting, they convince him to reverse the effect.

The scientist's laboratory is geometrically stylised, following the more elaborate design abstractions of the Soviet science fiction film *Aelita, Queen of Mars** (1924), made the year before *Paris qui dort*. Indeed, after all his lengthy and complex calculations on a blackboard to figure out how to reverse the ray's effects (comically, the characters who are awake fall asleep while waiting), the scientist simply pulls a stylised lever in reverse. As he shifts it, exterior shots play with slow motion and stop motion. Anticipating Fritz Lang's *Frau im Mond** (1929), in *Paris qui dort*, the scientist shows the group a diagram of his ray in relation to the Earth, animated with moving lines to explain that they escaped the ray's effect because they were at physical heights above its wavelength. Such techniques, even as they advance the story, draw attention to cinema as a medium, a concern *Paris qui dort* shares with the non-narrative experimental films of the era.

Clair's first sound films – especially the musicals *Sous les toits de Paris* (*Under the Roofs of Paris*, 1930)

DIRECTOR René Clair
PRODUCER Henri Diamant-Berger
SCREENPLAY René Clair
DIRECTOR OF PHOTOGRAPHY
Maurice Desfassiaux, Paul Guichard
EDITOR René Clair
PRODUCTION DESIGN André Foy,
Claude Autant-Lara
MAIN CAST Henri Rollan, Albert
Préjean, Antoine Stacquet, Marcel
Vallée, Louis Pré Fils, Charles
Martinelli, Madeleine Rodrigue,
Myla Seller
PRODUCTION COMPANY Films
Diamant

and *Le Million* (1931) – are notable for their inventive use of sound in combination with fluid camerawork. Although *Paris qui dort* is silent, Clair's distinctive visual style is amply evident in his treatment of the Eiffel Tower (a few years later, in 1928, Clair would make a short documentary on the Tower, *La Tour*), which is presented with the kind of detailed admiration with which Joris Ivens shows the mechanics of a drawbridge in *The Bridge* (1928). *Paris qui dort* also contains impressive moving shots between levels on the Tower that look forward to the camerawork of *Sous les toits de Paris*. On one level, then, the mad scientist's machine is like cinema itself, with its ability to capture and manipulate motion and entrance spectators.

Plan 9 from Outer Space
US, 1959 – 79 mins
Edward D. Wood, Jr

Ed Wood, Jr made a number of low-budget genre and exploitation films in the 1950s, remembered today mostly for their technical ineptitude. Ever since he was posthumously awarded a Golden Turkey Award as Worst Director of All Time by Harry and Michael Medved, Wood has been reviled – or revered, depending upon one's point of view – for his campy disregard of the basic rules of classical narrative cinema. The writer and/or director of *Night of the Ghouls* (1959), *Orgy of the Dead* (1965), *Bride of the Monster* (1955) – which, like *Plan 9 from Outer Space*, featured Bela Lugosi – and the writer, director and star of the infamous *Glen or Glenda* (1953), about the tortured soul of a transvestite (which Wood himself was in real life), Wood towards the end of his career turned to soft-core pornography and writing pulp novels. Today, the excessive 'badness' of Wood's films has earned him a significant cult following, and Tim Burton's biopic about the cult film maker, *Ed Wood* (1994), starring Johnny Depp in the title role, culminates with the making of *Plan 9 from Outer Space*.

Appropriately, the directorial credit of *Plan 9*, cited as 'the worst movie of all time' by the Medveds, begins with a flash of lightning and peal of thunder. Originally titled *Grave Robbers from Outer Space* (the final name came from Valiant Pictures, who released it two years after it was made), the film, shot in five days in 1956 with a budget of approximately $20,000, offers ample evidence of Wood's unfortunate reputation, as it is replete with bad dialogue and acting, continuity errors and crude special effects. 'That's nothing from this world', says Jeff Trent (Walcott), the airline pilot who sees the alien saucers – a line that also applies to everything about *Plan 9*.

The nonsensical plot involves alien beings who want to stop humans from eventually discovering 'solarbonite', a technology that has the ability to explode particles of sunlight and start a chain reaction that would destroy the entire universe. Because the governments of Earth steadfastly refuse to acknowledge their existence, the aliens decide to implement Plan 9, a strategy involving reviving the dead in order to guarantee the attention of the people of Earth. Supposedly, the hordes of these walking dead are to march on the capitals of the world's nations, but the aliens manage to raise only three people: an old man (Lugosi), his wife (Vampira, the first television horror host) and a police detective, Inspector Daniel Clay (professional wrestler Tor Johnson).

Perhaps the film's most comical lapse of continuity involves the character of the Old Man (or Ghoul Man, as he is billed in the credits). The footage of Lugosi had been shot earlier, for several of Wood's unrealised projects. When the actor died, Wood hired Tom Mason, his wife's chiropractor, as a stand-in for Lugosi, despite the fact that there was no physical resemblance between them. Mason goes through his scenes with no dialogue and his face obscured by his cape. The Amazing Criswell, a popular American psychic who appeared in several of Wood's films, provides a confused narration as an attempt to better link Lugosi's footage with the rest of the narrative.

DIRECTOR Edward D. Wood, Jr
PRODUCER Edward D. Wood, Jr
SCREENPLAY Edward D. Wood, Jr
DIRECTOR OF PHOTOGRAPHY
William C. Thompson
EDITOR Edward D. Wood, Jr
MAIN CAST Bela Lugosi, John Breckenridge, Lyle Talbot, Tor Johnson, Vampira (Maila Nurmi), Tom Keene, Gregory Walcott
PRODUCTION COMPANY Reynolds Pictures

In the 'climactic' confrontation before the nominal heroes destroy the spaceship, the alien emissary Eros (Manlove) explains that 'All of you on Earth are idiots', primitive minds unable to control the new technologies being discovered – the ostensible theme of many Atomic Age science fiction movies such as *Invaders from Mars** (1953). Gaffes such as crosses in the graveyard flopping like rubber when characters bump into them or the mismatched shots of Eros gazing out of the port in his ship at a cloudy daytime sky during the night might, for some viewers, seem to confirm the truth of his claim.

Planet of the Apes
US, 1968 – 112 mins
Franklin J. Schaffner

French writer Pierre Boulle became known internationally for *The Bridge over the River Kwai* (1952), made into a multiple Oscar-winning film by David Lean in 1957, but its success was surpassed by that of his 1963 novel *La Planète des singes* (originally published in the UK as *Monkey Planet*, and later changed to *Planet of the Apes* as a tie-in to the first film), which has inspired an ongoing franchise comprising seven films to date – an original series of five, a 2001 remake by Tim Burton and a 2011 reboot – as well as comic books, merchandising and two television series, one live action (*Planet of the Apes* [1974] and one animated (*Return to the Planet of the Apes* [1975–6]). All four sequels – *Beneath the Planet of the Apes* (1970), *Escape from the Planet of the Apes* (1971), *Conquest of the Planet of the Apes* (1972) and *Battle for the Planet of the Apes* (1973) – were produced by Arthur P. Jacobs and released by 20th Century Fox, although only the first was directed by Franklin J. Schaffner, who followed the success of *Planet of the Apes* with a series of blockbuster productions in the 1970s (*Patton* [1970], *Papillon* [1973]) that concluded with another science fiction film, *The Boys from Brazil* (1978). With groundbreaking prosthetic make-up by John Chambers (designer of the make-up for all five films in the series, winning an honorary Academy Award for outstanding make-up achievement on *Planet of the Apes*), the film's simple yet ingenious inversion of the relationship between humans and apes allowed for commentary about such issues as animal ethics, imperialism, war, religion and, for better or worse, racial relations in the US.

The misanthropic Taylor (Heston) and two other astronauts, travelling at light speed, crash on an unknown planet, having penetrated the time barrier to the year 3978. After trekking across barren land (later referred to as 'the Forbidden Zone' by the apes) to a jungle, they come across a band of primitive, mute humans and are quickly caught in an organised hunt of them conducted by intelligent gorillas. Here, Jerry Goldsmith's score, relying heavily on percussion, is perfectly suited to the shocking scene of apes beating the bushes to herd human animals into nets. In this world, Taylor discovers, humans are considered dumb animals and are used as slave labour or for scientific experimentation.

Caged and at first unable to speak because of an injury to his throat, Taylor eventually convinces two chimpanzee scientists, animal psychologist Zira (Hunter) and her fiancé Cornelius (McDowall), an archeologist, of who he is. However, their superior, the orangutan Dr. Zaius (Evans), refuses to accept that a human animal can be intelligent. Zira and Cornelius help Taylor and Nova (Harrison), a woman who had been given to him as a mate when encaged, to escape to an archaeological cave dig on the edge of the Forbidden Zone that shows evidence of a pre-simian human civilisation. Zaius arrives, and in a final confrontation with Taylor admits he knows that human society preceded apes, but that the truth would be too disruptive to the apes' quasi-religious worldview, and so he allows Taylor to leave.

In the film's famous twist ending, Taylor and Nova follow the shoreline and eventually discover the ruins

DIRECTOR Franklin J. Schaffner
PRODUCER Arthur P. Jacobs
SCREENPLAY Michael Wilson, Rod Serling, based on the 1963 novel by Pierre Boulle
DIRECTOR OF PHOTOGRAPHY Leon Shamroy
EDITOR Hugh S. Fowler
MUSIC Jerry Goldsmith
PRODUCTION DESIGN William Creber, Jack Martin Smith
MAIN CAST Charlton Heston, Roddy McDowall, Kim Hunter, Maurice Evans, Linda Harrison, James Whitmore
PRODUCTION COMPANY APJAC Productions, 20th Century Fox

of the Statue of Liberty, Taylor now realising that he has been on Earth all along. The screenplay for *Planet of the Apes*, which went through a number of rewrites, was initially written by Rod Serling, known for his television series *The Twilight Zone* (1959–64), episodes of which typically featured a twist ending with a moral lesson. The film's twist was Serling's invention, quite different from the twist ending of Boulle's novel, which is cast in the form of Taylor's journal and read by ape astronauts. Interestingly, in the first-season episode 'People Are Alike All Over', written by Serling, Roddy McDowall – who would star in four of the five *Apes* films in the series – plays an astronaut who is treated kindly by aliens only to discover that he has been placed in a 'natural habitat' along with other animals in a zoo. The ending of Tim Burton's remake, in which the apes are at once campier and creepier, contains a different twist ending wherein the protagonist (Mark Wahlberg) returns to Earth from the planet of the apes only to find that Earth too is now populated by intelligent apes.

Quatermass and the Pit/Five Million Years to Earth
UK, 1967 – 97 mins
Roy Ward Baker

Based on the BBC's six-part television mini-series of the same name, originally broadcast live during December 1958 and January 1959, *Quatermass and the Pit* was the third and last instalment of the series, preceded by the well-received *The Quatermass Experiment* in 1953 and *Quatermass II* in 1955, both made into feature films directed by Val Guest for Hammer in 1955 (as *The Quatermass Xperiment*) and 1957, respectively, and starring American actor Brian Donlevy as Professor Quatermass. All three series, and the film adaptations, were written by Nigel Kneale, whose other credits, in addition to the screenplays of two John Osborne plays, *The Entertainer* (1960) and *Look Back in Anger* (1959), include the scripts for Hammer's *The Abominable Snowman* (1967), also directed by Guest; the British film adaptation of Jules Verne's *First Men in the Moon* (1964); and the teleplay for the BBC's adaptation of George Orwell's *Nineteen Eighty-Four* for *Sunday-Night Theatre* in 1954. In *Quatermass and the Pit*, as in the two earlier series, Kneale concentrates less on action than on science and logic, resulting in a classic hybrid of science fiction and detective story.

The plot, largely faithful to the original television production, begins with the discovery by workers of the remains of human ancestors at least five million years old along with a mysterious object at the Hobbs End construction site for an extension to the London Underground. Thinking that it is an unexploded bomb from World War 2, they call in the army to dispose of it. Quatermass (played much more effectively than Donlevy by the Scottish Keir), accompanying them, deduces that the object is an ancient Martian spaceship and that the aliens, a dying race, decided to colonise Earth by proxy by boosting human intelligence. The genre's conventional debate between science and the military informs the conflict between the rational Quatermass and Col. Breen (Glover), the officer in charge, who refuses to believe the evidence presented to him, steadfastly maintaining that the spacecraft is in fact a Nazi propaganda scheme that had been intended to undermine the morale of the British people, even when, in the film's most chilling scene, they enter the spaceship for the first time to discover the desiccated remains of insectoid creatures with horned heads.

With an experimental machine, Quatermass makes a video recording of what Barbara Judd (Shelley), the paleontologist's assistant who has fallen under the ship's influence, is thinking. The recording, created by special effects supervisor Les Bowie with a combination of puppets and live locusts, shows masses of Martians seemingly conducting a racial purging of the weak. As the Martian ship is unearthed, it gathers power from the nearby equipment and begins to exert a growing influence over people around it, bringing to consciousness buried alien racial memories. Violence erupts in the streets of London, which are themselves ripped apart by the Martian force, but the crisis is ended when Quatermass figures out a plan and a building crane is swung into the ship, discharging its mounting energy.

As with the previous two Quatermass serials, the film rights to *Quatermass and the Pit* were purchased by Hammer. Kneale wrote the screenplay in 1961, but because of problems with arranging financing from

DIRECTOR Roy Ward Baker
PRODUCER Anthony Nelson Keys
SCREENPLAY Nigel Kneale
DIRECTOR OF PHOTOGRAPHY
Arthur Grant
EDITOR Spencer Reeve
MUSIC Tristram Cary
ART DIRECTOR Bernard Robinson,
Kenneth Ryan
MAIN CAST Andrew Keir, Barbara
Shelley, James Donald, Julian Glover,
Grant Taylor, Duncan Lamont, Bryan
Marshall, Peter Copley, Edwin
Richfield, Maurice Good
PRODUCTION COMPANY Associated
British-Pathé, Hammer Films

American distributors, the film was not made until six years later. Guest was originally slated to direct again, with Donlevy to be cast once more as Quatermass, but eventually Roy Ward Baker was assigned as director apparently because of his experience working on the technically complex *A Night to Remember* (1958), about the sinking of the *Titanic*. Although Baker made another science fiction film for Hammer, *Moon Zero Two* (1969), he subsequently worked mainly in horror, directing *The Vampire Lovers* (1970), *Scars of Dracula* (1970), *Dr. Jekyll and Sister Hyde* (1971) and *The Legend of the 7 Golden Vampires* (1974) for the studio, as well as *Asylum* (1972), *And Now the Screaming Starts!* (1973), *The Vault of Horror* (1973) and *The Monster Club* (1981) for Hammer's rival, Amicus Productions.

The Quiet Earth
New Zealand, 1985 – 91 mins
Geoff Murphy

Geoff Murphy, one of the most important figures of the New Zealand New Wave, also made the road movie *Goodbye Pork Pie* (1981) and the seminal *Utu* (1983), a variation on the Western, before making the move to Hollywood, where he floundered with *Freejack* (1992) and *Fortress 2* (1999). But his New Zealand films show Murphy's ability to adapt generic convention to national culture, and *The Quiet Earth* is his best work in this regard. Despite the occasional concessions to the conventions of American action movies, *The Quiet Earth*, a post-apocalyptic tale set in New Zealand, is thoroughly Kiwi in its concerns.

Research scientist Zac Hobson (Lawrence) wakes up early one seemingly routine morning for work. Amidst his daily routine, a solar event seems to take place, and gradually Zac realises that no one else is around. He comes across the fiery wreckage of a passenger jet, but there are no bodies. Living in a world devoid of people and animal life, Zac soon begins to crack – at one point he goes into a church and, pointing a rifle at a statue of Jesus, demands that God reveal himself or else 'I'll shoot the kid'. On the verge of suicide, Zac manages to pull himself together and search the deserted North Island until he meets a woman, Joanne (Routledge), and a Maori, Api (Smith), who have somehow also survived. Gradually, we discover that Zac is a scientist who had been working on Project Flashlight, an international initiative to create a global energy grid (DNA experiments in Craig Harrison's novel). The three determine that they survived what Zac calls 'The Effect' because when it occurred was the exact moment each of them had died (Zak from a suicidal overdose of pills because of his guilt about not resisting what he suspected was a dangerous experiment).

Zac calculates that The Effect will happen again with unpredictable consequences, and the three agree to destroy the lab where he worked in an attempt to stop it. They drive a truckload of explosives to the facility, but Zac discovers a high level of radiation around it, preventing them from getting close. Riddled with guilt for having failed to oppose the project, Zac sacrifices himself by driving the truck into the lab, detonating the explosives at the same time as the Effect reoccurs. In the ambiguous last images he is seen standing alone on a beach with odd cloud formations and a giant ringed planet (Saturn?) looming in the sky above. Has the Effect happened again? Has Zac gone to meet his maker? The film provides no answers, just as the only explanation of The Effect we are given is Zac's condescending comment to Joanne and Api that it began as an experiment involving the in-flight fuelling of war planes which has somehow set off a warping of the space-time continuum – 'a cosmic event, like creation, and no one's been able to explain that'.

Coming one year after New Zealand's anti-nuclear declaration, *The Quiet Earth* expresses clear anti-American sentiment and nuclear anxiety when Zac reveals that 'the Effect' is the result of American scientists having concealed information about the project from their Kiwi collaborators. The film also alludes to the insidious influence of American culture by invoking the cycle of American apocalyptic movies focusing on a

DIRECTOR Geoff Murphy
PRODUCER Sam Pillsbury, Don Reynolds
SCREENPLAY Bill Baer, Bruno Lawrence, Sam Pillsbury, based on the 1981 novel by Craig Harrison
DIRECTOR OF PHOTOGRAPHY James Bartle
EDITOR Michael Horton
MUSIC John Charles
PRODUCTION DESIGN Josephine Ford
MAIN CAST Bruno Lawrence, Alison Routledge, Pete Smith
PRODUCTION COMPANY Cinepro, Mr. Yellowbeard Productions

handful of survivors, such as Roger Corman's *Day the World Ended* (1956) and, most importantly, Ranald MacDougall's *The World, The Flesh and The Devil* (1959) with its trio of a black man (Harry Belafonte), white man (Mel Ferrer), and white woman (Inger Stevens). In Murphy's film, as in MacDougall's, racial and sexual tensions mount immediately with the appearance of the dark Other (at one point Zac calls Api his 'Man Friday'). Zac becomes the ultimate but unfortunate 'man alone', deflating a mythic ideal of New Zealand masculinity, and the film critiques science as, in Joanne's words, 'an exclusive all-male club playing God with the universe'.

The Road
US, 2009 – 111 mins
John Hillcoat

Post-apocalyptic films from Roger Corman's *Day the World Ended* (1955) to Ray Milland's *Panic in Year Zero!* (1962) to Albert and Allen Hughes's *The Book of Eli* (2010) share a common theme of the struggle to preserve civilised values and a sense of humanity in the face of social breakdown and the crucible of survival. *The Road*, based on the Pulitzer Prize-winning 2006 novel by Cormac McCarthy, largely eschews action to focus instead on the psychological effects of that struggle on its two protagonists, a man and his young son. Its sensitivity to the emotional impact of disaster nudges the apocalyptic science fiction movie into the more highbrow realm of the art film.

In the near future, after an unexplained global environmental disaster has destroyed civilisation – 'There were warnings,' an old man (Duvall) says, the nearest the film comes to an explanation of the catastrophe – an unnamed father (Mortensen) and his young son (Smit-McPhee) struggle to survive. All animal and plant life is gone, and the sun is either dying or almost completely obscured by the sullen and pervasive grey ash that constantly falls. The few people remaining alive scavenge for food and supplies, some indulging in cannibalism. The father and son are travelling southeast towards the coast, where they hope it will be warmer and more hospitable. The narrative follows their trek as they search for food and shelter while trying to avoid human predators. Flashbacks from the perspective of the father show the boy being born after the disaster began and the mother (Theron), overcome by hopelessness, wandering off to die in suicidal despair.

The man carries a revolver with two bullets (eventually he uses one to shoot a member of a marauding gang of cannibals), and takes it as his fatherly duty to teach the boy to commit suicide if necessary so as to avoid being captured and eaten. In the course of their journey, the man has come so far down the road from his past existence that, in one particularly poignant scene, he tosses his wallet over the railing of a crumbling highway overpass and leaves his wedding ring on its edge, the last concrete evidence of his civilised identity. His worsening tubercular symptoms are likewise an indication of his fading former self. Ironically, in trying to protect his son and be one of 'the good guys', the man is forced to kill and withhold sympathy and help from others, including the old man they meet and another man (Williams) who tries to rob them without harming them. The boy perceptively observes that it is becoming difficult to tell the good guys from the bad.

Australian director John Hillcoat brings the same sense of gritty implacability to the fallen world of *The Road* that marked his previous film, *The Proposition* (2005). In addition to the conventional shots of eroding highways and crumbling industrial parks, greenery was digitally removed from exterior shots and the sky made to seem 'like the colour of television, tuned to a dead channel', to borrow from the first sentence of William Gibson's *Neuromancer* (1984). In the end, after the pair reaches the sea – which turns out to be as dead as everything else – the man dies and, in a jarringly optimistic ending that is nevertheless consistent

DIRECTOR John Hillcoat
PRODUCER Paula Mae Schwartz, Steve Schwartz, Nick Wechsler
SCREENPLAY Joe Penhall, based on the 2006 novel by Cormac McCarthy
DIRECTOR OF PHOTOGRAPHY Javier Aguirresarobe
EDITOR Jon Gregory
MUSIC Nick Cave, Warren Ellis
PRODUCTION DESIGN Chris Kennedy
MAIN CAST Viggo Mortensen, Kodi Smit-McPhee, Molly Parker, Robert Duvall, Guy Pearce, Charlize Theron, Michael Kenneth Williams, Garrett Dillahunt
PRODUCTION COMPANY Dimension Films, 2929 Productions, Nick Wechsler Productions

with the novel, the son is approached by, and taken under the protection of, a family. Even as the planet is dying, the traditional nuclear family, complete with two children and a dog, somehow survives. One might read this ending as impossibly sentimental, although more cynical readers have suggested that the boy is being lured to his death by more cannibals. However, it should be pointed out that the film prepares for the possibility of salvation in the scene shortly before, which has no antecedent in the novel, where the man and boy find a living beetle, a suggestion that life might somehow be renewed or carry on even in this devastated world.

RoboCop
US, 1987 – 102 mins
Paul Verhoeven

RoboCop marked the first major Hollywood production for Dutch director Paul Verhoeven and the first in a series of science fiction films he made there that also includes *Total Recall** (1990), *Starship Troopers** (1997) and *Hollow Man* (2000), a variation of *The Invisible Man** (1933), to deal with questions of violence, masculinity, the media and corporate capitalism in a manner that is at once graphic and ironic. (*Basic Instinct* [1992] takes a similar approach to issues of sexual representation, as does, possibly, the infamous *Showgirls* [1995].) A hit at the box office, the story of a policeman who is made into a cyborg spawned a franchise that includes two sequels – *RoboCop 2* (1990), directed by Irvin Kershner, director of *The Empire Strikes Back* in the *Star Wars** series, and *RoboCop 3* (1993), directed by Fred Dekker – as well as live action and animated television series, video games, a novelisation, comic books and other merchandise. In short, the film has

DIRECTOR Paul Verhoeven
PRODUCER Arne Schmidt
SCREENPLAY Edward Neumeier, Michael Miner
DIRECTOR OF PHOTOGRAPHY Jost Vacano
EDITOR Frank J. Urioste
MUSIC Basil Poledouris
PRODUCTION DESIGN William Sandell
MAIN CAST Peter Weller, Nancy Allen, Dan O'Herlihy, Ronny Cox, Kurtwood Smith, Miguel Ferrer, Robert DoQui, Ray Wise, Felton Perry, Paul McCrane, Jesse Goins, Del Zamora
PRODUCTION COMPANY Orion Pictures Corporation

found a significant presence within American popular culture even as it satirises it, particularly its offhand treatment of violence.

Set in the near future in the decaying and crime-ridden city of Detroit, the story focuses on police officer Alex Murphy (Weller), who has just transferred to the tough inner city precinct. On his first patrol along with his new partner, Officer Lewis (Allen), he is brutally killed by crime kingpin Clarence Boddicker (Smith). The city is on the verge of collapse, and has privatised its police force by contracting with OCP (the ominous sounding Omni Consumer Products), which is seeking ways to make the force more efficient. Murphy becomes the unwilling test subject of OCP's cyborg program, and as the superhuman, armoured RoboCop, seems an ideal solution to the city's crime problems. But RoboCop is haunted by unerased memories of his former self, in part triggered by his partner, Officer Lewis (Allen), who recognises Murphy's mannerisms in the machine, prompting him to investigate and discover his human origin. A secretly programmed directive prevents RoboCop from arresting Dick Jones, OCP's vice-president, for whom Boddicker secretly works, when he confronts the executive during a corporate board meeting, but the Chairman of the Board (O'Herlihy), taken hostage by Jones, fires him, thus nullifying the directive and allowing RoboCop to shoot Jones. The film ends with the Chairman asking for the officer's name, to which RoboCop replies 'Murphy' as he leaves.

The metal-clad RoboCop, inspired in part by British comic book hero Judge Dredd, was created by Rob Bottin, whose many make-up and special effects include John Carpenter's The Thing* (1982). Bottin also was responsible for the melting skin effects when one of Boddicker's thugs crashes into a container of smoking toxic waste, while stop-motion animation was used for the lumbering ED-209, another OPC prototype droid. The ED's obvious impracticality (it is unable to negotiate stairs, for example) is an indication of the film's condemnation of corporate corruption – as Jones remarks, he had a large contract for the machines around the country, and whether it actually works or not is irrelevant. At the same time that the film satirises corporate callousness, it also shows, as does Carpenter's They Live* (1988), urban decline, a disturbing trend in the 1980s when the film was made. In RoboCop, unemployment, crime and violence dominate the mock news broadcasts which punctuate the narrative, all delivered by a duo of astonishingly vacuous anchors.

At once liberal and fascist in its ideology, RoboCop offers a compelling extrapolation of contemporary concerns in a postmodern science fiction action movie featuring a sacrificial victim of corporate machinations who himself becomes a product. Of course, RoboCop, an expensive Hollywood movie, is itself a corporate product, adding a further layer of irony to the film. Accordingly, when RoboCop was originally given an X-rating in the US, Verhoeven re-edited it several times, toning down the violence in such scenes as when the ED-209 malfunctions in a test demonstration and riddles one of OPC's junior executives with bullets and when Murphy's arm is blasted off by Boddicker before the latter kills him. (The original uncut version can be found on several DVD editions.)

Seconds
US, 1966 – 100 mins
John Frankenheimer

John Frankenheimer directed a series of taut thrillers that captured the social tensions and anxieties of the turbulent 1960s. *The Manchurian Candidate* (1962), *Seven Days in May* (1964) and *Seconds* are concerned with surveillance, paranoia, social control, conspiracy and media manipulation. Frankenheimer would later make two other science fiction films – *Prophecy* (1979), about environmental pollution, and the third adaptation of *The Island of Dr. Moreau* (1996), about genetic engineering – that continued to explore these thematic concerns. The fact that all of the director's science fiction thrillers are set in the present or very near future indicates that for Frankenheimer these Orwellian fears are already reality. None of his films conveys this more powerfully than *Seconds*, which offers a vision of bourgeois America in the 1960s that seems at once like documentary realism and Kafkaesque nightmare. The film did not fare well upon its release (perhaps because of the casting against type of Rock Hudson), although its reputation has grown over the years.

The story concerns Arthur Hamilton (Randolph), a successful middle-aged businessman who feels that his life has lost meaning. He receives a telephone call from a close friend who is supposedly dead, and is approached by representatives of a mysterious, secret organisation known as 'the Company', which offers unhappy clients new lives through a process that involves their faked deaths, extensive plastic surgery and the creation of a completely new identity. With understandable apprehension, Hamilton buys the Company's services, and is transformed into the more youthful-looking Tony Wilson (Hudson), a successful artist with a Malibu beach house and a continuous supply of paintings courtesy of the Company. Walking on the beach, he meets and begins a relationship with a woman named Nora (Jens), and although Wilson now seems to have everything that he thought he wanted and had missed, he cannot adjust to his new life. During a party that he hosts for his neighbours, Tony gets drunk and begins talking about his former identity, and as his guests collectively restrain him, he realises that they are all 'reborns' too, including Nora, there on behalf of the Company to monitor his progress.

Fleeing this completely manufactured life and posing as an acquaintance of the deceased Hamilton, Wilson visits his wife and learns that from her perspective he had devoted himself to his career rather than to his family. Wilson then returns to the Company and requests to start again with another new identity. Sitting with the other men waiting to trade in their identities, he is called for surgery, but as he is being wheeled down the hallway and a priest begins to read him the last rites, he, along with the viewer, realises that he is about to die. As a medicated and restrained Tony is rolled into the operating room ('requisitioned from day stock'), it becomes clear that he is going to become one of the cadavers that are used to fake the death of new clients.

Seconds reveals that the material trappings of the American Dream are but an illusion, superficial

DIRECTOR John Frankenheimer
PRODUCER John Frankenheimer, Edward Lewis
SCREENPLAY Lewis John Carlino, based on the 1965 novel by David Ely
DIRECTOR OF PHOTOGRAPHY James Wong Howe
EDITOR David Newhouse, Ferris Webster
MUSIC Jerry Goldsmith
ART DIRECTOR Ted Haworth
MAIN CAST Rock Hudson, Jeff Corey, Will Geer, John Randolph, Richard Anderson, Salome Jens, Karl Swenson, Khigh Dhiegh, Dodie Heath
PRODUCTION COMPANY Gibraltar Productions, Joel Productions, John Frankenheimer Productions

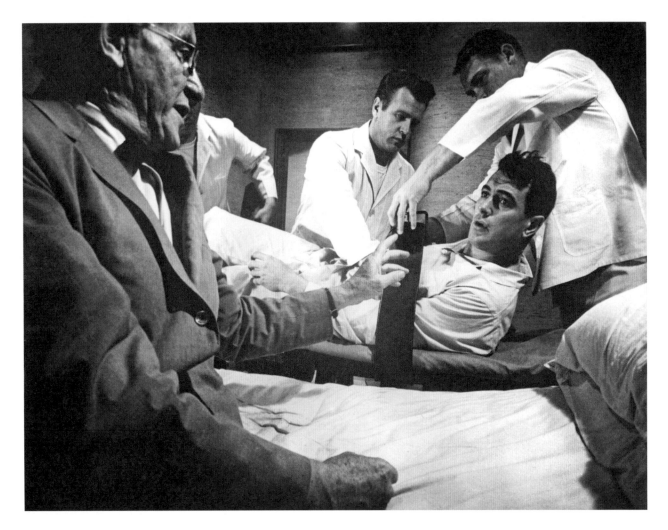

commodities that neither define a person nor necessarily fulfil the pursuit of happiness. Further, the film's cruel and crushing climax not only brings to an inevitable tragic end the life of a man unhappy with who he is, it also offers a savage critique of corporate capitalism as people themselves become consumable commodities while the Company continues to generate profits. Throughout, the film features the excellent cinematography of the prolific James Wong Howe, whose credits included the pioneering use of the hand-held camera in the fight scenes of the boxing movie *Body and Soul* (1947) while on roller skates. In *Seconds*, for which he received an Academy Award nomination, he also uses a hand-held camera that gives Tony's life of California Dreamin' the look of direct cinema, a style of documentary popular at the time, while also effectively using a fisheye lens to convey a sense of underlying unease.

Signs
US, 2002 – 106 mins
M. Night Shyamalan

A film about first contact, *Signs* is M. Night Shyamalan's most successful film after his breakthrough, *The Sixth Sense* (1999), and possibly his best film to date, avoiding the tendency towards the twist ending (*The Sixth Sense*, *The Village* [2004]) also characteristic of one of his primary influences, Rod Serling, who wrote the original screenplay for *Planet of the Apes** (1968) with its famous concluding twist. The title of Shyamalan's film alludes to a world that, despite the disturbing realisation that we are not alone, is nevertheless comforting because it, like everything, is all part of a grand design – evident immediately in the opening scene's shot of a wall with the faded outline where a cross used to hang – and to a self-reflexivity on the part of Shyamalan as aspiring auteur that to date has achieved its fullest treatment in *Lady in the Water* (2006). In the more fully realised *Signs*, Shyamalan shows an ability to balance cinematic suspense with metaphysical speculation in the tradition of Val Lewton's RKO horror cycle in the 1940s.

As the world witnesses the arrival of alien ships and videotaped glimpses of alien scouts – seen chiefly through CNN coverage on television – the story focuses on Graham Hess (Gibson), a former Episcopalian priest, and his family. Graham lost his faith in God and left the Church because of the apparent meaninglessness of his wife's death when she was struck by a truck whose devastated driver, Ray Reddy (Shyamalan), had fallen asleep at the wheel. They live in a farmhouse in Bucks Couny, Pennsylvania (where Shyamalan lives and where almost all of his films are set), along with Graham's younger brother, Merrill (Phoenix), who helps care for Graham's two children, Morgan (Culkin) and Bo (Breslin). One day they find crop circles in their cornfields, a few of the many that have appeared in places around the world. Eventually realising that the crop circles are navigational directions and landing points, they begin to barricade their house in preparation for invasion.

The aliens arrive and gain entry to the house, forcing the family into the basement, as in George Romero's influential *Night of the Living Dead* (1968). An alien momentarily grabs Morgan through the old farmhouse's coal chute, inducing an asthma attack in the boy, whose medicine was left in his bedroom upstairs. After a terrified evening in the dark, a radio news report indicates that the aliens are retreating after an as yet unknown weapon was discovered. The family leaves the basement but is confronted by a single alien, who snatches up the unconscious Morgan.

At this point the film brings together all the seemingly irrelevant character traits and plot points ('signs') to demonstrate an order beyond human understanding. The glasses of water that Graham's daughter has a habit of leaving about the house now become a weapon when they discover that water is harmful to the alien – a plot device borrowed from the 1962 film version (but not the novel) of John Wyndham's *The Day of the Triffids* – and Graham realises the meaning of his dying wife's final words that he should tell Merrill, a former champion minor league baseball player, to 'swing away' – which he does,

DIRECTOR M. Night Shyamalan
PRODUCER M. Night Shyamalan, Frank Marshall
SCREENPLAY M. Night Shyamalan
DIRECTOR OF PHOTOGRAPHY Tak Fujimoto
EDITOR Barbara Tulliver
MUSIC James Newton Howard
PRODUCTION DESIGN Larry Fulton
MAIN CAST Mel Gibson, Joaquin Phoenix, Rory Culkin, Abigail Breslin, M. Night Shyamalan, Cherry Jones, Patricia Kalember, Ted Sutton
PRODUCTION COMPANY Touchstone Pictures, Blinding Edge Pictures, The Kennedy/Marshall Company

splashing the water from the numerous glasses on the alien and killing him, thus saving Morgan.

In a key scene, as the family watches television coverage of developing events, Graham rejects Merrill's belief in signs, saying that ultimately we are all alone and that anyone who thinks otherwise only does so because they cannot confront their own fear in the face of the unknown. But after the dark night of the soul in his basement, and the defeat of the aliens and the saving of his son's life, in the coda Graham is seen donning his clerical collar once again. The film thus restores the father in several senses: Graham as father and Father, God the Father, and Shyamalan as artist-creator (it is he, as Ray, who provides both the catalyst for the test of Graham's faith and the clue for its reaffirmation when he hypothesises that the aliens fear water).

Silent Running
US, 1972 – 89 mins
Douglas Trumbull

Douglas Trumbull, the director of *Silent Running*, worked as special effects supervisor on several major science fiction films – *2001: A Space Odyssey** (1968), *The Andromeda Strain* (1971), *Close Encounters of the Third Kind** (1977), *Star Trek: The Motion Picture** (1979) and *Blade Runner** (1982) – and also directed the special effects showcase *Brainstorm* (1983), about a machine that records the sensory experiences of an individual and allows another to have the same experience during playback (an idea more interestingly explored in the SQUID device in *Strange Days** [1995]). Conceived partly in response to Stanley Kubrick's milestone movie *2001*, *Silent Running* emphasises human involvement instead of extraterrestrial intervention, endorsing what today might be called an act of eco-terrorism in one of the first environmentally conscious science fiction films.

In the future of *Silent Running*, Earth can no longer sustain plant and animal life. The last remaining flora and fauna have been preserved in giant geodesic greenhouse domes that are attached to a fleet of space freighters positioned near Saturn. Four crewmen work on the freighter *Valley Forge*, including Freeman Lowell (Dern), a botanist who maintains the forests in the six domes of the ship in anticipation of some indefinite time in the future when they might be brought back to Earth. Lowell has a limited camaraderie with the rest of the crew, who have no appreciation for the natural world. They view the forests merely as cargo, preferring the synthetic foods provided by the ship to the wholesome meals with natural ingredients lovingly prepared by Lowell, who worships the forests. While they amuse themselves racing through the ship's corridors in ATVs, the long-haired Lowell tends to the forests in a robe, looking like a cross between a monk in a monastery and a flower child in the garden.

When the order comes to destroy the domes so that the freighters can be returned to commercial service, the other crewmen celebrate their imminent return to Earth, but Lowell decides to take a stand against the company and save the forest habitats on his ship. After four of the domes are jettisoned and destroyed with nuclear charges, Lowell accidentally kills one of the other crewmen when he refuses to allow the next charge to be planted, and then traps the other two in the fifth dome when they plant a charge there, killing them when it separates and explodes. Lowell reprograms the ship's robot drones (whom he names Huey, Dewey and Louie), teaching them, among other things, how to care for the forest in the one remaining dome, all the while maintaining the pretence in radio contact that there has been an accident on the ship and that he is irretrievably drifting away to certain death in the rings of Saturn. When the fleet's lead ship manages finally to locate the *Valley Forge* and Lowell is about to be 'rescued', he deliberately jettisons the one remaining dome with Drone 1 (Dewey), the only drone still functioning, aboard and then blows up the ship, with himself in it, with one of the nuclear charges. The last poignant images show the brightly illuminated greenhouse dome drifting into space with Dewey tending the plants with a battered child's watering can.

DIRECTOR Douglas Trumbull
PRODUCER Michael Gruskoff, Douglas Trumbull
SCREENPLAY Deric Washburn, Michael Cimino, Steven Bochco
DIRECTOR OF PHOTOGRAPHY Charles F. Wheeler
EDITOR Aaron Stell
MUSIC Peter Schickele
CAST Bruce Dern, Cliff Potts, Ron Rifkin, Jesse Vint, Mark Persons, Steven Brown, Larry Whisenhunt
PRODUCTION COMPANY Universal Pictures, Trumbull/Gruskoff Productions

Unlike the technological aloofness of *2001*, *Silent Running* focuses on the emotional turmoil of its protagonist, highlighting Dern's intense performance with long close-ups as Lowell speaks passionately about nature or, later, when he begins to go mad alone on the ship. The three waddling drones (played by double-amputees) must have inspired George Lucas when creating R2-D2 and C-3PO in *Star Wars** (1977). Like faithful pets, they are especially endearing when Lowell repairs Huey after accidentally striking him with one of the ATVs and Dewey loyally refuses to leave him, and when Lowell teaches Huey and Dewey how to play poker. Despite their unarguable cuteness, though, *Silent Running* never lets us forget the threats of capitalism. In addition to the company's order to destroy the domes, product placement looms large (as in *2001*), with American Airlines, Dow Chemical and other actual corporate logos clearly emblazoned on the storage containers that fill the ship.

The Silent Star/Der schweigende Stern (First Spaceship on Venus)
GDR, 1960 – 85 mins
Kurt Maetzig

Based on *The Astronauts*, the first science fiction novel by Polish author Stanislaw Lem, author of *Solaris*, *The Silent Star* was a prestige production and the first science fiction film released by the East German studio DEFA. Shot in intense Agfacolor and in widescreen, it was directed by Kurt Maetzig, a major figure in the cinema of the German Democratic Republic. Crown International Pictures released a shortened version of the film in the US in 1962 under the title *First Spaceship on Venus* on a double bill with *Varan the Unbelievable*, the Americanised version of a 1958 *kaiju-eiga* by Ishirō Honda, who had also directed *Gojira** (1954). Unsurprisingly, *First Spaceship on Venus* was featured in an episode of *Mystery Science Theater 3000*, a show that mocks poorly made science fiction and horror movies, in 1990. But, despite *Silent Star*'s comparative technical deficiencies, it remains fascinating as a Socialist take on the genre.

The story begins in 1985, a future in which Socialism has triumphed and the Eastern bloc is leading the world in space exploration. During a massive engineering project to irrigate the Gobi Desert, a strange artefact is accidentally unearthed, as in *Quatermass and the Pit** (1967). Scientists determine that it is not of earthly origin, and link it to the extremely powerful explosion that actually occurred in Siberia in 1908 and which has been explained as most likely the result of a large meteorite, but in the film is newly determined to have been the crash site of a spaceship. Professor Harringway (Lukes) concludes that the alien ship came from Venus and that the artefact is a form of flight recorder.

An expedition with an international crew is sent on a new generation ship to Venus to discover the meaning of the information contained in the recorder. During the journey, the scientific team, with the help of the ship's computer, succeeds in partially translating the message and determines that it involves a Venusian plan to destroy humanity and invade Earth. The crew debates whether to return to Earth with this important news, but decides against it, concluding that rather than causing panic around the world even by radioing the news back home they instead will forge on to Venus to investigate. When they arrive on the planet, they discover that before the aggressive Venusians could carry out their invasion of Earth they had destroyed themselves in an apocalyptic nuclear explosion. However, although the Venusians are gone, their machinery, including the radiation weapon, has continued to function, and the scientists accidentally trigger it and also disturb the planet's gravitational force.

In the dramatic attempt to disarm the machine, several of the crew members are killed, but the survivors return to Earth to warn humanity about the dangers of atomic warfare, which is understood as a threat from the West. Criticism of Western aggression is clear in the film, particularly when the crew's Japanese member, a doctor, recalls the horrors of Hiroshima in a poignant monologue. Also, in sharp contrast to many classic American science fiction movies, Socialist ideals inform the ethnic and gender diversity of the ship's crew.

DIRECTOR Kurt Maetzig
SCREENPLAY Jan Fethke, Wolfgang Kohlhaase, Günter Reisch, and Günter Rücker, based on the novel *The Astronauts* (1951) by Stanislaw Lem
DIRECTOR OF PHOTOGRAPHY Joachim Hasler
EDITOR Lena Neumann
MUSIC Andrzej Markowski
MAIN CAST Yoko Tani, Oldrich Lukes, Ignacy Machowski, Julius Ongewe, Michail N. Postnikow, Kurt Rackelmann, Günter Simon, Tang Hua-Ta
PRODUCTION COMPANY DEFA (Deutsche Film-Aktiengesellschaft)

The East German/Soviet/Bulgarian co-production *Eolomea* (1972) offers a climax as stirring as Raymond Massey's speech regarding the necessity of personal sacrifice for space exploration at the conclusion of *Things to Come** (1936): eight commandeered spaceships containing a group of renegade scientists pass by Lunar Station 3 entering the uncharted vastness of space, rendered briefly as abstract imagery recalling the stargate sequence in Stanley Kubrick's *2001: A Space Odyssey** (1968), while they bid goodbye forever to their Earthly ties as they begin their 136-year journey to explore the possible existence of another planet. The ideology of *The Silent Star*, by contrast, is entirely earthbound, despite the bizarre Venusian landscape, the design of which is a combination of surrealism, psychedelia and Dr. Seuss.

Slaughterhouse-Five
US, 1972 – 104 mins
George Roy Hill

Cult science fiction writer Kurt Vonnegut, Jr introduced black humour to science fiction. George Roy Hill, who had seen active duty during both World War II and the Korean War, directed *Slaughterhouse-Five*, based on Vonnegut's most popular novel, between *Butch Cassidy and the Sundance Kid* (1969) and *The Sting* (1973), both multiple Academy Award winners starring Paul Newman and Robert Redford. However, *Slaughterhouse-Five*, a better film by far, earned none, perhaps because, in contrast to the other two films, it is unremittingly downbeat, with (as the alien Tralfamadorians in the movie insist), the concept of free will merely an illusion.

Like the novel, the film follows Billy Pilgrim (Sacks), who becomes 'unstuck in time' and so experiences his life in achronological fashion. Billy shuffles between scenes of his traumatic war experiences including the bombing of Dresden, a civilian target, in World War II (a horrific event that Vonnegut himself had witnessed), living on the planet Tralfamadore with porn starlet Montana Wildhack (Perrine) and his comfortable married life in Ilium, a fictitious town in upper New York State that also appears in a number of Vonnegut's other novels including *Player Piano* (1952), *Cat's Cradle* (1963) and *Galápagos* (1985). Visual rhymes and sound bridges, the work of editor Dede Allen, who brought jump cuts to Hollywood with her editing for Arthur Penn's *Bonnie and Clyde* (1967), brilliantly provide transitions from one phase of Billy's life to another and establish thematic links between them.

The narrative is ambiguous as to whether Billy, a pilgrim searching for meaning in the world, really is unstuck in time or whether he has embraced the idea and the existence of the Tralfamadorians as a fantasy escape from an intolerable existence, much as Connie Ramos does in Marge Piercy's later novel *Woman on the Edge of Time* (1976). At one point Billy does admit that 'If it weren't for Tralfamadore, I might have needed an institution'. Certainly his marriage is depicted as joyless and stifling, and his wife Valencia (Gans) is a screeching harridan from whom any man would wish to flee – thus also linking *Slaughterhouse-Five* with the masculinist sentiments of Hill's blockbuster buddy films.

Vonnegut praised the film soon after its release in his preface to *Between Time and Timbuktu* (1972), declaring that it was 'a flawless translation' of the novel that was 'so harmonious with what I felt when I wrote the book'. Curiously, though, the film contains nothing of what is perhaps the most cinematic passage in the novel, when Billy, killing time until the Tralfamadorian saucer will arrive to take him away, watches an unnamed Hollywood war film on television backwards, so that its meaning is reversed, the sequence now showing kindly Americans working feverishly to dismantle dangerous bombs rather than building them. Nor, oddly, is the Tralfamadorian response to the exigencies of existence, 'so it goes', ever spoken in the film – although Glenn Gould's doleful piano helps convey Vonnegut's absurdist vision of the individual trapped within larger social and cosmic forces barely comprehended, and the silver boots and woman's fur-lined coat

DIRECTOR George Roy Hill

PRODUCER Paul Monash

SCREENPLAY Stephen Geller, based on the 1969 novel *Slaughterhouse-Five or The Children's Crusade* by Kurt Vonnegut, Jr

DIRECTOR OF PHOTOGRAPHY Miroslav Ondricek

EDITOR Dede Allen

MUSIC Glenn Gould

PRODUCTION DESIGN Henry Bumstead

MAIN CAST Michael Sacks, Ron Liebman, Valerie Perrine, Holly Near, Eugene Roche, Perry King, Kevin Conway, Sharon Gans, Nick Belle, Sorrell Booke, Richard Schall

PRODUCTION COMPANY Universal Pictures, Vanadas Productions

Billy wears throughout his time as a prisoner of war serve as constant visual reminders of the comic indifference of the universe.

While Keith Gordon directed a feature adaptation of the novel *Mother Night* (1961) in 1996 and Alan Rudolph a version of *Breakfast of Champions* (1973) in 1999, and a few of Vonnegut's short stories have been adapted for television, including 'Harrison Bergeron' (1961), 'Who Am I This Time?' (1961) and a series, *Monkey House* (1991–3), that adapted three other stories collected in *Welcome to the Monkey House* (1968) – 'The Euphio Question' (1951), 'All the King's Horses' (1951) and 'Next Door' (1965) – *Slaughterhouse-Five* remains to date the best of the few of Vonnegut's science fiction novels to reach the big screen.

Sleep Dealer
US/Mexico, 2008 – 90 mins
Alex Rivera

Mexico produced some science fiction films in the 1950s and 60s, including *La momia Azteca contra el robot humano* (*The Aztec Mummy vs. the Human Robot*, 1958), in which a mad scientist builds a robot to steal an ancient Aztec treasure, and *Santo el enmascarado de plata contra la invasión de los marcianos* (*Santo vs. the Martian Invasion*, 1967), about the legendary masked wrestler's battle against a Martian attack. These were mostly B movies that were embarrassing as science fiction, but *Sleep Dealer* is a much more ambitious film in its production values, thematic depth and extrapolative imagination. Combining a cyberpunk sensibility with a Third World critique of American culture and influence, it depicts a near future in which the global digital network has made a number of advances, now exploiting virtual labour and moving social networking into memory sharing, that have destroyed local communities even as actual national borders become more entrenched.

A wall now separates the United States from Mexico (as in Gareth Edwards's *Monsters* [2010], which addresses similar border issues), and instead of attempting illegal immigration, Mexican labourers work robotic drones through virtual hookup, exploited until they burn out from the process. Memo Cruz (Peña) is a young man living with his peasant family in the remote village of Santa Ana del Rio, Oaxaca, his father (Macías) working a small *milpa*, or field. International corporations control natural resources such as water, and one such company, Del Rio Water, based in San Diego, has built a dam in the village's valley, cutting off the natural water supply to the local inhabitants and requiring them to buy water by the bag at the armed and patrolled dam facility. As a hobby, Memo has built a satellite antenna and hacks into conversations on the network, eventually tapping into the US Air Force communications system of remote drones operating in the area to protect the company from so-called 'aqua-terrorists'. The company, detecting the hack and assuming it is the work of terrorists, sends a drone operated by a Mexican-American pilot, Rudy Ramirez (Vargas), to destroy the Cruz house, killing Memo's father – all of which is shown live on the television show 'Drones' as entertainment with no thought of due process.

Leaving home to find work, Memo goes to Tijuana, where he has nodes implanted, like the bodily portals in *eXistenZ* (1999), and becomes a 'node worker' at Cybercero, one of the factories known as 'sleep dealers' because the workers tend to fall asleep or collapse from exhaustion during their long shifts. There, he is plugged into the network, in virtual space operating a robot worker high atop a skyscraper in San Diego. He meets Luz Martínez (Varela), a writer who inputs her memories to an online site called 'TruNode' ('the world's number one memory market') in hopes that others will purchase her memories. Meanwhile, Ramirez, a Mexican-American, has had misgivings about having carried out his orders, and, after buying Luz's online memories involving Memo, he tracks him down. To atone for his actions, Ramirez convinces Memo to sneak him into Cybercero, where he connects remotely to his Air Force drone and blasts a hole in the Santa

DIRECTOR Alex Rivera
PRODUCER Anthony Bregman
SCREENPLAY Alex Rivera, David Riker
DIRECTOR OF PHOTOGRAPHY Lisa Rinzler
EDITOR Julie Carr, Madeleine Gavin, Alex Rivera, Jeffrey M. Werner
MUSIC tomandandy
MAIN CAST Leonor Varela, Jacob Vargas, Luis Fernando Peña, José Concepción Macías, Metztli Adamina, Tenoch Huerta, Guillermo Ríos
PRODUCTION COMPANY Likely Story, This is That Productions

Ana dam, causing the water to flow freely to the people there. In the end, Ramirez and Memo acknowledge that their terrorist act may not have liberated the water permanently, that it was, in effect, a small blow to the empire, before the former disappears into the interior and the latter continues as a node worker in Tijuana.

Director and co-writer Alex Rivera, born and raised in the US, is an artist and film-maker whose work, including *Sleep Dealer*, addresses Latino political issues. The film critiques the exploitation of immigrant labour in the US in its premise of global virtual technology which allows for migrant workers without actual migration. As Memo's boss tells him, this is the American Dream, giving Americans 'what they've always wanted – all the work without the workers.' Tellingly, the technology requires node workers to wear contact lenses that obscure their irises and a face plate that seems to muzzle their mouths. As the initially naïve Memo observes after working at Cybercero for a while, 'The more time I spend connected, the harder it is to see'. Over time workers go blind or experience cardiac arrest as the technology seems to suck their souls from them. Ultimately, Memo and the other workers are a natural resource to be drained away by gringos, like the Santa Ana river.

Sleeper
US, 1973 – 89 mins
Woody Allen

Everything You Always Wanted to Know about Sex* But Were Afraid to Ask (1972) made clear Woody Allen's debt to genre film-making. A series of comic vignettes responding loosely to questions from David Reuben's 1969 bestselling book of the same name, each offers a generic parody, including a horror film with John Carradine as a mad scientist and the culminating *tour-de-force*, a science fiction parody of *Fantastic Voyage** (1966) in which technicians inside the brain and body of an Allenesque nebbish struggle to coordinate signals in order to succeed in seducing the man's dinner date. Allen has often incorporated elements of the fantastic genres into his films – *Love and Death* (1975), *Stardust Memories* (1980), *Zelig* (1983), *The Purple Rose of Cairo* (1985), *Alice* (1990) and *Midnight in Paris* (2011), most notably – but *Sleeper* is his only science fiction feature to date, and its humour is firmly rooted in the conventions of the genre.

The plot, which borrows from such classics of science fiction literature as Edward Bellamy's *Looking Backward* (1888), H.G. Wells's *The Sleeper Awakes* (1910) and George Orwell's *Nineteen Eighty-Four* (1949), involves the owner of a Greenwich Village health food store, Miles Monroe (Allen), who is cryogenically frozen (in aluminum foil) without his knowledge in 1973 and revived in a totalitarian world 200 years later by scientists working with the underground Resistance. In order to escape capture, Miles disguises himself as a robot butler and is deployed at the home of vapid socialite Luna Schlosser (Keaton). As they begin to develop a romantic relationship, circumstances send them on the run together; and while Miles is captured and brainwashed into being a model citizen, Luna is radicalised by the underground. She rescues and helps to deprogram Miles, and together they infiltrate the government, where they discover that the Leader had been killed in an attack and that all that remains intact is his nose, which the State hopes to clone into a reconstituted Leader. Pretending to be scientists, Miles and Luna enter the operating room, steal the nose, and squash it under a passing steamroller.

The plot's futuristic premise allows Allen considerable opportunity for gags, both verbal and visual. So, for example, a Volkswagen Beetle hidden in a cave for two centuries starts instantly, a robot pooch defecates batteries, and a newspaper from the 1990s carries the headline 'Pope's Wife Gives Birth to Twins'. Much of the humour is dependent on Allen's persona as a sexually insecure neurotic. When he is regaining his wiped memory, for example, he imagines himself as Blanche DuBois from *A Streetcar Named Desire*, depending on the kindness of strangers. To escape the police, at one point Miles hides for a time in the Orgasmatron, a cylindrical stall into which one steps to obtain the feeling of sexual satisfaction, emerging finally in a comic euphoria. In the climactic set-piece, Miles and Luna, mistaken for the cloning scientists, attempt to stall for time even as they claim they are going to clone the Leader from his nose directly into his clothes while the calm voice of the monitoring computer in the operating room is that of Douglas Rain, who supplied a similar relaxed voice for the HAL 9000 computer in Stanley Kubrick's *2001: A Space Odyssey** (1968).

DIRECTOR Woody Allen
PRODUCER Jack Grossberg
SCREENPLAY Woody Allen, Marshall Brickman
DIRECTOR OF PHOTOGRAPHY David M. Walsh
EDITOR O. Nicholas Brown, Ron Kalish, Ralph Rosenblum
MUSIC Woody Allen
PRODUCTION DESIGN Dale Hennesy
MAIN CAST Woody Allen, Diane Keaton, John Beck, Mary Gregory, Don Keefer, John McLiam, Bartlett Robinson, Chris Forbes, Marya Small, Peter Hobbs
PRODUCTION COMPANY Rollins-Joffe Productions

Allen suggests the timelessness of slapstick in the depiction of government stormtroopers like the Keystone Kops, piling out of their futuristic paddy wagons and blowing themselves up with their supposedly advanced weaponry, and when Miles and a pursuer slip on the huge peels from genetically modified giant bananas. In addition to the film's reflections on comedy, it is serious in that the awakening sleeper, as with the protagonist of Wells's novel, wakes to political awareness and commitment. At the same time, *Sleeper* suggests that the comic schlemiel, with all his foibles, is necessary to maintain a sense of the human in an increasingly technologised world in which hedonistic pleasure is paramount.

Solaris (*Solyaris*)

USSR, 1972 – 165 mins
Andrei Tarkovsky

The first film adaptation of the novel by Polish science fiction author Stanislaw Lem (who also wrote *The Astronauts* [1951], upon which the East German film *The Silent Star** [1960] was based), about the human inability to comprehend and communicate with an alien Other, eschews action and special effects to focus instead on the psychological complexities of space travel and first contact. Although it has more of a plot on which to hinge its exploration of character than Andrei Tarkovsky's other foray into the genre, *Stalker* (1979),

DIRECTOR Andrei Tarkovsky
PRODUCER Vyacheslav Tarasov
SCREENPLAY Fridrikh Gorenshtein, Andrei Tarkovsky, based on the 1961 novel by Stanislaw Lem
DIRECTOR OF PHOTOGRAPHY Vadim Yusov
EDITOR Lyudmila Feiginova, Nina Marcus
MUSIC Eduard Artemiev
PRODUCTION DESIGN Mikhail Romadin
MAIN CAST Donatas Banionis, Natalya Bondarchuk, Jüri Järvet, Anatolii Solonitsyn, Sos Sarkisyan, Nikolai Grinko
PRODUCTION COMPANY Creative Unit of Writers & Cinema Workers, Mosfilm, Unit Four

about a trio of characters exploring The Zone for artefacts supposedly left by alien visitors, *Solaris* nevertheless is one of the most cerebral of science fiction films. The film premiered at the Cannes Film Festival, where it won the Grand Prix Spécial du Jury and was nominated for the Palme d'Or and, its reputation growing over the years, inspired a undeservedly underrated 2002 remake written and directed by Steven Soderbergh and starring George Clooney.

The narrative is set primarily aboard a space station orbiting the planet Solaris, the surface of which is covered by one large, apparently sentient ocean. Scientists have been studying this ocean planet for generations, producing exhaustive volumes of data and theoretical tomes about it, but thus far have been unsuccessful in the attempt to make contact with it. Now, something mysterious is occurring on the station, with the crew becoming unresponsive to attempted communications. Kris Kelvin (Banionis), a psychologist, travels to the station at the request of one of the crew members, who has since committed suicide, to evaluate the situation.

Once on the station, which has fallen into disarray and neglect and which now contains a crew of only three, he encounters the same mysterious phenomenon that the others there have all experienced: at night, while asleep, the ocean has probed his memories and sent him a 'visitor' – in his case, a replica of his wife Hari (Bondarchuk), who had committed suicide after a domestic argument and over which he has thus been carrying a burden of guilt. The ocean, it seems, is providing each person with a replica of someone from his or her past with whom they had an intense emotional connection. Its motives, whether benevolent or sinister, are never made clear, but only speculated upon by Kelvin and the other crew members. Kelvin at first destroys his visitor, horrified by it, but when she is reconstituted each night with a developing consciousness, eventually Kelvin accepts, then embraces, the simulation of his wife as a gift from the ocean and a wondrous opportunity to erase their tragic past and begin their relationship anew.

Lem collaborated with Tarkovsky on the screenplay, but there were creative differences, and Tarkovsky does take some liberties with Lem's narrative. The novel ends with Kelvin in existential stasis, unable to tear himself away from Solaris, while the film, more visually, concludes with a scene of Kelvin back home visiting his father (where the film begins) as the camera pans up and away to eventually reveal Kelvin living in an illusory environment created by Solaris. Tarkovsky takes up Lem's primary concern with the limits of human science and understanding confronted by the truly alien ('We don't need other worlds. We need mirrors', says Snaut, one of the scientists on the station) and the place of humanity in the cosmos, but also devotes considerable time to the psychological conflict within Kelvin, who suffers from both personal trauma and the harsh environment of space, which is contrasted with the lush, natural world of the Russian countryside. Even before Kelvin begins his journey, our collective alienation from the natural world is vividly depicted in the lengthy tracking shots, filmed through the windscreen, of the modern concrete highway as former astronaut Henri Berton (Dvorshetsky) returns in his self-navigating vehicle from Kelvin's family home in the country.

Soylent Green
US, 1973 – 97 mins
Richard Fleischer

Set in New York City in 2022, 50 years from the time of its making, *Soylent Green* was one of the first science fiction films to extrapolate on the problems of overpopulation, global warming and the growing corporate control of food production. The film's opening montage of still images of increasing urbanisation and industrialisation since the nineteenth century anticipates the ecological consciousness of later documentaries such as *Koyaanisqatsi* (1982), although the narrative is essentially a police procedural set in a dystopian future. Directed by Richard Fleischer (*20,000 Leagues Under the Sea** [1954], *Fantastic Voyage** [1966]), the film, with a screenplay by Stanley R. Greenberg, sharpens the focus and ecological critique of Harry Harrison's more rambling and didactic source novel.

In the sweltering metropolis of 40 million people, most sleep in stairways and streets, and there are chronic shortages of goods and services. Real food is a luxury few can afford, and the general population lives on rations of wafers produced by the monopolistic Soylent Corporation, the newest of which is Soylent Green, supposedly made from plankton. There are frequent food riots in the streets, but the privileged elite have luxury apartments with real food, in one of which the murder of a wealthy and influential tenant brings investigating detective Ty Thorn (Heston) to a world that offers new material pleasures but hides a terrible secret. Thorn lives in a small, dilapidated apartment with Solomon 'Sol' Roth (Edward G. Robinson), a former professor who is now a 'book', an intellectual who searches through old documents to assist in Thorn's investigations and who speaks, like a wise elder, of what it was like in an earlier era when food was abundant. In conversation with other 'books' at the 'Supreme Exchange', Roth realises the terrible truth about Soylent Green and, crushed by it, decides to commit suicide at a government facility, an invention of the film but perhaps inspired by Kurt Vonnegut's 1953 story 'Tomorrow and Tomorrow and Tomorrow'. Thorn arrives too late to save his friend, whose dying words prompt the detective to surreptitiously follow Roth's body as it is loaded, along with the many corpses of other suicides, onto trucks which take them to a guarded waste disposal plant, where he discovers that the bodies are being processed into Soylent Green wafers.

Soylent Green was Robinson's last movie. The actor knew he was dying of cancer (he passed away less than two weeks after shooting finished), making his death scene particularly poignant. The scene is also cannily self-reflexive. As Roth dies, he is treated to IMAX-like panoramic video clips of a verdant and pristine Earth teeming with animal and plant life while listening to (his choice) 'light classical music'. The intruding Thorn is overwhelmed when he sees these images of animals in the wild, fields of flowers and babbling streams ('How could I know? How could I ever imagine?') – a demonstration of the affective power of the film medium and a celebration of the camera's ability to capture the real world.

It is ironic, then, that while the screenplay mostly improves on Harry Harrison's novel by streamlining the plot and eliminating its often preachy prose, *Soylent Green* itself often seems stiff and uninspired,

DIRECTOR Richard Fleischer
PRODUCER Walter Seltzer, Russell Thacher
SCREENPLAY Stanley R. Greenberg, based on the novel *Make Room, Make Room!* (1966) by Harry Harrison
DIRECTOR OF PHOTOGRAPHY Richard H. Kline
MUSIC Fred Myrow
PRODUCTION DESIGN Edward C. Carfagno
MAIN CAST Charlton Heston, Edward G. Robinson, Leigh Taylor-Young, Chuck Connors, Joseph Cotten, Brock Peters
PRODUCTION COMPANY MGM

qualities it shares with director Richard Fleischer's other forays into the fantastic including *20,000 Leagues Under the Sea*, *Fantastic Voyage*, *Amityville 3-D* (1983), and *Conan the Destroyer* (1984). The crowd scenes are especially disappointing, and the idea of giant scoops used for crowd control – another invention of the film – is rather unconvincing (although the idea does follow from the premise of Soylent Green being made of people). Still, particularly provocative is the film's depiction of gender relations in this new world order. In this world of scarcity, masculine privilege has once again asserted itself, and women, like the murder victim's mistress (Taylor-Young), are sexual objects who come with luxury apartments along with other mod cons and are referred to dismissively as 'furniture' in the film's futuristic slang, making an idea only touched upon discreetly in the novel more brutally explicit.

Star Trek: The Motion Picture
US, 1979 – 132 mins
Robert Wise

Created by Gene Roddenberry, *Star Trek* began as a television series that was first broadcast on NBC from 1966–1969. Set in the 23rd century, *Star Trek* envisions a world in which humanity has achieved peace on Earth and belongs to the United Federation of Planets, dedicated to exploration rather than expansionism in space. The show developed a strong fan base – devoted fans of the show are the subject of the documentary *Trekkies* (1997) and are genially mocked in *Galaxy Quest** (1999) – and has since expanded to become a franchise second only to *Star Wars** (1977). The show's success generated *Star Trek: The Motion Picture*, featuring the same cast as the TV show, and five sequels, all following the same characters – *Star Trek II: The Wrath of Khan* (1982), *Star Trek III: The Search for Spock* (1984), *Star Trek IV: The Voyage Home* (1986), *Star Trek V: The Final Frontier* (1989) and *Star Trek VI: The Undiscovered Country* (1991) – as well as four spin-off television shows, five other films (including *Star Trek* [2009], J.J. Abrams's reboot with the characters of the

DIRECTOR Robert Wise
PRODUCER Gene Roddenberry
SCREENPLAY Harold Livingston
DIRECTOR OF PHOTOGRAPHY
Richard H. Kline
EDITOR Todd Ramsay
MUSIC Jerry Goldsmith
PRODUCTION DESIGN Harold
Michelson
MAIN CAST William Shatner,
Leonard Nimoy, DeForest Kelley,
James Doohan, George Takei, Majel
Barrett, Walter Koenig, Nichelle
Nichols, Persis Khambatta, Stephen
Collins
PRODUCTION COMPANY Century
Associates, Paramount Pictures

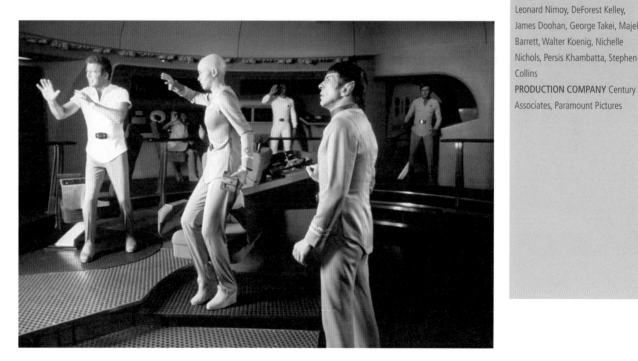

original show as young men on their first assignment), video games, numerous novels and other merchandising. (After *Star Trek VI*, the films were no longer numbered for their North American and UK releases, although in Europe they continued to be numbered until *Star Trek: Nemesis* [2002], one of the later films focusing on the characters from *Star Trek: The Next Generation* [1987–94]). *Star Trek: The Motion Picture* is very much like an extended episode of the show, and provides the same pleasures as viewers expected of it.

The plot involves a mysterious energy cloud that is heading from deep space directly towards Earth. The force destroys three Klingon warships and a Starfleet monitoring station in its path and seems unstoppable. All of Starfleet's other ships are too distant to intercept it before it reaches Earth, except for the USS *Enterprise*, orbiting Earth in 'drydock' for an upgrade. Given the emergency, the ship's former captain, now Admiral Kirk (Shatner), takes command of the refitting ship from Capt. Willard Decker (Collins), causing predictable tension between them. The *Enterprise* intercepts the cloud, which sends an energy probe to the ship's bridge, targeting Vulcan science officer Spock (Nimoy) and abducting the navigator, Ilia (Khambatta), who is returned to the ship as an android to gather information for 'V'ger'. Spock 'mind melds' with V'ger and discovers that it is a living machine, which is ultimately revealed to be the terrestrial space probe Voyager 6, which had been sent three centuries ago into space to gather information and which was found by an alien race of machines that reprogrammed it, allowing it to develop consciousness and to fulfil its mission of learning everything in order to report back to 'the Creator'. When the Creator doesn't answer V'ger's antiquated radio signal, it becomes intent on destroying Earth, which has become 'infested' with 'carbon units' which it does not at first realise are in fact the Creator.

Star Trek has resonated so deeply within the popular imagination in large part because it depicts an appealing mythic harmony between the human and technology. This tension is enacted in the relationship of the three main characters: the conflicted half-human Spock, who initially seeks the Vulcan ideal of pure logic devoid of emotion; the impetuous emotionalism of Dr. McCoy (Kelly); and Kirk, the Captain, who seeks to balance the extremes of the other two men in order to maintain safe and smooth functioning of the microcosmic spaceship of state. *Star Trek: The Motion Picture* exploits the same themes, paralleling V'ger's search for purpose and meaning in the universe despite having gained vast knowledge with Spock's personal conflict. In the climax, Decker, who had been involved in a romantic relationship with Ilia in the past, literally joins with the machine, agreeing to be absorbed by it as together they become a new life form and continue on its journey. The film's lack of action and slow pace, with many languorous tracking shots such as, for example, when the Enterprise is released from its orbital moorings and when it penetrates the numerous layers of V'ger, was a deliberate stylistic choice by director Robert Wise (*The Day the Earth Stood Still** [1951], *The Andromeda Strain* [1971]), for depicting the show's respectful regard for the universe.

Star Wars (*Star Wars Episode IV: A New Hope*)
US, 1977 – 121 mins
George Lucas

Reinvigorating the conventions of several genres including war movies, Westerns and space opera, *Star Wars* became an international phenomenon, providing a nostalgic return to the bygone pleasures of Hollywood serials such as *Flash Gordon** (1936), with their melodramatic morality and rousing action. It became the top-grossing film of all time (until displaced five years later by Steven Spielberg's *E.T.: The Extra-Terrestrial** [1982]), and generated an elaborate and thus far unsurpassed merchandising franchise. Waiving his up-front fee as director, creator George Lucas instead negotiated to retain the licensing rights for merchandising, which the studio deemed largely worthless, thus earning a fortune.

Star Wars was followed by two sequels, *The Empire Strikes Back* (1980, directed by Irvin Kershner), and *Return of the Jedi* (1983, directed by Richard Marquand), each released three years apart. Sixteen years after *Jedi* came the second trilogy – *Star Wars Episode I: The Phantom Menace* (1999), *Star Wars Episode II:*

DIRECTOR George Lucas
PRODUCER Gary Kurtz
SCREENPLAY George Lucas
DIRECTOR OF PHOTOGRAPHY Gilbert Taylor
EDITOR Richard Chew, Paul Hirsch, Marcia Lucas
MUSIC John Williams
PRODUCTION DESIGN John Barry
MAIN CAST Mark Hamill, Alec Guinness, Harrison Ford, Carrie Fisher, Kenny Baker, Anthony Daniels, Peter Mayhew, James Earl Jones (voice of Darth Vader), David Prowse, Peter Cushing
PRODUCTION COMPANY Lucasfilm, 20th Century Fox

Attack of the Clones (2002) and *Star Wars Episode III: Revenge of the Sith* (2005) – all directed by Lucas (*THX 1138** [1971]) and again released three years apart. (The re-release of *Star Wars* in 1981 added the subtitle *Episode IV: A New Hope* to establish its position in relation to the projected new films.) The six *Star Wars* films together were nominated for 25 Academy Awards, winning ten, including Best Original Score for John Williams. Collectively, the films have earned billions at the box office, and as a series rank behind only the Harry Potter and James Bond franchises.

The story of the films is set, as the opening title crawl of *Star Wars* announces, 'a long time ago, in a galaxy far, far away'. The evil Darth Vader, overseeing the completion of the Death Star, the ultimate weapon of the Galactic Empire to destroy the Rebel Alliance, captures Princess Leia Organa (Fisher), who has hidden the plans of the Death Star in the 'droid R2-D2 (Baker). R2, along with another robot, C-3PO (Daniels), escape to the planet Tatooine, where they are bought by Luke Skywalker (Hamill), a young farm boy, and his uncle and aunt, setting in motion the epic action. Luke joins with Obi-Wan Kenobi (Guinness), a Jedi Knight, one of a select group of skilled warriors who are able to use the mystical power of 'The Force', freewheeling smuggler Han Solo (Ford) and his Wookie co-pilot Chewbacca (Mayhew), on a mission to rescue Leia. In the climax, they join the rebel assault on the Death Star, and Luke fires the fatal shot at its one conveniently vulnerable point, destroying it.

The sequels reveal that Darth Vader is in fact a former Jedi, Anakin Skywalker, and father of Luke and Leia, adding a darker Oedipal overtone to the traditional hero quest. As well, *Star Wars'* production design, informed by a sense of a 'used future' rather than the pristine look of so many futuristic films before it, anticipates such later and grittier films as Ridley Scott's *Alien** (1979) and *Blade Runner** (1982). The prequel series begins 19 years earlier and follows the life of Anakin as a young man and his gradual fall to the dark side of the Force as he fights in the Clone Wars.

After *Star Wars*, Lucas concentrated on the film's many spinoffs in cinema, television, radio and other media such as amusement park rides (in partnership with the Walt Disney Corporation). Hundreds of *Star Wars* novels have been written since the 1976 novelisation of the film, which predated the film's release and was credited to Lucas but ghost-written by Alan Dean Foster (who also wrote *Splinter of the Mind's Eye*, one the first novels set in the *Star Wars* 'Expanded Universe', in 1978). *Star Wars* has also been the source of numerous parodies, most notably Mel Brooks's *Spaceballs* (1987) and, on television, *Family Guy's* three-episode riffing on the original trilogy, beginning with 'Blue Harvest' (2007). Lucas did not direct a film again until *The Phantom Menace* two decades later, although in the interim he produced other films, some very successful (the *Indiana Jones* series, which he convinced Spielberg to direct), and others embarrassing failures (*Howard the Duck* [1986]). In 1997, Lucas enhanced scenes and added others to the original trilogy using newly available digital technology, and released them theatrically as the *Star Wars Trilogy: Special Edition*. The films were further tweaked for DVD release in 2004. *The Phantom Menace* was re-released in theatres in 3-D in 2012, with 3-D conversion planned for the other five films as well.

Starship Troopers
US, 1997 – 129 mins
Paul Verhoeven

Robert Heinlein's controversial yet influential novel *Starship Troopers*, first published in 1959, is an embarrassingly didactic and militaristic, if not fascistic, work. Following the maturation of a boy, Juan Rico, into a man and a soldier in a future when an intergalactic war breaks out between humans and intelligent arachnids, it contains many long disquisitions by characters such as the retired officer who is now Rico's high school instructor on 'History and Moral Philosophy' and who, standing in for Heinlein, explains the Federation's views on society, history and war, emphasising the importance of individual responsibility and, if necessary, sacrifice for the common good. One looks in vain in the novel for any sense of ironic distance between the author and his pro-militaristic mouthpieces. The film, however, virtually reverses the politics of the novel. The third in a series of Hollywood science fiction movies by Dutch director Paul Verhoeven, following *RoboCop** (1987) and *Total Recall** (1990), it uses similar strategies of ironic excess to comment on the human inclination towards violence generally and within American culture specifically.

DIRECTOR Paul Verhoeven
PRODUCER Jon Davison, Alan Marshall
SCREENPLAY Ed Neumeier, from the 1959 novel by Robert A. Heinlein
DIRECTOR OF PHOTOGRAPHY Jost Vacano
EDITOR Mark Goldblatt, Caroline Ross
MUSIC Basil Poledouris
PRODUCTION DESIGN Allan Cameron
MAIN CAST Casper Van Dien, Dina Meyer, Neil Patrick Harris, Denise Richards, Michael Ironside, Jake Busey, Clancy Brown, Patrick Muldoon
PRODUCTION COMPANY TriStar Pictures, Touchstone Pictures, Big Bug Pictures

The story follows Johnny Rico (Van Dien), a young soldier in the Mobile Infantry, part of the Terran space army fighting the 'Bugs' from the planet Klendathu. After graduating high school in Buenos Aires, Rico, his girlfriend Carmen Ibanez (Richards) and friends Carl Jenkins (Harris) and Dizzy Flores (Meyer) all enlist in Federation military service. When an asteroid propelled by the arachnids destroys Buenos Aires, killing millions, their training kicks into high gear and we follow Rico and Diz in the infantry, Carmen as she becomes a space pilot and Carl, who is assigned to military intelligence. In the climax, one of the arachnid 'brain bugs', the intelligent beings that seem to control a variety of other giant insects, is captured, and Carl reassuringly explains that victory for humans is in sight now that they will be able to learn about the brain bug. Interlaced with this action plot – replete with numerous and elaborate CGI shots of giant bugs, some of epic proportions with hundreds of articulated arachnids, accounting for much of the film's massive $105 million budget – is a romantic melodrama involving Rico, Carmen, Diz and Rico's former school sports rival, Zander Barcalow (Muldoon).

The casting of young, handsome actors who begin as innocent youths and who seem to be in a soap opera as much as a science fiction action movie suggests how anyone is capable of becoming violent toward others. The film provides the kinetic pleasures of action, but along with the many spectacular and graphic battles with the bugs, it critiques the human propensity toward violence. The term 'bugs' to describe the arachnids may be understood as a racial slur, like 'prawns' in *District 9** (2009). The arachnids may resemble lowly terrestrial insects, but they are clearly intelligent, more than once in the film luring the gung-ho humans into traps where their ranks are decimated. The idea that the arachnids are hostile because humans have disturbed their natural habitat, and that humanity should seek peaceful coexistence with them, is never entertained by any of the film's characters, who assume human superiority to their insectoid foe.

The film signals this intolerance towards the Other in the look of the costumes and props of the Federation's military. Unambiguously recalling that of Nazi Germany, Allan Cameron's production design connects Heinlein's starship troopers and Fascist storm troopers. The video reports on the war that appear periodically in the film, continuing the technique employed by Verhoeven and writer Ed Neumeier in *RoboCop*, wittily combine references to both Leni Riefenstahl's glorification of Nazi ideology, *Triumph of the Will* (1934), and Frank Capra's series of American war propaganda films entitled *Why We Fight* (1942–5). Ultimately, to enjoy *Starship Troopers* is thus, in a sense, to stand accused by it. Although its reception was, as might be expected, mixed, it was popular enough to generate two sequels – *Starship Troopers 2: Hero of the Federation* (2004) and *Starship Troopers 3: Marauder* (2008), both direct-to-video releases with which Verhoeven had no involvement – as well as an animated television series, *Roughnecks: Starship Troopers Chronicles* (1998), board and video games and comics.

Strange Days
US, 1995 – 145 mins
Kathryn Bigelow

Writer/director Kathryn Bigelow has established herself as the only female film-maker specialising in action films who, at least to this point, can claim the status of auteur. Her films *Near Dark* (1987), *Blue Steel* (1989), *Point Break* (1991), *Strange Days* and *The Hurt Locker* (2008) are characterised by astonishing action sequences featuring both rapid editing and lengthy Steadicam shots, providing all the expected pleasures of action films. Yet at the same time they also work within the various action genres – cop film, buddy and road movie, Western, horror film and war film – to question their traditional and shared ideological assumptions about gender and violence. Much as Douglas Sirk approached melodrama and Paul Verhoeven science fiction in *RoboCop** (1987), *Total Recall** (1990) and *Starship Troopers** (1997), providing the generic pleasures while critiquing the ideology that underpinned them, so Bigelow works within the action film. *Strange Days*, which Bigelow has called her most personal film, was co-written and produced by her one-time spouse, James Cameron, who also wrote *Point Break* as well as making his own science fiction action movies *The Terminator** (1984), *Aliens* (1986), *The Abyss* (1989) and *Avatar** (2009).

Strange Days is set just a few years in the future of the film's release, in Los Angeles on the day before New Year's Eve, 1999. Lenny (Fiennes) is a black market dealer in 'clips', an outlawed form of total cinema (SQUID – 'Superconducting Quantum Interference Device') produced by a new technology that taps directly into the cerebral cortex for both recording and playback. The self-pitying Lenny must learn to move beyond the simulated memories of his former girlfriend (Lewis), however realistic, and embrace a new life in the real world with Mace (Bassett). Through this metacinematic metaphor, violent action and eroticism are critiqued as voyeuristic, sadistic, and decidedly masculine.

The film begins by positioning us as viewers of one of these clips, although it is only in retrospect that we realise this, since no exposition precedes it. We are thrust immediately into the viewing dynamic, our identification fully mobilised, the camera in the physical perspective of one of a gang of robbers in what seems like one lengthy, technically breathtaking shot (there are actually a couple of disguised cuts) that ends, joltingly, when 'we' die by plunging from a rooftop trying to escape the police. This astonishing opening sequence exposes the subjective camera common to such genres as action and slasher movies as nothing less than a tool of naked male aggression, and many of the violent action sequences that follow in *Strange Days* involve the victimisation of women with the SQUID apparatus, in the infamous manner of Michael Powell's *Peeping Tom* (1960).

In the climax, Lenny and Mace are saved by the honest white police commissioner when they try to deliver to him a clip that has recorded the killing of a popular militant black rock star by two racist white cops. The two policemen confront Mace during the wild celebration on the eve of the millennium and begin to assault her with their nightsticks, the scene invoking the infamous tape of the Rodney King beating, which

DIRECTOR Kathryn Bigelow
PRODUCER James Cameron, Steven-Charles Jaffe
SCREENPLAY James Cameron, Jay Cocks
DIRECTOR OF PHOTOGRAPHY Matthew F. Leonetti
EDITOR Howard E. Smith
MUSIC Graeme Revell
PRODUCTION DESIGN Lilly Kilvert
MAIN CAST Ralph Fiennes, Angela Bassett, Juliette Lewis, Tom Sizemore, Michael Wincott, Vincent D'Onofrio, Glenn Plummer, Brigitte Bako, Richard Edson, William Fichtner, Josef Sommer
PRODUCTION COMPANY Lightstorm Entertainment

occurred in the same city four years before the release of *Strange Days*. But in the movie, unlike the real world, the crowd of onlookers responds by actively banding together to fight an act of racial oppression, and the honest commissioner, brandishing the evidence in his raised hand, parts the suddenly compliant crowd and calls for the arrest of the two rogue cops. Power, ultimately, is thus retained in the (literal) hands of the white male – the putative viewer which the film had been criticising. If this narrative closure contradicts what has come before, the confusion nevertheless speaks to the tensions inherent in the situation of a woman making commercially successful yet self-reflexive action movies, emphasising the still limited place and power of women in mainstream cinema, whether in front of the camera or behind it.

Superman (*Superman: The Movie*)
US, 1978 – 143 mins
Richard Donner

The archetypal superhero Superman (and his alter ego, mild-mannered reporter Clark Kent) began as a comic strip created by writer Jerry Siegel and artist Joe Shuster, who sold it to Detective Comics (later DC Comics) in 1938. 'The Man of Steel' made his first comic book appearance in *Action Comics* #1 in June that year, and was given a self-titled comic a year later. Superman subsequently appeared in a range of media formats including radio, television, the Broadway stage, film and video games. The first radio show, *The Adventures of Superman* (1940–51), was followed by a series of animated cartoons produced by the Fleischer Brothers Studios and two live-action serials, *Superman* (1948) and *Atom Man vs. Superman* (1950), with Kirk Alyn, the first actor to portray Superman on screen. The several live-action television series featuring Superman or his younger teenage Superboy self began with *Adventures of Superman* (1952–8), starring George Reeves, who also starred in *Superman and the Mole Men* (1951), the first Superman feature film, while the various animated shows began with *The Adventures of Superman* in 1966. Most recently, *Man of Steel* (2013), directed by Zack Snyder (*Watchmen* [2009}, *Sucker Punch* [2011]), reboots the story just as Christopher Nolan's *Batman Begins* did for the Caped Crusader in 2005.

Superman boasted Oscar-winning, state-of-the-art special effects, which were done before the advent of digital technology (the film's promotional tagline was 'You'll believe a man can fly') and created through a deft combination of wire work, matte shots and front projection. Released after *Star Wars** (1977) and *Close Encounters of the Third Kind** (1977) but begun before them, *Superman* marked the pivotal transition of the media's treatment of the superhero from camp to serious, a transitional tension everywhere apparent in the film, beginning with the seemingly interminable opening credits, at once epic and excessive.

The opening sections on the doomed planet Krypton and in the rural American town of Smallville, where Jonathan and Martha Kent (Ford, Thaxter) raise the infant Kal-El, are presented earnestly, but once Clark leaves home, moves to the big city (named for Fritz Lang's influential 1927 film *Metropolis**) and becomes a reporter for the Daily Planet, the plot becomes increasingly silly. While Marlon Brando plays Jor-El, Superman's father, as if in a Shakespearean tragedy, Gene Hackman's portrayal of Superman's arch enemy Lex Luthor, aided for some unexplained reason by an inept assistant, Otis (Beatty), is as campy as any of the star villains on the *Batman* television show (1966–8) a decade earlier. The film's overblown production values, featuring a crystal motif for Krypton and the Fortress of Solitude, seem arbitrary, and Superman's ability to fly backwards in time and alter the course of history, which he does to bring Lois Lane (Kidder) back to life after she dies in a landslide caused by Luthor's ridiculously nefarious scheme, unnecessarily violates the narrative universe of the original Superman comic.

The producers added approximately 45 minutes of footage for the television broadcast of *Superman*, a version also available on DVD. *Superman* was a box-office hit and Warner Bros.' most successful production

DIRECTOR Richard Donner
PRODUCER Alexander Salkind, Pierre Spengler
SCREENPLAY Mario Puzo, David Newman, Leslie Newman, Robert Benton
DIRECTOR OF PHOTOGRAPHY Geoffrey Unsworth
EDITOR Stuart Baird, Michael Ellis
MUSIC John Williams
PRODUCTION DESIGN John Barry
MAIN CAST Christopher Reeve, Marlon Brando, Gene Hackman, Margot Kidder, Ned Beatty, Jackie Cooper, Glenn Ford, Jack O'Halloran, Terence Stamp, Valerie Perrine, Phyllis Thaxter, Susanna York
PRODUCTION COMPANY Alexander Salkind, Dovemead Films, Film Export A.G

at the time of its release. The film's commercial success generated three sequels, *Superman II* (1980), *Superman III* (1983) and *Superman IV: The Quest for Peace* (1987), and elevated Christopher Reeve to stardom. Initially, *Superman* and *Superman II* were shot simultaneously, but differences between director Richard Donner and the producers resulted in Richard Lester replacing Donner, who had already shot most of the second film, a version of which is available as *Superman II: The Richard Donner Cut* (2006). *Superman* also opened the door for bringing other comic book superheroes to the big screen, beginning in 1989 with Tim Burton's *Batman*, DC's second most popular superhero, followed by the glut of Marvel Comics adaptations featuring, among others, The Hulk (2003, 2008), Iron Man (2008, 2010), Spider-Man (2002, 2004, 2007) , Fantastic Four (2005), the *X-Men* films (2000, 2003, 2006, 2009, 2011) and the mother of Marvel adaptations, *The Avengers* (*Avengers Assemble*, 2012).

The Terminator

UK/US, 1984 – 108 mins

James Cameron]

The second feature film written and directed by James Cameron, who would go on to make *Aliens* (1986), *The Abyss* (1989), *Avatar** (2009) and write the screenplay for Kathryn Bigelow's futuristic thriller *Strange Days** (1995), *The Terminator* set the bar for the resurgent action film of the 1980s and helped establish Arnold Schwarzenegger as the genre's top star during the decade. The Terminator of the title is an emotionless cyborg that looks human but is programmed for killing – a role for which the inexpressive Schwarzenegger, whose acting ability is less Method than muscle, was perfectly cast. The film generated three sequels: *Terminator 2: Judgment Day* (1991), co-written and also directed by Cameron; *Terminator 3: Rise of the Machines* (2003); and *Terminator Salvation* (2009); as well as a short-lived television series, *Terminator: The Sarah Connor Chronicles* (2008–9), a novelisation, a comic book and several video games.

After a future nuclear apocalypse in 2029 triggered by a computerised defence system, Skynet, that became self-aware, machines are deployed to wipe out the remaining pockets of human resistance. Skynet sends a terminator back in time to the then present to kill a woman named Sarah Connor, in order to prevent her from giving birth to a son, John, who will grow up to lead the Resistance against the machines in the future. The situation is explained to Sarah by Kyle Reese (Biehn), a Resistance fighter who has also come back in time for the purpose of protecting her. Kyle saves Sarah from the Terminator's attack in a night club, but the cyborg attacks again. When Kyle and Sarah are arrested after a car chase with the Terminator, it attacks the police station (prefaced by Schwarzenegger's famous line, 'I'll be back') on a killing rampage, but the pair escapes and hides out in a motel.

The Terminator tracks Kyle and Sarah to the motel, where they have made love (and, as we later learn, Sarah has become pregnant with John), beginning the climactic battle in which Kyle is killed and the Terminator is damaged in a factory explosion. Still pursuing her, the Terminator is led by Sarah into a hydraulic press, where it is finally crushed. In the coda, the pregnant Sarah, keeping a low profile, is travelling through Mexico towards approaching symbolic storm clouds. Cameron provides a breathless pace to the action sequences and some truly memorable images, such as the shots of human skulls being crushed underfoot by the machines in the world of the future. Linda Hamilton became buff for her role as the now hardened Sarah Connor, training for future Terminator attacks, and was championed as a female if not feminist take on the masculine hardbodies such as Schwarzenegger who dominated movie screens at the time. The film's premise was similar enough to 'Soldier', a 1964 teleplay for the original *Outer Limits* television series (1963–5), that its author, science fiction writer Harlan Ellison (who also wrote the novella on which *A Boy and His Dog** (1975) was based, as well as episodes for several other science fiction television series including *Star Trek*, *Logan's Run* and *Babylon 5*), filed a lawsuit against the film's production company, Hemdale, and distributor Orion Pictures, which was settled out of court. An acknowledgment to Ellison was added to the

DIRECTOR James Cameron
PRODUCER Gale Anne Hurd
SCREENPLAY James Cameron, Gale Anne Hurd
DIRECTOR OF PHOTOGRAPHY Adam Greenberg
EDITOR Mark Goldblatt
MUSIC Brad Fiedel
ART DIRECTOR George Costello
MAIN CAST Arnold Schwarzenegger, Linda Hamilton, Michael Biehn, Paul Winfield, Lance Henriksen, Bess Motta, Earl Boen, Rick Rossovich, Dick Miller, Shawn Schepps
PRODUCTION COMPANY Helmdale Film, Cinema 84, Euro Film Funding

film's credits, against Cameron's wishes.

　　Terminator 2, like the first film, again offered fast-paced action combined with cutting-edge special effects, particularly in those scenes involving the upgraded T-1000 Terminator (played by Robert Patrick), a shape-shifting machine composed of liquid metal, that becomes the new villain. Schwarzenegger's Terminator had become so popular that in the sequel he is cleverly presented as heroic, a father figure to young John who has been reprogrammed to protect the boy and who in the end sacrifices himself for the sake of humanity.

　　T3, directed by Jonathan Mostow, and *T4*, directed by McG, offered diminishing returns, yet their success at the box office suggests that the franchise itself may not yet be terminated.

Tetsuo (*Tetsuo: The Iron Man*)
Japan, 1989 – 67 mins
Shin'ya Tsukamoto

Science fiction or experimental film, speculative extrapolation regarding the direction of Japanese society or the extended nightmare of a businessman having a nervous breakdown? The Japanese cyberpunk film *Tetsuo: The Iron Man* manages to be all of these at once – an anguished statement about the dwindling of the human in a technological world and a hysterical depiction of masculine panic. *Tetsuo* is also a dark cinematic joke, and it is no accident that the film periodically cuts to a shot of a laughing face on an omnipresent television set – a more technologised version of the painting of the laughing clown seen three times in Alfred Hitchcock's *Blackmail* (1929). Quickly developing a cult following, *Tetsuo* was followed by two further films, *Tetsuo II: Body Hammer* (1992) and *Tetsuo: The Bullet Man* (2009, filmed in English), both also written and directed by Shin'ya Tsukamoto.

The obscure narrative, an excuse for the stunning montages of metal, begins with a man, the 'Metal Fetishist' (Tsukamoto), cutting open his thigh and inserting a steel rod into the wound. Later, he discovers that the wound is infested with maggots, and in a panic runs into the street and is hit by a car. The driver, a Japanese businessman (Taguchi), and his girlfriend (Fujiwara) dump the body into a ditch, but the intended victim enacts a bizarre revenge by somehow forcing the businessman's body to metamorphose into a fusion of human and metal. At first the businessman finds a small piece of sharp metal protruding from his cheek while shaving in the morning. On his way, presumably, to work, with a bandage over his cheek, the businessman sits next to a nondescript woman on a train station bench who apparently is taken over by the Metal Fetishist, becoming partially metal and pursuing the businessman through the station like *The Terminator** (1984) until he finally defeats her.

There follows a dream sequence involving the businessman and his girlfriend in which she dances provocatively with a large snake attached to her groin and then rapes him. But this may be a dream within a dream, just one indication of the businessman's besieged masculinity, as all that ensues might be read as a compensatory fantasy, an imaginary 'armouring' of the male body that provides the potency lacking in his quotidian life. Thus in the next scene, the businessman continues to mutate, more and more metal emerging through his flesh everywhere on his body, including a huge working power drill that pokes through his pants from his crotch and which, after a physical struggle with his girlfriend, she willingly straddles and dies. With the businessman now almost completely metamorphosed into an Iron Man, the Metal Fetishist reappears, emerging from the body of the dead girlfriend, and shows the Iron Man his hellish vision of a 'new world' in which metal is everywhere – a blasted landscape of twisted iron, blackened earth and curling smoke. The two battle in an abandoned industrial building, both of them acquiring more metal as they fight and taking on a variety of fused forms, until, in the end, they merge into one giant two-headed metal monster that sets out to transform the world into one rusting heap of metal.

DIRECTOR Shin'ya Tsukamoto
SCREENPLAY Shin'ya Tsukamoto
PRODUCER Shin'ya Tsukamoto
DIRECTOR OF PHOTOGRAPHY
Shin'ya Tsukamoto, Kei Fujiwara
EDITOR Shin'ya Tsukamoto
MUSIC Chu Ishikawa
ART DIRECTOR Shin'ya Tsukamoto
CAST Tomorowo Taguchi, Shin'ya Tsukamoto, Kei Fujiwara, Nobu Kanaoka
PRODUCTION COMPANY Japan Home Video, K2 Spirit, Kaijyu Theater

A heterogeneous mix of cinematic influences from Sergei Eisenstein and French surrealist cinema to David Lynch (*Dune** [1984]) and David Cronenberg (*Videodrome** [1983], *The Fly* [1968]), *Tetsuo* is not unlike the scrapheaps of metal it surveys in the many panning shots of industrial decay; it is, perhaps even more than Jean-Luc Godard's *Weekend* (1967), a film 'found on a scrapheap'. Yet with his astonishing metal sculptures and techniques such as stop-motion animation, Tsukamoto imbues the film's chaos of machine parts with a fascinating beauty impossible to deny. The film ends with the image of a television screen filled with electronic 'snow' and the words 'game over' (rather than 'The End'), alluding one final time to its darkly comic nature and maintaining the emphasis on technology to the last. Ultimately, the monstrous Iron Man is in its way as apt an image of post-industrial Japan on the cusp of the millennium as the giant dinosaur *Gojira** (1954) was for postwar Japan nearly half a century earlier.

Them!
US, 1954 – 94 mins
Gordon Douglas

Them!, about an invasion of giant carnivorous mutated ants, was the first and the best of the giant bug cycle of the 1950s, inspiring such subsequent oversized insects as *Tarantula* (1955) and *The Deadly Mantis* (1957), among a plague of others. The original story was written by George Worthing Yates, who would go on to write the screenplays for *It Came from Beneath the Sea* (1955), *The Amazing Colossal Man* (1957) and *Attack of the Puppet People* (1958), all of which also depend on premises of altered scale. *Them!* is generally seen as a paranoid parable about Communist subversion burrowing from within, as in *Invaders from Mars** (1953), a frightening scenario of Sen. Joseph McCarthy's warnings that Communists were 'invading' and 'infesting' America. The film is in black and white, but the opening title credit, significantly, is printed in blood red letters.

From the opening scene, when two state policemen find a little girl wandering alone in the New Mexico desert in shock, the film effectively balances a semi-documentary, police procedural style and its fantastic premise. The policemen investigate a series of bizarre murders in the area, beginning with that of the little girl's parents. One of their puzzling clues, a large unidentifiable footprint, attracts the attention of FBI agent Robert Graham (Arness) and a father/daughter team of government entomologists, Dr. Harold Medford (Gwenn) and his daughter, Patricia (Weldon). Investigating the scene, the group is attacked by an ant as large as an elephant, mutated as a result of atomic testing. They manage to kill it with the sage advice of Dr. Medford ('Shoot the antennae!'), after which the US military locates the nest and destroys it with poison gas. A young queen which had earlier hatched and flown away is tracked to the Los Angeles storm drain system, a location which inspired the later South Korean monster movie *The Host** (2006). The Army declares martial law and launches a search and destroy mission in the drain tunnels, wiping out giant worker ants as they move toward the egg chamber, which they torch with flamethrowers, destroying all the new queens and thus preventing the development of any further colonies.

Director Gordon Douglas made *I Was a Communist for the FBI* (1951) for Warner Bros. just three years before *Them!*, suggesting that he may have been inclined to see the latter as a conservative political parable. In any event, Douglas, whose extensive directorial credits include no other science fiction films (although he did direct the horror comedy *Zombies on Broadway* [1945]), succeeds here in making the desert seem more eerie than even Jack Arnold, thus raising *Them!* above the level of mere right-wing propaganda. In the desert sequences, Joshua Trees frequently twist into the frame, making for an unsettling *mise en scène* abetted by an effective soundtrack that includes the whipping winds of a desert sandstorm and the distinctive electronic ululations emitted by the giant ants.

The ants, while not very convincing by today's standards, are nevertheless impressive for a time before animatronics, and the film was acknowledged with an Oscar nomination for special effects. Douglas skilfully shows only parts of the insects, their shadows, or signals their presence just through their sound. Two scenes

DIRECTOR Gordon Douglas
PRODUCER David Weisbart
SCREENPLAY Russell Hughes, Ted Sherdeman, based on the story by George Worthing Yates
DIRECTOR OF PHOTOGRAPHY Sid Hickox
EDITOR Thomas Reilly
MUSIC Bronislau Kaper
ART DIRECTOR Stanley Fleischer
MAIN CAST James Whitmore, Edmund Gwenn, Joan Weldon, James Arness, Onslow Stevens, Sean McClory, Chris Drake, Sandy Descher
PRODUCTION COMPANY Warner Bros.

are especially chilling: first, when the near-catatonic little girl (Sandy Descher, also featured in Arnold's *The Space Children* [1958]) suddenly snaps awake at the smell of formic acid, her face moving in tight to the camera as she screams 'Them!' and runs off to cower in the corner of the room; and second, when we glimpse an ant coming out of its nest rolling a human ribcage down the slope of the entrance, the camera following until it comes to a stop by a couple of skulls.

Early in the film, the two policemen search a destroyed general store as a radio broadcasts a news report in which we hear an upbeat item about the conquering of several diseases. But, the film asks, what new plagues await humanity in the atomic age? In the final shot of the young queens burning in their nest, Graham asks the question everyone in the audience was undoubtedly wondering: if these mutated ants are the result of the first atomic test, what about all the other tests? In response, Medford ominously muses that 'When man entered the atomic age, he opened a door to a new world. What we eventually find in that new world, nobody can predict'.

They Live
US, 1988 – 93 mins
John Carpenter

John Carpenter, writer and/or director of *Dark Star** (1974), *The Thing** (1982), *Halloween* (1978) and *Starman* (1984), among other films, wrote *They Live* under the pseudonym Frank Armitage. The surname is also that of the librarian in H.P. Lovecraft's 1929 short story 'The Dunwich Horror', and is an apt reference, for *They Live*, which, as Carpenter himself has noted, shares with Lovecraft's fiction a concern with a hidden world below the quotidian. Playing on contemporary anxieties regarding economic recession, rising unemployment, the decline of the United States as an industrial power and even global warming, *They Live* imagines a vast and secret extraterrestrial conspiracy in which the resources of the nation and the world are being depleted while at the same time people are being made apathetic to their deteriorating conditions in an illusory world, like an analogue variation of *The Matrix** (1999).

The plot follows an anonymous, unemployed blue collar worker (Piper), referred to as 'Nada' (Spanish for 'nothing') in the credits, who, looking for a construction job in Los Angeles, discovers that aliens have infiltrated all aspects of society and are controlling human affairs, in part through subliminal messages in the media. Nada stumbles onto a box containing sunglasses made by the underground Resistance which, when put on, allows the wearer to see through the surface text to the subliminal messages ('Obey', 'Consume', 'Watch TV', 'Marry and Reproduce') hidden within magazines, advertising billboards, food packaging, and so on. The aliens, who are humanoid with heads like skulls, realise that Nada is able to see them, and they pursue him. Nada kills two alien police officers, takes their guns and begins shooting aliens in a bank – uttering, as he enters, the film's immortal line, 'I've come here to chew bubblegum and kick ass … and I'm all out of bubblegum'. Together with fellow worker Frank (David), he discovers details of the alien conspiracy from the Resistance and an elaborate underground infrastructure of the alien society, including a space port. They learn that a broadcast signal from their antenna, disguised as a satellite dish of a local cable television station, makes them look human. In a final battle Nada destroys the antenna, revealing to all the aliens' real appearance, but he dies heroically in the process.

The power of the media to manufacture consent is a theme that informs Carpenter's work – *In the Mouth of Madness* (1994), for example, is about a horror writer who gains terrible powers through the sheer magnitude of his popularity – but in *They Live* it is most explicit. The film offers a critique of the mass media and calls for the necessity to see through its obfuscating ideological haze. The aliens have created what Frankfurt School cultural theorists would call a 'false consciousness' (their television signals create, according to the words of a subversive hacker, 'an artificially induced state of consciousness that resembles sleep'). They are, not unlike the Martians in H.G. Wells's *War of the Worlds*, merely monstrous capitalists – as one human collaborator explains, free market entrepreneurs for whom the Earth is 'just another developing planet. We're their Third World.' That the aliens pass for human yet really look like death is a trenchant comment about

DIRECTOR John Carpenter
PRODUCER Larry Franco
SCREENPLAY John Carpenter (as Frank Armitage), based on the story 'Eight O'Clock in the Morning' (1963) by Ray Nelson
DIRECTOR OF PHOTOGRAPHY Gary B. Kibbe
EDITOR Gib Jaffe, Frank E. Jimenez
MUSIC John Carpenter, Alan Howarth
ART DIRECTOR William J. Durrell, Jr, Daniel Lomino
MAIN CAST Roddy Piper, Keith David, Meg Foster, Raymond St. Jacques, Peter Jason, Sy Richardson, George 'Buck' Flower
PRODUCTION COMPANY Alive Films, Larry Franco Productions, Universal

the inhumanity of capitalism and the profit motive in Reaganite America.

The blues-inflected musical score, co-written by Carpenter, who frequently composes the music for his own films, alludes to hard times for the common man while insistently driving the narrative forward.

Yet the film's emphasis on action sequences also offers the main argument against a progressive view of *They Live*, for, as the narrative unfolds, the film sacrifices its radical cultural critique for a conventional action movie – presumably the very kind of popular entertainment of which the film warns.

The Thing from Another World
US, 1951 – 87 mins
Christian Nyby

On the one hand a paradigm of the cinema's debasing treatment of science fiction and, on the other, an effectively atmospheric monster movie, *The Thing from Another World* is one of the touchstone films that established the tone and conventions of the genre. The film makes significant changes from John W. Campbell, Jr's source story, 'Who Goes There?' (originally published in *Astounding Science Fiction* in August, 1938), nor does it much resemble John Carpenter's much more faithful adaptation, *The Thing** (1982). Campbell's alien telepathic shape-shifter is changed here into a grunting, inarticulate vegetable monster (Arness) – a 'super carrot', in the vivid phrase of Scotty (Spencer), the journalist on the scene. With a compelling conflict between the scientists and the military representing the debate between reason and action, *The Thing* served as the model for many of the monster movies that appeared later in the decade, including *Gojira** (1954).

The plot involves an Air Force crew which, when dispatched to a scientific base in the Arctic to investigate a strange fluctuation in the magnetic field, discovers a spacecraft buried in the ice. When they try to dislodge it, the ship is accidentally destroyed, but the alien pilot is found embedded in a block of ice. They bring the ice block back to the base, where it thaws accidentally, reviving the alien, who proceeds to kill a number of the men, driven by its vampiric need for human blood and the desire to propagate. Some of the scientists, led by Dr. Carrington (Cornthwaite), want to communicate with the Thing, but the military personnel are convinced of the necessity to destroy it, and in the final confrontation the alien is electrocuted. Unlike Campbell's creature, who merely seeks to survive, the film's Thing seems distinctly malevolent, and it strains one's willing suspension of disbelief to accept the idea that such a vegetable monster could have invented the technology necessary for interplanetary travel. Certainly Carrington's desire to communicate with the Thing is depicted as futile and foolish, and the film ends with Scotty speaking by radio to the world, and directly to the audience, warning us all to 'keep watching the skies'.

Although the film's direction is credited to Christian Nyby, it clearly bears the stamp, both stylistically and thematically, of its producer, Howard Hawks, in its fast-paced, overlapping dialogue and depiction of an isolated group of male professionals intent on doing their job. Further, the film features a romantic subplot involving the crew's leader, Captain Hendry (Tobey) and Dr. Carrington's lovely assistant, Nikki (Sheridan) that, with its comic repartee, is of a piece with Hawks's screwball comedies. Nyby worked for Hawks from 1944–52, editing four films for him including the classic Western *Red River* (1948). The relative involvement of Hawks and Nyby, who subsequently went on to a prolific career as a television director, on *The Thing from Another World* has been a matter of some debate, although it is generally accepted that Hawks gave directorial credit to Nyby as a favour to his dependable editor.

Hawks was comfortable working within the constraints of genre, and he forayed into most of them, including the gangster and war film, musicals, film noir, Western, Biblical epic and screwball comedy. But

DIRECTOR Christian Nyby (Howard Hawks, uncredited)
PRODUCER Howard Hawks
SCREENPLAY Charles Lederer, based on the novella 'Who Goes There?' (1938) by John W. Campbell, Jr
DIRECTOR OF PHOTOGRAPHY Russell Harlan
MUSIC Dimitri Tiomkin
EDITOR Roland Gross
MUSIC Dimitri Tiomkin
ART DIRECTOR Albert S. D'Agostino, John Hughes
MAIN CAST Kenneth Tobey, Margaret Sheridan, Robert Cornthwaite, Douglas Spencer, James Arness, Dewey Martin
PRODUCTION COMPANY Winchester Pictures

with the exception of *The Thing* and the comic *Monkey Business* (1952), in which a scientist and his wife ingest a newly developed youth drug which causes them to regress with humorous results, Hawks otherwise avoided the genre of science fiction. If Hawks's action films are preoccupied with the theme of masculine professionalism, then perhaps the quintessential Hawksian moment occurs in *The Thing* when the men spread apart and with outstretched arms trace, to their amazement, the shape of the circular spaceship in the ice. The image at once expresses the solidarity of the masculine group and its simultaneous exclusion of the Other, whether woman or alien 'super-carrot'.

The Thing/John Carpenter's The Thing
US, 1982 – 109 mins
John Carpenter

The first film by John Carpenter (*Dark Star** [1974], *Escape from New York* [1981], *Prince of Darkness* [1987], *Starman* [1984], *They Live** [1988], *Ghosts of Mars* [2001]) for a major studio, *The Thing* is the second adaptation of John W. Campbell, Jr's novella *Who Goes There?*, after Howard Hawks and Christian Nyby's *The Thing from Another World** (1951), about an alien creature that has the ability to assimilate other lifeforms and imitate them. While it is often regarded as a remake of the earlier film, and despite the fact that Carpenter has frequently stated his admiration for Hawks's work – the children in Carpenter's *Halloween* (1978) are watching *The Thing from Another World* on television – his version is in fact a much more faithful adaptation of Campbell's story than a remake.

Although Carpenter's film did not perform especially well at the box office when it was first released (it opened on the same day as Ridley Scott's *Blade Runner** and two weeks after Steven Spielberg's *E.T.: The*

DIRECTOR John Carpenter
PRODUCER David Foster, Lawrence Turman
SCREENPLAY Bill Lancaster, based on the novella 'Who Goes There?' (1938) by John W. Campbell, Jr
DIRECTOR OF PHOTOGRAPHY Dean Cundey
EDITOR Tom Ramsay
MUSIC Ennio Morricone
PRODUCTION DESIGN John J. Lloyd
MAIN CAST Kurt Russell, Keith David, Wilford Brimley, T.K. Carter, Richard Dysart, David Clennon, Peter Maloney, Richard Masur, Donald Moffat, Joel Polis, Thomas Waites
PRODUCTION COMPANY David Foster Productions, Turman-Foster Company, Universal Pictures

*Extra-Terrestrial**), over time *The Thing* has gained a cult reputation, particularly for the prosthetic effects by Rob Bottin (*Total Recall** [1990]), showing the creature morphing into a variety of forms. The film has spawned a novelisation by Alan Dean Foster, a series of comic books, several action figures and a 2002 survival horror third-person shooter video game sequel. A prequel, also entitled *The Thing* (directed by Matthijs van Heijningen, Jr, 2011) focuses on the Norwegian crew in Antarctica that first discovers the alien, several days before it arrives at the American base in the form of a dog.

In Carpenter's *The Thing*, a Norwegian helicopter lands at an American Antarctic research station, then explodes, and a crewman insistently shoots at a dog they were tracking until he is killed by the Americans. The dog is put in with their own team by Clark (Masur), and R.J. MacReady (Russell), a helicopter pilot, flies to the Norwegian camp to seek an explanation, but finds the station burned out and no one alive. The dog mutates and attacks, but is incinerated with a flamethrower. Investigating the records at the Norwegian station, they find the creature's spacecraft, and Dr. Blair (Brimley) estimates that if the creature were to reach civilisation, it would be able to absorb life on Earth within three years. Since anyone could be an alien, paranoia overtakes the men, and in turn they are assimilated, discovered and killed. In one of the film's most suspenseful scenes, MacReady develops a blood test to determine if someone is infected. After several uneventful tests, suddenly the dish with one of the men's blood samples screeches and leaps up. As Blair, the creature attempts to build a ship to escape, and MacReady dynamites the base to stop it. In the ruins of the complex, MacReady finds Childs (David), the only other survivor. Facing certain death from the elements if not the alien, who could be either one of them, they resign themselves to sharing a bottle of Scotch.

Ultimately Carpenter's vision is fundamentally different from that of the first version. In both, a group of men is faced with an important and difficult job while isolated from society at large, but now the threat isolates the members of the group rather than brings them together. In Carpenter's version, the characters do not unite but rather, turn on each other. His film ends not, as the first version does, with the injunction to 'keep watching the skies' – that is, to be on guard against the alien Other – but with the image of MacReady and Childs, a black man and a white man, armed and eyeing each other warily across the icy expanse of the widescreen frame. An extremely loaded image, it fails to resolve its narrative dilemma (has the Thing been defeated? Is either or both of the men a Thing?) and arouses rather than assuages anxiety about race relations in the United States.

Things to Come
UK, 1936 – 96 mins (original US release)/108 minutes (original UK release)
William Cameron Menzies

Things to Come was the first of only two of his novels that H. G. Wells would adapt himself, the second being *The Man Who Could Work Miracles* (1937), also produced by Alexander Korda and for which Wells co-wrote the screenplay. In his introduction to the 1934 collection of five of his early 'scientific romances', Wells wrote that 'The world in the presence of cataclysmal realities has no need for fresh cataclysmal fantasies. That game is over'. Who wants invented catastrophes, he asked, 'when day by day we can watch Mr. Hitler in Germany?' Accordingly, the book is presented within a narrative frame as if it were written by a diplomat, Dr. Philip Raven, who has had visions of a future history textbook which he has transcribed and

DIRECTOR William Cameron Menzies
PRODUCER Alexander Korda
SCREENPLAY H.G. Wells, based on his novel *The Shape of Things to Come* (1933)
DIRECTOR OF PHOTOGRAPHY Georges Périnal
EDITOR Charles Crichton, Francis Lyon
MUSIC Arthur Bliss
PRODUCTION DESIGN William Cameron Menzies
MAIN CAST Raymond Massey, Edward Chapman, Ralph Richardson, Margaretta Scott, Cedric Hardwicke, Maurice Braddell, Sophie Stewart, Derrick De Marney, Ann Todd
PRODUCTION COMPANY London Film Productions

given to Wells to edit. The film eliminates this frame, quickly launching into its alternate history of the world from 1940 to 2036, a century after the year the film was released, focusing on the British city of 'Everytown' as a microcosm for world events.

The story begins on Christmas Day, 1940, as John Cabal (Massey), along with his guests Harding (Braddell) and Passworthy (Chapman), hears news of impending war. Bombing follows that night, and global war begins. Cabal becomes a pilot but decries the madness of the war, which continues for decades as civilisation is destroyed and humanity is plunged into a new dark age. By 1970, local warlords have risen to power, with the blustering 'Chief' or 'Boss' (Richardson) in charge of Everytown. His plan to conquer 'the hill people' for their resources is disrupted by the landing of a futuristic airplane piloted by Cabal, who explains that the few surviving engineers and scientists have united to created a new social order, Wings Over the World, which has outlawed war and the existence of independent nations. Wings Over the World drops gas bombs ('the gas of peace') on Everytown, peacefully conquering it.

A dizzying montage, accompanied by Arthur Bliss's strident score, quickly shows decades of impressive technological progress, concluding with the construction of the new Everytown as an underground city in 2036. In this apparent utopia the sculptor Theotocopulos (Hardwicke) incites the people to demand a halt to the burden of continual progress by rushing to destroy the council's new space gun – an improbable technological throwback to Jules Verne's From the Earth to the Moon (1865) – forcing Oswald Cabal, council

head and great grandson of John Cabal, to rush the launch of the ship with his daughter and her boyfriend Horrie Passworthy in it despite the risk. In the stirring conclusion, in response to Horrie's father's hesitation about the benefits of technology, the camera dollies in to Raymond Massey's chiselled, determined face, stars twinkling behind him, as he asks regarding human destiny, 'All the universe or nothing. Which shall it be, Passworthy? Which shall it be?'

Wells, who, alas, was only 16 months off in predicting the outbreak of World War II, exerted considerable control over the film's production. He particularly disliked Metropolis* (1927), with its depiction of workers as oppressed brutes exploited by a managerial elite (an idea he had already turned on its head in The Time Machine [1895]), and admonished cast and crew that they were to do everything the opposite of Fritz Lang's film. Things to Come, like the book, is emphatic in stating Wells's belief in a technocratic society, the global Modern State. But if Wells's screenplay (published, along with selected production notes, in 1935) tends toward the didactic, the film, directed and designed by William Cameron Menzies, who also designed and directed the stylish Invaders from Mars* (1953), is visually thrilling from start to finish, imaginatively translating Wells's ideas into cinematic drama. The rough cut reputedly ran to 130 minutes, but the British release version was shortened to 108 minutes and the American version to 96 minutes, with subsequent cuts producing yet more versions. A digitally-restored 134-minute cut, also containing script extracts and production photographs to provide a 'virtual extended edition', was released in 2007.

THX 1138
US, 1971 – 86 mins
George Lucas

A sophisticated depiction of an ironic utopian future, *THX 1138* was the first feature directed by George Lucas, who would direct *Star Wars** (1977) six years later. It was expanded from a 1967 student film, *Electronic Labyrinth: THX 1138 4EB*, which he made while enrolled at the University of Southern California. Science fiction writer Ben Bova authored a novelisation the same year. Warner Bros co-produced the film with American Zoetrope, which Francis Ford Coppola founded with Lucas as an alternative to the constraints of the studio system, but the film's abstruse style hampered its commercial success.

As its narrative unfolds, *THX 1138* provides no exposition, no explanation of where, when or how the world has evolved to this point where people live in a sterile hi-tech city (it is only revealed at the end that the city is entirely underground) in which everyone is constantly monitored and every aspect of life regulated by mandatory doses of drugs to suppress emotion and desire. The dense electronic soundscape of the monitoring equipment and voices that fills the soundtrack was designed by Walter Murch (editor and/or sound editor for several of Coppola's most important films, including *The Conversation* [1974], a film about sound recording). The eponymous THX 1138 (Duvall) works in a factory making the android policemen that patrol the city and ensure its smooth functioning. His female roommate, LUH (McOmie), decides to violate the law by ceasing to take her various medications, as does THX who, as a result, begins to experience authentic emotions and sexual desire for the first time. THX is followed by SEN (Pleasence), who wants THX for his roommate. When their sex crimes are discovered, THX and LUH are arrested.

Imprisoned in a featureless white space that seems boundless and where prisoners are prodded with lances like cattle prods, THX, along with the disillusioned SRT (Colley), who had appeared in ubiquitous propaganda holograms, attempts to flee the city. During their escape, THX discovers that LUH has been 'reassigned' as a fetus. They steal two vehicles, and while SRT quickly crashes into a concrete abutment, dropping out of the story, THX flees to the edge of the city, finds an escape ladder, and begins climbing, all the while followed by the android police. However, at the last minute the police robots are ordered to cease their pursuit because the budget of 14,000 credits allotted for their recapture has been spent. THX continues to climb until he emerges to the surface, and in the film's ambiguous last shot he is seen silhouetted against a huge red setting sun as some birds fly past. The red sky suggests that some sort of disaster had taken place in the past, forcing humans underground, yet the presence of the birds indicates that life above ground is still possible.

Alternatively, people, or at least this particular society, may have chosen at some point to move underground and restructure. This interpretation is a possibility because, although the film withholds exposition about its science fictional premises, there are several indications that the world the film depicts is merely an extrapolation of contemporary American culture. The citizens of the underground city pray to

DIRECTOR George Lucas
PRODUCER Larry Sturhahn, Francis Ford Coppola
SCREENPLAY George Lucas, Walter Murch
DIRECTOR OF PHOTOGRAPHY Albert Kihn, David Myers
EDITOR George Lucas
MUSIC Lalo Schifrin
ART DIRECTOR Michael D. Haller
MAIN CAST Robert Duvall, Donald Pleasence, Maggie McOmie, Don Pedro Colley, Ian Wolfe, Marshall Efron, John Pearce, Irene Forrest, Gary Marsh
PRODUCTION COMPANY American Zoetrope, Warner Bros.

OMM 0910, a deity whom they worship in 'Unichapels' like telephone booths. The prerecorded responses of OMM satirise the Christian ritual of confession even as the booths in which the people pray comment on the drive-through lifestyle of contemporary California. THX's escape and pursuit by android policemen on motorcycles was filmed in the yet to be completed Bay Area Rapid Transit (BART) tunnel, and other actual locations including the San Francisco International Airport were also used in the film. Like *Logan's Run* (1976), which was shot in Dallas, Texas, and with which it shares a similar narrative involving an underground city of the future from which the protagonist attempts to escape, the location photography underscores the sense of continuity with the actual present.

The Time Machine
US, 1960 – 103 mins
George Pal

During the 1940s, Hungarian-born George Pal produced more than three dozen animated shorts for children, and then moved on to producing important science fiction features. *The Time Machine*, based on H.G. Wells's first novel, followed *Destination Moon** (1950), *When Worlds Collide** (1951), *The War of the Worlds** (1953) and *Conquest of Space* (1955) for Pal, and was the first to be directed as well as produced by him. Although the film, Pal's most commercially successfully venture, retains the novel's Victorian setting, unlike *War of the Worlds*, it drains much of Wells's critique of British class society, envisioned as the division between the bestial Morlocks and wan Eloi, recasting it instead as another Cold War parable.

In a town in southern England on January 5, 1900, four friends arrive for dinner, their host, H. George Wells (Taylor), staggering in late, dishevelled and exhausted. George claims that he can travel into the past and future, and begins to recount his adventures since they last met a week ago. His friends scoff at the idea, except for David Filby (Young). They agree to meet again the following week. After their departure, in his basement laboratory, George mounts his machine and begins moving into the future, watching time pass at an increasingly accelerated rate. He moves through the twentieth century, characterised by advances in the technology of warfare, until a nuclear war unleashes a volcano that buries his house in lava and pushes him to travel much further into the future, to the year 802,701, until the lava has worn away and freed him.

Here he discovers a simple people, the Eloi, who seem to have no emotion or intellectual capacity. From Weena (Mimieux), a woman whose life he saves, he learns of the Morlocks, and at an ancient museum, still functioning 'talking rings' explain that as the result of a prolonged nuclear war the atmosphere had become polluted, prompting some survivors to move underground, eventually becoming the Morlocks, while those on the surface evolved into the Eloi. After an air-raid siren lures many of the conditioned Eloi, including Weena, into the Morlocks' lair, George descends underground to rescue them, and, finding human bones, realises that the Morlocks have become cannibals. He fights off the Morlocks, one of the Eloi showing a spark of life by helping him. They escape to the surface as the fire they start causes the Morlocks' caves to implode. Fighting off Morlocks, he manages to remount the time machine and return to 1900. His disbelieving friends depart, but Filby hesitates and hears George leaving again on his time machine. His housekeeper notes that George took three books with him – which ones we are left to speculate – to help the Eloi rebuild their civilisation.

Wells's description of the experience of time travel was likely inspired in part by the contemporaneous invention of cinema. Shortly after the novel's publication, British motion picture pioneer Robert Paul filed a patent for a moving picture ride inspired by Wells's novel that would provide the illusion of motion through time. Despite some backdrops that look as palpably false as those in the films of Georges Méliès (see *Le Voyage dans la lune** [1902]), Pal exploits the cinematic potential of George's trips in the machine with

DIRECTOR George Pal
PRODUCER George Pal
SCREENPLAY David Duncan, based on the 1895 novel by H.G. Wells
DIRECTOR OF PHOTOGRAPHY Paul C. Vogel
EDITOR George Tomasini
MUSIC Russell Garcia
PRODUCTION DESIGN George Davis, William Ferrari
MAIN CAST Rod Taylor, Yvette Mimieux, Alan Young, Sebastian Cabot, Tom Helmore, Whit Bissell, Doris Lloyd
PRODUCTION COMPANY MGM, George Pal Productions, Galaxy Films

creative time-lapse and stop-motion photography that earned an Oscar for special effects. The now-iconic early steampunk design for the time machine has appeared in a number of other films, including Nicholas Meyer's delightful *Time After Time* (1979), in which Jack the Ripper (David Warner) uses Wells's time machine to flee to the late twentieth century, where he is pursued by the author (Malcolm McDowell). A reboot of the novel was directed by Wells's great-grandson, Simon Wells, starring Guy Pearce as the Time Traveller, in 2002. Both versions omit entirely Wells's pessimistic ending, in which the Time Traveller glimpses a dying Earth far in the future, Pal's film providing instead a decidedly upbeat ending in which George goes back to the future to impart Victorian values.

Total Recall
US, 1990 – 113 mins
Paul Verhoeven

The original script for *Total Recall* was written by Ronald Shusett and Dan O'Bannon (the writers of *Alien**
[1979]) and directed by Paul Verhoeven, the second in his series of Hollywood science fiction blockbusters
between *RoboCop** (1987) and *Starship Troopers** (1997). Involved in the production at one point was David
Cronenberg (*Videodrome** [1983], *The Fly** [1986]), who contributed the idea of the mutants on Mars,
which has no basis in Philip K. Dick's source story 'We Can Remember It for You Wholesale'. Despite being
one of the last Hollywood blockbusters to be made before the CGI revolution, the film's special effects,
including the makeup effects by Rob Bottin (*The Thing** [1982]), justly earned it a Special Academy Award.
The film's box-office success, along with that of the earlier *Blade Runner** (1982), based on Dick's 1968 novel
Do Androids Dream of Electric Sheep? and directed by Ridley Scott (who also directed *Alien**), initiated an
ongoing spate of film adaptations of Dick's fiction, including Peter Weir's *The Truman Show* (1998), based
on the novel *Time Out of Joint*; Steven Spielberg's *Minority Report*, (2002), based on the short story 'The
Minority Report'; John Woo's *Paycheck* (2003) from the story of the same name; Richard Linklater's
rotoscoped feature *A Scanner Darkly* (2006), based on the novel of the same name; *The Adjustment Bureau*
(2011), from the short story 'Adjustment Team'; and a disappointing 2012 remake of *Total Recall* starring
Colin Farrell that is little more than one extended chase. Verhoeven's *Total Recall*, like several of these other
works by Dick, problematises questions of perception, subjectivity, memory, identity and reality.

In the year 2084, construction worker Doug Quaid (Schwarzenegger) unexpectedly finds himself in the
middle of interplanetary intrigue. Quaid dreams of travelling to Mars, but decides upon a virtual vacation
from a company called 'Rekall' that implants memories. At Rekall, he spices up the parameters of his vacation
by casting himself as a secret agent who discovers alien technology. As the implantation procedure begins,
something seems to go wrong and Quaid is quickly thrust into exactly the kind of non-stop adventure he had
just purchased, including meeting an attractive woman ('demure *and* sleazy', Quaid had requested),
precipitated by the attempted procedure itself, which has uncovered Quaid's buried identity as Hauser, who
had once worked for Mars's top administrator, Cohaagen (Cox).

Quaid/Hauser finds himself fighting for his life, even with his wife Lori (Stone), who suddenly tries to
kill him (claiming to be a secret agent only pretending to be his wife), in a series of high-octane chases and
shootouts. He travels to Mars, meets the sleazy and demure Melina (Ticotin) and mutants, the result of
inferior radiation shielding, including Kuato, a small humanoid growth on another man. From Kuato, Quaid
learns about the discovery of an alien reactor that has the capability of providing oxygen to the entire planet.
Quaid/Hauser and Melina are captured by Cohaagen, who has kept the discovery secret in order to maintain
power, but eventually Quaid/Hauser defeats Cohaagen and turns on the oxygen machine. In the final shots,
as the oppressed populace emerges into the new blue sky of Mars, Quaid is about to kiss Melina, but

DIRECTOR Paul Verhoeven
PRODUCER Buzz Feitshans, Ronald
Shusett
SCREENPLAY Dan O'Bannon,
Ronald Shusett, Gary Goldman, John
Povill, based on the short story 'We
Can Remember It for You Wholesale'
(1966) by Philip K. Dick
DIRECTOR OF PHOTOGRAPHY Jost
Vacano
EDITOR Carlos Puente, Frank J.
Urioste
MUSIC Jerry Goldsmith
PRODUCTION DESIGN William
Sandell
MAIN CAST Arnold Schwarzenegger,
Rachel Ticotin, Sharon Stone, Ronny
Cox, Michael Ironside, Marshall Bell,
Ray Baker
PRODUCTION COMPANY Carolco
International N.V., Carolco Pictures,
TriStar Pictures

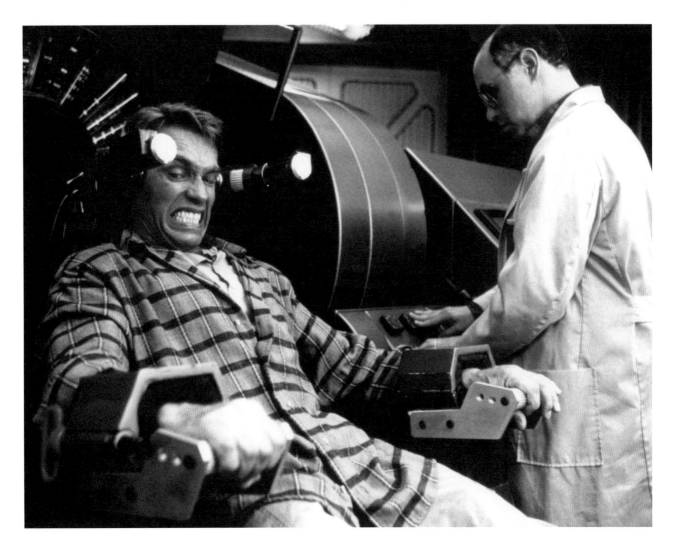

wonders if this is still part of his Rekall program.

Like *The Matrix** (1999), *Total Recall* raises many of the issues of postmodern theory, including Baudrillard's ideas of the simulacrum. With postmodern irony, the film deconstructs the ideal action movie even as it gives it to us. All the parameters of the science fiction action movie are programmed in for Quaid, and for us as spectators. At the same time, however, the film questions whether the plot we are watching is 'really' happening or is just 'a movie' – the programmed exciting vacation that Quaid had paid for. The convincing special effects help place the viewer in the same ambiguous position as Quaid, the film cleverly allowing for both interpretations.

Tribulation 99: Alien Anomalies Under America
USA, 1992 – 48 mins
Craig Baldwin

Craig Baldwin is an American experimental film-maker who makes collage films using found footage to present mockumentaries that offer a provocative commentary on international politics, particularly the dynamics of colonialism and imperialism, and their ideological coding by the media. In the 1980s Baldwin studied with Bruce Conner, a pioneer of the collage film form whose best-known film, *Report* (1967), reworks the Zapruder footage of the assassination of President John F. Kennedy. Like Conner's films, Baldwin's work is concerned with the mass media and its relation to cultural consciousness. His *Wild Gunman* (1978), for example, deconstructs the masculine image of the Western and connects it with consumerism and American imperialism abroad. Given Baldwin's interest in B movies as source material, it is no surprise that *Spectres of the Spectrum* (1999) and *Mock-Up on Mu* (2008), like *Tribulation 99,* perhaps his most well-known film, posit science fiction premises.

According to *Tribulation 99*, in the year 1000, aliens from their dying planet Quetzalcoatl came to Earth, seeking refuge underground. Then, disturbed by American atomic tests in the 1950s, the Quetzals retaliate by hatching a variety of plots against the United States, including the substitution of a replicant Fidel Castro and a scheme involving Marxist president Salvador Allende in Chile to shift the Earth's axis. Covert action by the CIA becomes necessary in order to stop the aliens' nefarious plans. Like Baldwin's other films, *Tribulation 99* recycles an astonishing range of pre-existing footage, including educational and industrial films, television commercials, newsreels and B movies, especially horror and science fiction, at a mind-numbing pace; at the same time, the soundtrack also pastiches a wide range of pre-existing music from Richard Strauss's 'Thus Spake Zarathrustra' (accompanied by a close-up of what looks like a newt fetus that recalls, hilariously, the shot of the Star Child in *2001: A Space Odyssey** [1968]) to, of course, 'Ghost Riders in the Sky', a traditional western folk tune recorded by dozens by artists over the years. Obviously familiar with the editing strategies of Soviet film makers during the silent era, Baldwin employs a rapid pace of editing, juxtaposing and connecting images and ideas, offering visual rhymes and counterpoints, in a non-stop rapid flow that almost convinces, despite the ludicrousness of its premise, through the avalanche of 'evidence' presented.

Tribulation 99 is structured, in a matter recalling a Peter Greenaway film, in ninety-nine sections, each introduced with a sensationalised title in capital letters. The film begins with the bold title 'WARNING: This film is not fiction. It is the shocking truth about the coming APOCALYPSE. And the events that have led up to it', then a title informing us that the film is 'reported' (not 'narrated', giving it an extra ring of truth), after which the reporter begins his incredible tale, his hushed conspiratorial tone underscoring the urgency of the terrible secrets he is about to reveal.

Yet, at the same time, the film builds its paranoid plot on much that is actual documented history of

DIRECTOR Craig Baldwin
SCREENPLAY Craig Baldwin
DIRECTOR OF PHOTOGRAPHY Bill Daniel
EDITOR Craig Baldwin
MUSIC Dana Hoover

postwar American intervention in Central and South America. The CIA apparently did try some of the crackpot plots to kill Castro mentioned in the film, but it is unlikely that, as a conclusion, as the reporter explains, 'After thirty-three failed assassination attempts, entailing two thousand people, and fifty million dollars, they are horrified to realise that you can't kill something that isn't alive'. *Tribulation 99* loosely mixes fact with the fantastic, but unlike such documentaries as, say, *Chariots of the Gods?* (1970), based on Erich von Däniken's 1968 book which popularised the' ancient astronaut' thesis, and similar non-fiction shows such as *Ancient Aliens* (2009–12) that use the techniques of documentary to persuade viewers, Baldwin's pseudo-history forces viewers to question how images are presented as visual evidence in the first place. Baldwin has rightly called *Tribulation 99* a 'pseudo pseudo documentary', in that it presents a patently false and manipulated argument disguised as a documentary that ultimately tells truths through misdirection about American covert operations of destabilisation in Latin America while at the same examining the nature of visual signification itself.

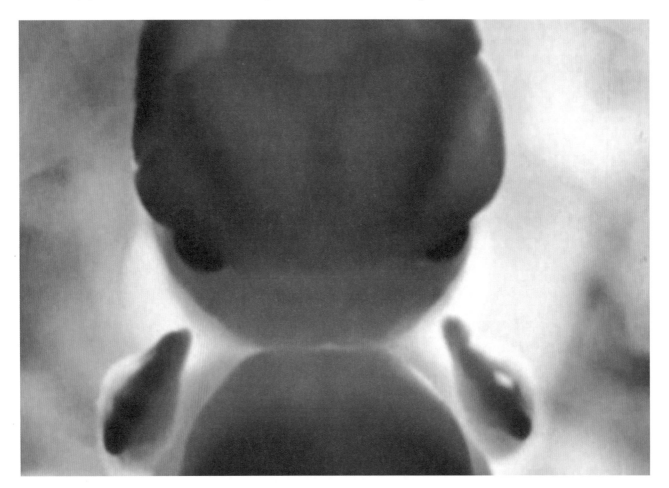

Tron
US/Taiwan, 1982 – 96 mins
Steven Lisberger

One of the first movies to rely to a significant degree on computer animation, *Tron* marked a new phase in film technology. With a narrative involving a software engineer, Kevin Flynn (Bridges), who is transported inside the world of a mainframe computer, it was a pioneering depiction of virtual space. *Tron* was a moderate box-office success when first released, but over time became a cult hit, eventually generating a franchise consisting of comic books, an animated television series, *Tron: Uprising* (2012), a novelisation (1982) written by science fiction author Brian Daley and, of course, an arcade game and several video games. A sequel, *Tron: Legacy* (2010), directed by Joseph Kosinski, a director of television commercials for several video games, follows Flynn's son Sam, who, following a message he receives from his lost father, like him enters a virtual reality, the Grid, where he meets his father (Bridges) and fights another renegade program. *Tron* was nominated for Academy Awards for Best Costume Design and Best Sound, and won neither, although years later, in 1997, Ken Perlin was awarded an Oscar for Technical Achievement for Perlin Noise, a computer-generated special effect that he invented for *Tron*.

Flynn is a former hotshot software engineer now running a video arcade where he rules with 'Space Paranoids', one of the games he designed when he worked for Encom but which was stolen from him by Ed

DIRECTOR Steven Lisberger
PRODUCER Donald Kushner
SCREENPLAY Steven Lisberger,
Bonnie MacBird
DIRECTOR OF PHOTOGRAPHY
Bruce Logan
EDITOR Jeff Gourson
MUSIC Wendy Carlos
PRODUCTION DESIGN Dean
Edward Mitzner
MAIN CAST Jeff Bridges, Bruce
Boxleitner, David Warner, Cindy
Morgan, Barnard Hughes, Dan Shor,
Peter Jurasik, Tony Stephano, Craig
Chudy, Vince Deadrick, Sam Schatz
PRODUCTION COMPANY
Walt Disney Productions,
Lisberger/Kushner

Dillinger (Warner), now chief executive of the company. Flynn has been trying to hack into Encom's computer system to get evidence of Dillinger's theft of his programs but has been prevented by the Master Control Program (MCP), a new artificial intelligence program that controls all the company's computer systems and which, recalling the eponymous computer in *Colossus: The Forbin Project** (1970), has been hacking into other programs. Growing in strength, it is now planning to hack the computers at the Pentagon and the Kremlin because it can operate more efficiently than humans. An Encom programmer, Alan Bradley (Boxleitner), and his girlfriend Lora Baines (Morgan), who also works at Encom developing an experimental laser that breaks down matter and reassembles it, warn Flynn that Dillinger is aware of his hacking attempts and sneak him into the company lab to try again, but MCP protects itself by using the laser to bring Flynn into the Encom mainframe.

In the mainframe, computer programs, which have the faces of their designers, are absorbed by MCP, while those who are resistant, who claim loyalty to the mythic 'users', are forced by MCP and his disciplinary program, Sark (Warner), to play like gladiators in martial arts video games in which the losers are destroyed. Flynn is forced to play, but along with the interface program Tron (Boxleitner), escapes. Eventually Tron communicates with his designer Bradley and, with Bradley's help, they destroy MCP. Flynn is reconstituted in the real world, gains the evidence of Dillinger's guilt, and replaces him as executive of ENCOM.

Multiple designers and software companies were involved in creating the look of the computer world in the film. French comic book artist Jean Giraud ('Moebius'), who also worked on *Alien** (1979) and *The Fifth Element** (1997), designed the sets and costumes. Most of the virtual vehicles were designed by Syd Mead, who also designed *Blade Runner** (1982). Frank Serafine, who did the sound design for *Star Trek: The Motion Picture** (1979), created the film's computer sounds, and the soundtrack includes original electronic music by Wendy Carlos, whose other film credits include Stanley Kubrick's *A Clockwork Orange** (1971) and *The Shining* (1980). *Tron*'s special effects, which involved not only computer-generated images but a number of other techniques as well because the technology for combining CGI and live action images did not yet exist, was clearly the primary interest of director and co-screenwriter Steven Lisberger, as the human characters are uninteresting. However, this flatness of character is certainly consistent with the numerous shots in the 'real world' of the film, beginning immediately with the opening shot of lights on a grid that fades into an image of a city street, which echo design elements of the virtual world and together suggest the extent to which contemporary life had already been shaped by computer logic even before the home computer revolution.

The Tunnel/Transatlantic Tunnel
UK, 1935 – 94 mins
Maurice Elvey

The Tunnel (*Transatlantic Tunnel* in the United States) is about the epic struggle in the near future to build a transatlantic tunnel between Britain and the United States. The fourth adaptation of Bernhard Kellermann's 1913 novel *Der Tunnel*, it was preceded by a silent German version, *Der Tunnel*, in 1915, and two sound films, the German *Der Tunnel* and the French *Le Tunnel*, both released in 1933 and both directed by Curtis Bernhardt (as Kurt Bernhardt). Maurice Elvey, director of *The Tunnel*, was the most prolific film director in the history of British cinema, with more than two hundred feature films and numerous shorts to his credit made over five decades. In the same year as *The Tunnel*, Elvey also directed *The Clairvoyant* (1935), a thriller starring Claude Rains, who had made his American debut in James Whale's *The Invisible Man** two years earlier.

DIRECTOR Maurice Elvey
PRODUCER Michael Balcon
SCREENPLAY Clemence Dane, L. Du Peach, Curt Siodmak, based on the 1913 novel *Der Tunnel* by Bernhard Kellermann
DIRECTOR OF PHOTOGRAPHY Günther Krampf
EDITOR Charles Frend
MUSIC Hubert Bath
PART DIRECTOR Ernö Metzner
MAIN CAST Richard Dix, Leslie Banks, Madge Evans, Helen Vinson, C. Aubrey Smith, Basil Sidney, Henry Oscar, George Arliss, Walter Huston
PRODUCTION COMPANY Gaumont British Pictures

The script for *The Tunnel* was co-written by Curt Siodmak, who would became a prolific writer of horror and science fiction films, his extensive credits including, among the former, *The Wolf Man* (1941) and *I Walked with a Zombie* (1943), and among the latter, *The Invisible Man Returns* (1940), *Riders to the Stars* (1954) and *Earth vs. the Flying Saucers* (1956).

The film begins with a gathering of several wealthy industrialists arranged by a millionaire, Mr. Lloyd (Smith), who introduces them to McAllan (Dix), the engineer who had overseen the successful construction of the Channel Tunnel in 1940. McAllan explains that, as a result of the combination of his newly developed 'Allanite steel' and the 'radium drill' invented by Frederick 'Robbie' Robbins (Banks), he believes it is possible to achieve the engineering miracle of building a transatlantic tunnel. Lloyd's willingness to invest in the project wins over the others, who are initially sceptical but who eventually agree, giving McAllan the financial backing necessary to begin the mammoth undertaking.

The film then follows the personal and professional problems that plague the project and threaten its completion, including an encounter with a dangerous new gas that blinds McAllan's wife Ruth (Evans), resulting in a lengthy estrangement; a submarine volcano; and the financial machinations of some of the investors. In the climax, an explosion of volcanic gases forces the closure of a section of the tunnel, resulting in the deaths of many workers including McAllan's

son Geoffrey, who had just reunited with his father during his first day on the job. McAllan and Robbins put aside the personal differences that had developed between them and together take the radium drill through the extremely hot volcanic rock to rescue the surviving men, breaking through to the American side in the process and thus completing the tunnel.

Like the sweeping *Things to Come** (1936), released the following year, *The Tunnel* preaches an inevitable gospel of scientific progress as an altar upon which the fates of individuals must unfortunately but inevitably be sacrificed. Dix provides the same indomitable spirit he brought to his Oscar-nominated role as the pioneer Yancey Cravat in the epic Western *Cimarron* (1931), while George Arliss as the British Prime Minister and Walter Huston as the American president (who, speaking in Congress, puzzlingly stands in front of an American flag with only 36 stars) lend equal gravitas to the importance of the project, emphasising the tunnel's significance for the establishment of world peace by uniting the two great English-speaking nations in the face of what the Prime Minister refers to as the growing threat of 'the Eastern federation of powers'. Clearly this was an important and urgent message given the aggressive militarisation of Germany at the time. Appropriately, some of the shots in the film, featuring excellent special effects and model work of the tunnel and its various machinery, invoke the epic quality of Fritz Lang's *Metropolis** (1927).

20,000 Leagues Under the Sea
US, 1954 – 127 mins
Richard Fleischer

The *voyages extraordinaires* of Jules Verne, the first author in the genre recognised today as science fiction, have been adapted to the screen many times, beginning with Georges Méliès's silent *Le Voyage dans la lune** (*A Trip to the Moon*, 1902), which was inspired by both Verne's *From the Earth to the Moon* (1865) and H.G. Wells's *The First Men in the Moon* (1901). There are several versions of *A Journey to the Centre of the Earth* (1864), including two Hollywood adaptations, one in 1959 and another in 2008; two versions of *From the Earth to the Moon*, one in 1958 directed by Byron Haskin (*The War of the Worlds**, [1953]), and a comic take, *Rocket to the Moon* (1967); two versions of *Around the World in Eighty Days* (1873), in 1956 and 2004, with the former, directed by Michael Anderson (who also directed the first version of Orwell's *Nineteen*

DIRECTOR Richard Fleischer
PRODUCER Walt Disney
SCREENPLAY Erle Fenton, based on the 1870 novel (*Vingt mille lieues sous les mers*) by Jules Verne
EDITOR Elmo Williams
MUSIC Paul Smith
DIRECTOR OF PHOTOGRAPHY Franz Planer
PRODUCTION DESIGN Harper Goff
MAIN CAST Kirk Douglas, James Mason, Peter Lorre, Paul Lukas, Robert J. Wilkie, Ted de Corsia, Ted Cooper
PRODUCTION COMPANY Walt Disney Company

Eighty-Four [1956]), winning five Oscars including Best Picture; a version of *Master of the World* (1961), starring Vincent Price with a script by Richard Matheson (*The Incredible Shrinking Man** [1957]) and featuring special effects by Ray Harryhausen (*The Beast from 20,000 Fathoms** [1953]); and at least five versions of *The Mysterious Island* (1874), a loose sequel to *Twenty Thousand Leagues Under the Sea*, including Cy Endfield's *Mysterious Island* in 1961, featuring special effects by Harryhausen and starring Herbert Lom as Nemo.

Twenty Thousand Leagues Under the Sea, published in 1870, was filmed several times, beginning with a version by Méliès in 1907, and also inspired a number of spinoffs including *Captain Nemo and the Underwater City* (1969) starring Robert Ryan, several animated movies and an updated version, *30,000 Leagues Under the Sea* (2007), produced by The Asylum studio. Disney's *The Black Hole* (1979) is based in part on the book, with Maximilian Schell's Dr. Hans Reinhardt a variation of Verne's misanthropic Nemo. Of these several versions, Disney's, directed by the usually stolid Richard Fleischer (*Fantastic Voyage** [1966], *Soylent Green** [1973]), is justifiably the most well-known, successfully balancing the serious concerns of science fiction with the studio's mandate of family entertainment, complete with the irrelevant addition of a trained seal. The first science fiction film produced by Walt Disney Productions and the first of its features to be released through its distribution arm, Buena Vista Pictures, *20,000 Leagues Under the Sea* featured two memorable performances: Kirk Douglas as the plucky harpooner Ned Land, and an early animatronic giant squid that attacks the *Nautilus*, a complex

scene that contributed to making it one of the most expensive films ever made up to that time. With excellent production design, an early example of steampunk that admirably captures Verne's vision of the *Nautilus,* the film won two Academy Awards, for Art Direction (John Hench) and Special Effects (Joshua Meador).

In 1868, Prof. Pierre M. Aronnax (Lukas) and his assistant, Conseil (Lorre), join an American expedition to determine the existence of a rumoured sea-monster. Eventually they spot the monster as it rams the ship, throwing harpooner Ned Land and Aronnax overboard, with Conseil following. They are taken aboard the *Nautilus*, a submarine boat mistaken for the monster, by Nemo (Mason), who introduces them to the various wonders of the ship, including walking on the seabed in suits with oxygen tanks. However, they are Nemo's prisoners, subject to his autocratic rule and forbidden from returning to the surface world and society, which Nemo has renounced. Among their various adventures as they explore Earth's oceans is the hand-to-hand fight with the giant squid and its eight flailing tentacles when the ship's protective electrical shield fails to dislodge its grip. The novel concludes with the *Nautilus* being sucked into a whirlpool with all hands aboard, their fate left ambiguous, while only the trio of plucky protagonists escapes. The film, by contrast, finds Nemo going down with his crew after he is shot by pursuing soldiers when he blows up his lair containing his technological secrets in what seems like a nuclear explosion, linking the film's message about the humane use of technology to the real world of contemporary viewers.

2001: A Space Odyssey
UK/US, 1968 – 141 mins
Stanley Kubrick

Commonly regarded as one of the greatest science fiction films ever made – indeed, one of the greatest films ever made – *2001: A Space Odyssey* was a resounding commercial success, and opened the way for the science fiction blockbusters of the next decade such as *Star Wars** and *Close Encounters of the Third Kind** (both 1977). The screenplay was co-written by Kubrick (*Dr Strangelove or: How I Learned to Stop Worrying and Love the Bomb* [1964], *A Clockwork Orange** [1971]) and Arthur C. Clarke, an important science fiction writer whose work frequently considered the impact of human contact with superior alien beings, and was inspired in part by Clarke's 1948 short story, 'The Sentinel'. Relying heavily on scientific knowledge and accuracy, on the one hand, and on ambiguity in both narrative and imagery, on the other, *2001* comes as close as any film to eliciting the 'sense of wonder' often associated with science fiction.

The slim story, arranged in four sections, depicts humanity's technological evolution involving a series of encounters with black monoliths that remain, as Dr. Heywood Floyd (Sylvester) puts it in the last line of the film's sparse dialogue, 'a total mystery'. In the first section, 'The Dawn of Man', a tribe of primitive humans finds a black monolith, and soon after one of them (Richter) touches it, he discovers how to use a bone as both a tool and a weapon, killing the leader of a rival tribe with it in order to take possession of a water hole. As he throws the white bone into the air in triumph, a match cut, one of the most famous edits in the history of cinema, takes us to a space station in the year of the film's title, where Dr. Floyd has a

DIRECTOR Stanley Kubrick
PRODUCER Stanley Kubrick
SCREENPLAY Stanley Kubrick, Arthur C. Clarke
DIRECTOR OF PHOTOGRAPHY Geoffrey Unsworth
EDITOR Ray Lovejoy
MUSIC Richard Strauss, György Ligeti, Aram Khachaturyan
PRODUCTION DESIGN Ernest Archer, Harry Lange, Tony Masters
MAIN CAST Keir Dullea, Gary Lockwood, William Sylvester, Daniel Richter, Leonard Rossiter, Douglas Rain (voice of HAL 9000)
PRODUCTION COMPANY MGM, Stanley Kubrick Productions

stopover en route to a US outpost on the Moon, for a meeting regarding the discovery of another monolith, buried four million years ago.

In the 'Jupiter Mission' section, 18 months later, astronauts David Bowman (Dullea) and Frank Poole (Lockwood) are on the American spaceship Discovery One bound for Jupiter, along with three other scientists in cryogenic hibernation for the journey. 'Hal', the HAL9000 computer responsible for the ship's operations, seems to malfunction and kill all those aboard, except Bowman, who disconnects it. A pre-recorded video message from Floyd explains that the mission is to follow the signal emitted by the monolith on the moon at Jupiter. In the final section, 'Jupiter and Beyond the Infinite', Bowman leaves the ship in an emergency pod and enters the 'stargate' where, thanks to the work of visual effects supervisor Douglas Trumbull (who would go on to direct Silent Running* in 1972), he hurtles across vast and strange landscapes and mysterious cosmic phenomena to find himself in a strange bedroom where he sees progressively older versions of himself. As an elderly man, he sees another monolith at the foot of his bed and is then transformed into a fetus-like 'star-child' that floats in space above the Earth.

In a bold reversal of convention, Kubrick abandoned the original score by composer Alex North (who had written the music for the director's earlier Spartacus [1960] and worked on Dr. Strangelove) in post-production and substituted instead classical music such as Johann Strauss's Blue Danube Waltz during the docking at the space station and Richard Strauss's Thus Spake Zarathustra during the climatic creation of the star child, as well as contemporary compositions by György Ligeti. Kubrick's choices lend an elegant beauty to the film's breathtaking images of space, evoking the celestial music of the spheres. There is no dialogue at all in the opening and closing sequences, the film relying instead on the visual images and the music as it strives to provide the experience of expanding human consciousness.

Clarke worked on the novel simultaneously with the screenplay. In 1972, he published The Lost Worlds of 2001, containing his account of the film's production history which he had documented in his diary. Clarke also wrote three sequel novels: 2010: Odyssey Two (1982), 2061: Odyssey Three (1987), and 3001: The Final Odyssey (1997). A less inspiring sequel to Kubrick's film, 2010: The Year We Make Contact, based on the first of these, was directed by Peter Hyams, whose other science fiction credits include Capricorn One (1978), Outland (1981), and Timecop (1994). The film answers some of 2001's questions, making it clear that the monoliths are purposefully directing human destiny.

Videodrome
Canada, 1983 – 87 mins
David Cronenberg

As a film about media and globalisation, *Videodrome,* despite coming early in David Cronenberg's career, remains one of his most relevant. In *Shivers* (aka *They Came from Within/ The Parasite Murders*, 1975), Cronenberg's first theatrical feature, a mad scientist invents a parasite that creates an insatiable sexual appetite in its human host. The parasite, which enters any bodily orifice, escapes into an ultra-modern apartment building, spreading to the point that all the tenants become infected and indulge in a frenzied mass orgy. In the end, the residents of Starliner Tower leave in their cars *en masse*, driving off to spread the infection throughout Canada and, presumably, the world. The film is a clever reversal of the more conventional depiction of foreign infection as alienated and affectless behaviour in, for example, *Invasion of the Body Snatchers** (1956). In *Shivers'* scenario of uninhibited free love, the so-called sexual revolution happening south of the border in the United States becomes the source of anarchy and horror, infiltrating

DIRECTOR David Cronenberg
PRODUCER Claude Héroux
SCREENPLAY David Cronenberg
DIRECTOR OF PHOTOGRAPHY
Mark Irwin
EDITOR Ronald Sanders
MUSIC Howard Shore
ART DIRECTOR Carol Spier
MAIN CAST James Woods, Sonja
Smits, Deborah Harry, Peter Dvorsky,
Les Carlson, Jack Creley
PRODUCTION COMPANY Canadian
Film Development Corporation,
Famous Players, Filmplan
International

orderly Canadian society. Similar fears animate *Videodrome*, a science fiction-horror film about the medium of television and its desensitising effects on viewers, depicted here in terms of bodily invasion characteristic of Cronenberg's early horror films like *Rabid* (1977), *The Brood* (1979) and *Scanners* (1981), as well as *Shivers*.

An opportunistic television producer, Max Renn (Woods), looking for something new to push the envelope of permissible entertainment in order to attract viewers to his station, learns of a mysterious signal possibly emanating from an unknown pirate station in the United States containing a sadistic programme entitled 'Videodrome'. Renn grows increasingly obsessed with the show, which has no narrative and consists simply of a stationary camera showing naked people being tortured. On a television talk show he meets the media guru Prof. Brian O'Blivion (Creley), clearly modelled on the influential Canadian media scholar Marshall McLuhan (McLuhan taught at the University of Toronto in the early 1970s, when Cronenberg was a student there), who only appears on a TV monitor, and psychiatrist and radio personality Nikki Brand (Harry), with whom he begins a sadomasochistic sexual relationship.

Psychically stimulated by watching 'Videodrome', Renn begins hallucinating, imagining videocassettes pulsating like living creatures and a vaginal slit in his abdomen into which the cassettes can be inserted that program him. As Renn tries to sort through the truth of his hallucinations, he discovers that O'Blivion has been dead for years, a result of exposure to the hallucinogenic 'Videodrome' signal which causes brain tumours and which he himself had helped develop. O'Blivion's daughter Bianca (Smits) now edits his videotaped 'appearances' to keep alive his work, which involves ideological combat with Spectacular Optical, a military-industrial weapons manufacturer that, as part of a government conspiracy, is planning to expose the 'Videodrome' signal to North Americans in order to eliminate all the 'lowlifes' who enjoy violent entertainment.

As Renn's hallucinations grow more intense, the distinction between fantasy and reality begins to collapse for him, as well as for the viewer, since the film withdraws any narrational markers that might distinguish between them. Viewers might well ask themselves the question Seth Brundle poses to his sceptical girlfriend Veronica Quaife (Geena Davis) in Cronenberg's remake of *The Fly** (1986): 'Is it real or is it Memorex?' Cronenberg later employed a similar approach in *Naked Lunch* (1991), an adaptation of William S. Burroughs's drug-infused science fiction novel; in *eXistenZ* (1999), about the enveloping seductiveness of virtual reality; and in *Spider* (2002), a psychological study of a schizophrenic man. In *Videodrome*, the immoral television programmer himself becomes programmed, first by Spectacular Optical and then by Bianca O'Blivion. Anticipating the more overtly ideological treatment of the media in John Carpenter's *They Live** (1988), *Videodrome* shows Renn suffering the fate of all those whose imagination, in the words of Wim Wenders, has been colonised by foreign popular media – a theme also treated in Cronenberg's *Crash* (1996), an adaptation of the novel by J.G. Ballard.

Village of the Damned
UK, 1960 – 77 mins
Wolf Rilla

Despite its unnecessarily lurid title, *Village of the Damned* is a generally faithful adaptation of *The Midwich Cuckoos* by John Wyndham, one of the most widely read of British science fiction writers. (His most well-known work, the 1951 catastrophe novel *The Day of the Triffids*,was adapted as a series for both radio and television and as a feature film in 1962.) The film's premise, involving the impregnation of all fertile women in one British village by an alien intelligence, was especially resonant during the Cold War, when the novel was written and the film made, and when fears of infiltration and subversion were rife. Wolf Rilla's unremarkable but solid direction and the considerable gravitas of George Sanders provide an effective balance to the

DIRECTOR Wolf Rilla
PRODUCER Ronald Kinnoch
SCREENPLAY Stirling Silliphant, Wolf Rilla, Ronald Kinnoch, based on the novel *The Midwich Cuckoos* (1957) by John Wyndham
DIRECTOR OF PHOTOGRAPHY Geoffrey Faithfull
EDITOR Gordon Hales
MUSIC Ron Goodwin
ART DIRECTOR Ivan King
MAIN CAST George Sanders, Barbara Shelley, Martin Stephens, Michael Gwynn, Laurence Naismith
PRODUCTION COMPANY Metro-Goldwyn-Mayer

gradually unfolding threat represented by the children that may or may not have been designed to bring about the end of humanity. The intelligent screenplay was co-written by Stirling Silliphant, who also wrote *Charly*, the 1968 film adaptation of Daniel Keyes's novel *Flowers for Algernon* (1966), about a mentally challenged man who through experimental surgery temporarily becomes a genius, for which Cliff Robertson won an Oscar for Best Actor.

One day, without warning, all the people and animals of Midwich fall unconscious, as does anyone else attempting to enter the town from outside. Shortly after the military arrives and seals off the town, everyone wakes as suddenly as they had fallen asleep. Soon the women, some of whom insist that they are virgins, discover that they are pregnant. The fetuses develop abnormally quickly, and all the women give birth on the same day. The children have a few unusual features – odd hair (straight and nearly white), striking eyes, curious fingernails – and they develop, both physically and intellectually, at an unprecedented speed. Professor Gordon Zellaby (Sanders), the 'father' of one of them, soon realises that they also have telepathic abilities and share a hive consciousness.

The children act remotely, without emotion, dressing alike and walking together. In addition to the ability to read minds, the children develop the power to control people through their collective will, signalled by an eerie glow from their eyes. (Some prints of the film exist without the glow effect, the children merely widening their eyes instead. The variation was possibly due to the elimination of the glow effect from initial prints, deemed as too horrific by British censors.) There are a number of suicides and accidental deaths, but no evidence that the children are responsible, although we see their eyes glow when, in full view of Zellaby and his wife, the children glare at a reckless driver and make him fatally crash into a brick wall.

The brick wall image returns later when Zellaby, despite his earlier plea that we should seize the opportunity to learn from them rather than fear them, realises that they must be destroyed. In the climax, the film's best sequence, he brings a time bomb in his briefcase to the school where he has been giving the children private lessons, trying to block their mental probing by thinking of a brick wall until the bomb detonates. The children, eyes aglow, concentrate on probing Zellaby's mind to learn what he is keeping from them; as Zellaby struggles to focus on the mental image of a brick wall, in a magnificent montage sequence we see a brick wall begin to buckle, bits of mortar and then bricks falling away. Just as the children break through the mental wall and discover the truth of the hidden bomb, it explodes, destroying the school (in a long shot featuring unconvincing model work), killing them all.

Children of the Damned, directed by Anton M. Leader and released in 1963, was billed in the credits as a sequel to *Village of the Damned*, although it is actually more of a loose remake, this time in an urban setting. In 1995 John Carpenter (*Dark Star** [1974], *The Thing** [1982], *They Live** [1988]) directed a remake, keeping the original title but changing the plot somewhat. In Carpenter's version, there is more graphic violence and the children are decidedly more malevolent in motivation. However, one of them develops human emotions and is spared from the explosion by Dr. Chaffee (Christopher Reeve), surviving at the film's end – presumably to reappear in a sequel that was never made.

Le Voyage dans la lune (*A Trip to the Moon*)
France, 1902 – 14 mins
Georges Méliès

A pioneering film-maker in the medium's infancy, Georges Méliès made trick films that exploited cinematic effects such as stop action, reverse motion, dissolves, multiple exposures and (hand-painted) colour. Méliès, a successful stage magician before turning to film, conceived of cinema as an extension of magic, exploiting the medium's possible techniques for perceptual misdirection. One could, for example, make characters or objects appear or disappear much more easily than on the stage through editing, simply by splicing two shots together. However, his sense of scene construction quickly became outdated as film-makers began to develop the dramatic strategies of classic narrative editing. Méliès always conceived of the action before the camera as a series of theatrical tableux and the camera invariably positioned front row centre. Yet his films, which he called 'Artificially Arranged Scenes', vividly demonstrated cinema's ability to show the marvellous

DIRECTOR Georges Méliès
PRODUCER Georges Méliès
SCREENPLAY Georges Méliès, loosely based on the novels *From the Earth to the Moon* (1865) by Jules Verne and *The First Men in the Moon* (1901) by H.G. Wells
DIRECTOR OF PHOTOGRAPHY Michaut, Lucien Tainguy
EDITOR Georges Méliès
PRODUCTION DESIGN Georges Méliès
MAIN CAST Georges Méliès, Bleuette Bernon, Víctor André, Henri Delannoy
PRODUCTION COMPANY Star Film

as well as the mundane. 'The Wizard of Montreuil', named for the town where he established his studio, directed more than 500 short films between 1896 and 1914, many of them in the categories of the fantastic. If *Le Manoir du diable* (*The House of the Devil*, 1896) is perhaps the first horror film, *Le Voyage dans la lune*, which Méliès wrote, designed and directed, is often acknowledged as the first science fiction film.

Méliès's most famous film – it contains the now iconic image of the spaceship landing in the eye of the Man in the Moon – *Le Voyage dans la lune* was loosely based on both Jules Verne's *From the Earth to the Moon* (1865) and H.G. Wells's *The First Men in the Moon*, published the year before the film was made. *Le Voyage* is comprised of sixteen shots, each equalling a scene except for three quick shots that depict the capsule's return through space, splashdown in the sea and sinking to the bottom before being rescued by a steamer. It begins with a meeting of astronomers where the president (played by Méliès) proposes the lunar flight. There is much consternation at the idea, but five other astronomers agree to go along. After their construction, a gigantic cannon blasts the space shell toward the moon. The idea of a space capsule being launched from a giant gun like a bullet was introduced in Verne's novel (Méliès would later film a version of another Verne novel, *20,000 Leagues under the Sea*, in 1907) and subsequently revived by Wells in his screenplay for *Things to Come**

(1936), adapted from his own *The Shape of Things to Come* (1933). After landing on the moon's surface, the intrepid astronomers take refuge in a crater, where they discover a new world of giant mushrooms and Selenites that conveniently explode when struck with their umbrellas. Dispatching the King of the Selenites in this way, the astronomers are pursued back to their capsule, with which they manage to escape in the nick of time and return to Earth. A final shot, missing from many prints of the film, shows a parade celebrating the travellers' return.

Despite the theatricality of Méliès's narrative construction, the film was an astonishing achievement for its time. When most films of the period were of a minute or two in duration, by comparison *Le Voyage* was epic in length and concept. The inclusion of a bevy of bathing beauties as 'Marines' to load and launch the shell seems particularly silly, while the exploding Selenites is merely an excuse for some stop-action trickery. Nevertheless, such moments as the moon growing larger as the shell approaches it, and the relatively long take showing the lunar landscape changing as the Earth rises on the horizon, followed by shooting stars, anthropomorphised constellations and a snowstorm, are remarkable given the technical limitations with which Méliès worked. With *Le Voyage dans la lune* Méliès revealed the cinema's affinity with science fiction, even if it did at the same time establish film's ability to emphasise sensation over sense.

WALL-E
US, 2008 – 98 mins
Andrew Stanton

A computer-animated feature produced by Pixar Animation Studios, *WALL-E* is a family film that also uses science fiction concepts to offer a critique of consumer culture. Indeed, it may be the darkest of Disney's animated features in its social vision. The film follows a robot named WALL-E (Waste Allocation Load Lifter – Earth Class), a waste collector centuries in the future when the Earth has been ruined by garbage and pollution. The extraordinarily expressive robots in the film continue Pixar's speciality of anthropomorphising mechanical objects, as with the tensor lamp in its second short film *Luxo Jr.* (1986), and automobiles in *Cars* (2006). Communicating with body language and robotic sounds resembling human vocal intonations designed by Ben Burtt, who worked on the sound design of, among others, George Lucas's *Star Wars** films and Steven Spielberg's *Indiana Jones* films and *E.T: The Extra-Terrestrial** (1982), the film relies on minimal dialogue to depict machines that are far more sympathetic than the wasteful humans who, after all, have despoiled the planet.

In the year 2805, Earth is uninhabitable due to continued mass consumption encouraged by the giant corporation, Buy N Large (BnL). In 2105, BnL had evacuated Earth's population in fully automated galactic cruise ships, leaving behind small, mobile trash compactor robots with solar power and all-terrain treads, shovel hands and retractable binocular eyes, looking similar to Johnny 5 in *Short Circuit* (1986). All have

DIRECTOR Andrew Stanton

PRODUCER Jim Morris

SCREENPLAY Andrew Stanton, Jim Reardon

EDITOR Steven Schaffer

MUSIC Thomas Newman

PRODUCTION DESIGN Ralph Eggleston

VOICE CAST Ben Burtt, Elissa Knight, Jeff Garlin, Sigourney Weaver, and Fred Willard (live-action) as the BnL CEO

PRODUCTION COMPANY Pixar Animation Studios, Walt Disney Pictures apparently ceased functioning except for one, which learns about humans by watching videos of old musicals like *Hello, Dolly!* (1969). One day a spaceship lands and deploys an Extraterrestrial Vegetation Evaluator ('EVE') robot – coded feminine with its egg-shaped body as opposed to WALL-E's angular shape – sent automatically from the *Axiom*, one of the cruise ships, to search for vegetation on Earth. WALL-E seeks to befriend EVE, who at first ignores him but gradually begins to interact with him. When 'he' shows EVE his collection of artefacts, including a recently discovered seedling plant, the first he has found, the appositely named EVE inserts it and enters standby mode until 'she' is gathered up by the ship, the loyal WALL-E following her into space by clinging to its hull.

On the *Axiom*, the human descendants of the ship's original passengers have grown obese and torpid after centuries in their luxurious but hermetic ship, floating on moving deck chairs and relying on automated systems for almost everything. The Captain learns that once the ship's computer verifies the existence of plant life, it will automatically return the ship to Earth for recolonisation. However, Auto, the bridge's main computer, initiates a secret directive never to return to Earth, which BnL had already deemed beyond reclamation. After the Captain (who literally learns to stand on his own two feet), and the robots defeat Auto, whose unblinking red eye recalls the rogue HAL

computer in *2001: A Space Odyssey** (1968), the ship returns to Earth and EVE repairs WALL-E, who has been damaged in the fight. They touch hands, as do the characters Wally has watched in *Hello, Dolly!* The implied fate of the people on the ship is similarly upbeat, with the final shot zooming away to reveal more vegetation growing elsewhere and a closing credits sequence showing humans and robots working together to rebuild civilisation – although their future success is debatable, given their physical condition and plans to grow 'pizza plants'.

WALL-E was nominated for six Academy Awards, winning Best Animated Feature, and was one of the top grossing films of the year. Director Andrew Stanton has worked with Pixar Studios on a number of its successful projects: in addition to *WALL-E*, he co-wrote the three *Toy Story* movies (1995, 1999, 2010) and *Monsters, Inc.* (2001), co-wrote and co-directed *A Bug's Life* (1998) and co-wrote and directed *Finding Nemo* (2003). After this string of hits, Stanton's first live-action feature as director was, unfortunately, *John Carter* (2012), a big-budget adaptation of the first of Edgar Rice Burroughs's 11-volume *Barsoom* series (1912–43) that flopped for Disney. Pixar, initially a branch of Lucasfilm, was bought by the Walt Disney Company in 2006. It is, then, rather ironic that *WALL-E* seems to criticise exactly the kind of people who patronise resorts, cruise lines, and theme parks – all of which the Disney Company owns.

The War Game
1965, UK – 48 mins
Peter Watkins

British film-maker and media activist Peter Watkins produced a series of pioneering docudramas that are science fiction stories with Orwellian overtones of totalitarian social engineering and media manipulation. Mixing documentary techniques and fictional narratives, *Privilege* (1967), *The Gladiators* (1969) and *Punishment Park* (1971) are all set in the near future and extrapolate from contemporary political and media realities. *The War Game*, about a hypothetical nuclear strike on Britain, is perhaps his most powerful film. It expertly melds science fiction and documentary and is often discussed in the context of both traditions.

DIRECTOR Peter Watkins
PRODUCER Peter Watkins
SCREENPLAY Peter Watkins
DIRECTOR OF PHOTOGRAPHY Peter Bartlett, Peter Suschitzsky
EDITOR Michael Bradsell
CAST Michael Aspel, Peter Graham
PRODUCTION COMPANY BBC Television

The War Game was Watkins's second film for the BBC after Culloden (1964), about the Jacobite uprising of 1745 and the crushing of Scottish highlander identity by the English army, presented as if television news reporters were embedded with the English forces, interviewing participants and covering the scene of the battle. Using a similar approach in The War Game, Watkins combines pseudo-vérité footage, mock interviews with authorities and people on the street, talking-head shots of actors quoting actual passages from official documents, and voice-over narration providing contextual information to create a thoroughly convincing hypothetical documentary. Shot on grainy, handheld 16mm, the film's convincing realism is also due in part to the work of its two cinematographers, one of whom, Peter Suschitzky, was later director of photography for, among others, Star Wars*: Episode V – The Empire Strikes Back (1980), Mars Attacks* (1996), Red Planet (2000) and numerous films for David Cronenberg, including Naked Lunch (1991) and eXistenZ (1999).

In the film's faux history, building from contemporary Cold War tensions, a Chinese invasion of South Vietnam is followed by the escalation of hostilities between the nuclear superpowers, leading to NATO's use of tactical nuclear weapons in response to the Soviet invasion of West Germany. As war breaks out, the Soviet Union launches a limited nuclear strike against Britain. We see the wholly inadequate attempt by authorities to evacuate urban populations, separate families and billet them with other families elsewhere in preparation for a nuclear strike, and what follows from just one nuclear airburst over the town of Rochester in Kent. A horrific firestorm ensues, followed by the inevitable breakdown of civil institutions as rioting occurs in response to food shortages, and looters are executed by police. The survivors are shown suffering from radiation sickness and psychological trauma. All of these events are presented in stark documentary-like scenes of individualised examples that seem authentic. The final scene, showing a miserable group of survivors gathered for Christmas dressed in tattered clothing and with radiation burns on their faces, as a priest hand-cranks a turntable to play a scratchy recording of 'Silent Night' while traumatised children look on with blank faces, is more chilling than any abstract apocalypse conjured by Hollywood CGI-infused visions of nuclear disaster.

The film's harrowing depiction of the complete inadequacy of civil defence plans disturbed government officials, and it was banned from television broadcast. A statement was issued declaring that 'the effect of the film has been judged by the BBC to be too horrifying for the medium of broadcasting'. Nevertheless, The War Game did get limited distribution in art cinemas and it went on to win the Academy Award for Best Documentary Feature in 1966. Still, the film was not shown in full on British television until 1985. When the film was withdrawn, Watkins left the BBC and, after Privilege, about the government's manipulation of the iconic power of a rock star, he also left the country, making his subsequent films elsewhere: the United States (Punishment Park), Sweden (The Gladiators), Norway (Edvard Munch, 1974) and France (La Commune (Paris, 1871), 2000), while The Journey (1987), a 14-hour film cycle about the threat of nuclear war, was shot in ten different countries.

By the time The War Game was shown on British television, several other docudramas about nuclear holocaust had been broadcast, including The Day After (1983) and Threads (1984), a BBC production that recalled Watkins's style. In 1967 Watkins published a book based on the film, 'for those who would further consider the deeply disturbing implications of The War Game'.

The War of the Worlds
US, 1953 – 85 mins
Byron Haskin

The third of producer George Pal's significant science fiction films (following *Destination Moon** [1950] and *When Worlds Collide** [1951]), *The War of the Worlds* is noteworthy as one of the few American films of the genre in the 1950s, along with *Earth vs the Flying Saucers* (1956), which was clearly influenced by it, to depict an all-out attack by aliens. Just as H.G. Wells's source novel may be read as the nightmarish unleashing of guilt upon an imperialist society, so the film may be understood on one level as articulating the more contemporary fear pervading the American postwar empire of being invaded by cold-blooded Communists.

DIRECTOR Byron Haskin
PRODUCER George Pal
SCREENPLAY Barré Lyndon, based on the 1898 novel by H.G. Wells
DIRECTOR OF PHOTOGRAPHY George Barnes
EDITOR Everett Douglas
MUSIC Leith Stevens
ART DIRECTOR Albert Nozaki, Hal Pereira
MAIN CAST Gene Barry, Ann Robinson, Les Tremayne, Sandro Giglio, Lewis Martin, Robert Cornthwaite
PRODUCTION COMPANY Paramount Pictures

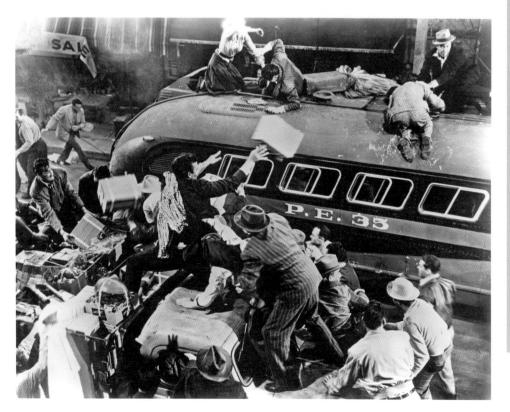

The movie retains the basics of Wells's plot, although Barré Lyndon's screenplay does make some significant changes, including altering the time and location from Victorian England to contemporary California and adding a typical Hollywood love interest. A meteor lands in a small town, and when several people attempt to investigate, they are disintegrated by a death ray. Similar meteors land elsewhere around the globe, and soon the Martian war machines launch their orchestrated assault. Wells's carefully described tripod machines are here replaced by a type of flying saucer, a revision apparently prompted more by financial than thematic reasons, although they do reflect the rash of actual UFO sightings at the time and then depicted in many science fiction movies during the period. The invaders' death rays incinerate both humans and hardware, while terrestrial (that is to say, American) military weaponry, including an atomic bomb detonated as a last resort, proves completely ineffective against the Martians' force fields.

In the climax, as the defeat of Earth seems certain, the scientist-hero (Barry) and his girlfriend (Robinson) gather with other survivors in a church. While everyone is 'praying for a miracle', the Martians burst through the church walls – and then suddenly die, the result, we learn, of infection by terrestrial bacteria. Thus the world is saved by a literal *deus ex machina* since, as Cedric Hardwicke's voice-over explains, it was God who thoughtfully put the microbes on the Earth in the first place. Although the reason for the failure of the Martian invasion is the same in both novel and film, the church location and the prayer are the invention of the latter. By invoking faith rather than biology, the movie is more conservative in its vision than is Wells's shocking subversion of comfortable British society. At the same time, however, the film strays from convention by disturbingly depicting the military as impotent against the alien aggressors.

From another perspective, the ending's biological salvation of humanity resonates with other films by director Byron Haskin, who remains a largely underrated auteur of science fiction cinema. In his *Conquest of Space* (1955, also produced by Pal) and *Robinson Crusoe on Mars* (1964), nature and ecology also play a significant role, while in *From the Earth to the Moon* (1958), based on the novel by Jules Verne, industrialist Stuyvesant Nicholl (George Sanders), initially collaborating on the rocket project with inventor Victor Barbicane (Joseph Cotten), loses his sanity when he thinks the scientific advance the rocket portends has violated God's intelligent design. Perhaps Haskin's most vivid depiction of nature's power is *The Naked Jungle* (1954), based on Carl Stephenson's famous short story 'Leiningen versus the Ants', about a European plantation owner in Brazil (Charlton Heston) who battles an invading horde of omnivorous ants. It also shares with *The War of the Worlds* a vision of the coloniser besieged.

Like both Orson Welles's famous radio adaptation, broadcast on Halloween night in 1938, and Haskin's film version, Steven Spielberg's 2005 remake also taps into contemporaneous concerns, in this case post-9/11 fears of terrorism. Its biggest departure from the two earlier texts is the premise that the Martian machines have been buried under the earth for aeons, animated by aliens parachuted into them like terrorist 'sleeper' cells suddenly awakened. Not coincidentally, the attack begins in New York City, site of the 9/11 attacks on the World Trade Center, and then spreads to the world beyond. And while Spielberg's version restores the terrifying machines of Wells's vision, as well as other plot points omitted in the first version, it also reworks the narrative into another Spielbergian Oedipal melodrama, ending with the protagonist father (Cruise) becoming a responsible father and restoring his children to their mother.

Westworld
US, 1973 – 88 mins
Michael Crichton

Westworld, about a future amusement park that becomes deadly, was the first feature directed by Michael Crichton, who would go on to write and direct *Coma* (1978) and *Looker* (1981), among others. With a background in medical training, Crichton created the award-winning television series *ER* (1994–2009) and also wrote other science fiction novels which were adapted as films, including *The Andromeda Strain* (1971), directed by Robert Wise (*Star Trek: The Motion Picture** [1979]); *The Terminal Man* (1974), directed by Mike Hodges; *Timeline* (2003), directed by Richard Donner (*Superman** [1978]); and the screenplays for *Jurassic Park** (1993) and the sequel, *The Lost World: Jurassic Park* (1997, both directed by Steven Spielberg. The first

DIRECTOR Michael Crichton
PRODUCER Paul Lazarus III
SCREENPLAY Michael Crichton
DIRECTOR OF PHOTOGRAPHY Gene Polito
EDITOR David Bretherton
MUSIC Fred Karlin
ART DIRECTOR Herman Blumenthal
MAIN CAST Richard Benjamin, Yul Brynner, James Brolin, Norman Bartold, Victoria Shaw, Alan Oppenheimer, Dick Van Patten, Linda Scott, Steve Franken, Sharyn Wynters
PRODUCTION COMPANY MGM

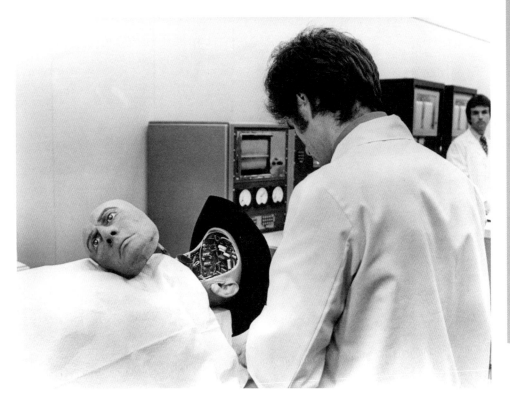

feature film to use digital imaging technology, in this case to show the pixellated perspective of the robot gunfighter (Brynner), *Westworld* is a generic hybrid that cleverly plays with the conventions of the Western within a science fiction context decades before the less imaginative *Cowboys and Aliens* (2011).

The film's plot and theme are essentially the same as in Crichton's later *Jurassic Park* – the folly of the human attempt to create and control our environment, denying the power of nature in the process, and its deadly consequences when things inevitably get out of control. Sometime in the near future, Peter Martin (Benjamin) and John Blane (Brolin), two friends from Chicago, are among a group of guests arriving at the high-tech amusement park Delos, a resort that, for $1,000 a day, allows guests to act out their fantasies with realistic looking androids in one of three simulated environments: Roman World, set in pre-Christian Rome; Medieval World, set in Europe; and Westworld, based on the American Wild West in the 1880s and the chosen destination of Martin and Blane. A group of technicians monitoring the guests in these themed environments discovers that a malfunction is spreading among the robots that causes them to ignore their programmed parameters. As the problem spreads, an android servant in Medieval World rejects a guest's sexual proposition and a robot rattlesnake bites Blane on the arm.

When a robot knight impales a guest during a swordfight in Medieval World, the park technicians decide to shut down Delos's power, hoping that a reboot will solve the glitches in the programming. However, they end up trapped in the control room, suffocating to death while the robots massacre each other and the guests. Martin and Blane, unaware of the technical problems besetting the park, engage The Gunslinger in another gunfight, but this time, to their surprise, the robot kills Blane and then, like Arnold Schwarzenegger's T-800 robot in *The Terminator** (1984) or the Mark-13 in *Hardware* (1990), implacably pursues Martin. It follows Martin into the other two worlds of Delos and finally into the park's underground control bunker where Martin, seemingly the sole survivor in the resort, manages to defeat it.

In a period when Hollywood was revisiting all its major genres, the Western, once the mainstay of Hollywood genre film-making, received particular attention. It is no coincidence that Mel Brooks's *Blazing Saddles* (1974) was released only one year after *Westworld*, and although *Westworld* lacks the self-reflexive humour of *The Cabin in the Woods** (2012), it does presume generic knowledge on the part of viewers to understand the rules of Westworld. Most obviously, Yul Brynner's role as The Gunslinger is modelled on his character Chris Adams, the professional gunfighter who leads *The Magnificent Seven* (1960), as indicated by their similar black outfits. Blane and Martin quickly become familiar with the conventions of the resort, and the film's dramatic suspense is generated by their violation. Given its pronounced generic qualities, it is no surprise that *Westworld* was followed by a sequel, *Futureworld* (1976), involving a conspiracy to replace world leaders with robot replacements and in which Brynner reprised his role as The Gunslinger, and a short-lived television series, *Beyond Westworld*, in 1980.

When Worlds Collide
US, 1951 – 83 mins
Rudolph Maté

Cecil B. DeMille had considered making a film based on *When Worlds Collide* soon after the novel's publication in 1932, but it was producer George Pal who ultimately got it made two decades later as the follow-up to his successful first venture in science fiction, *Destination Moon** (1950). Pal also considered making a sequel based on *After Worlds Collide*, Balmer and Wylie's sequel published in 1934, but was prevented from doing so by the box-office failure of *Conquest of Space* (1955), which he produced after *The War of the Worlds** (1953) and *The Naked Jungle* (1954), all three directed by Byron Haskin. Although the plot of *When Worlds Collide*, which involves a rogue planet on a collision course with Earth, focuses on only a few characters in one place, it provided the template for such later movies as Michael Bay's *Armageddon* (1998), Mimi Leder's *Deep Impact* (1998), and Roland Emmerich's *2012* (2009).

DIRECTOR Rudolph Maté
PRODUCER George Pal
SCREENPLAY Sidney Boehm, based on the 1932 novel by Philip Wylie and Edwin Balmer
DIRECTOR OF PHOTOGRAPHY W. Howard Greene, John F. Seitz
EDITOR Arthur Schmidt
MUSIC Leith Stevens
ART DIRECTOR Albert Nozaki, Hal Pereira
MAIN CAST Richard Derr, Barbara Rush, Hayden Rorke, Peter Hansen, John Hoyt, Larry Keating, Judith Ames, Stephen Chase, Frank Cady, Sandro Giglio
PRODUCTION COMPANY Paramount Pictures

In the course of the story, pilot David Randall (Derr), who is initially interested only in being paid for his services as a courier, becomes selflessly committed to the frantic attempt to build a spaceship in a race against time to transport a handful of people to Zyra, a planet orbiting around Bellus that will pass close to the Earth, and thus prevent the extinction of humanity. Randall's change of attitude shows man rising above the mere animal instinct for self-preservation that the self-centered industrialist Sidney Stanton (Hoyt), who funds the completion of the ship, correctly predicts will overcome the workers on the project designated to be left behind after the passengers for the space ark are chosen by lottery. The ship takes off at the last minute, amidst rioting workers and the approach of Bellus, and Randall successfully flies it to a rough but safe landing on Zyra, where the small band of survivors of Earth's destruction exit the ship to a brave and promising new world.

The novel was co-written by Philip Wylie, whose many science fiction credits include co-authoring *Island of Lost Souls** (1932), the first screen adaptation of H.G. Wells's *The Island of Dr. Moreau*. The film culminates with the arrival of the select all-white group in a new Eden, giving the story (which begins with a quote from Genesis in which God tells Noah that he is going to destroy the Earth because it is corrupt) distinct Christian overtones. Still, the evidence of an (uninhabited?) alien city is, in the last shot, clearly visible in the distance and thus disturbing for fundamentalists. The film is one of the

first of the decade's science fiction apocalyptic parables, with the 'worlds' of the title obliquely referring to the potential for mutually assured destruction that would result from a nuclear war between the two superpowers, the collision of ideologically different worlds separated by the Iron Curtain.

Rudolph Maté, director of the fine film noirs *Union Station* (1950) and *D.O.A.* (1950) and cinematographer of *Gilda* (1946), as well as Fritz Lang's *Liliom* (1934) and Carl Dreyer's *The Passion of Joan of Arc* (1928) and *Vampyr* (1932), among others, handles the narrative in workmanlike fashion, although he cannot conceal the budgetary compromises imposed by the studio on Pal's vision despite Academy Award-winning special effects. The few shots of public panic and martial law when the world realises its inevitable fate are stock black-and-white footage in an otherwise colour film. The montage of destruction when Bellus passes Earth, with volcanoes, rending glaciers and tsunamis – including one passable shot of a giant wave crashing through Times Square in New York City – is curiously devoid of human victims, and the ultimate destruction of Earth by Bellus is shown in one anticlimactic shot. The final scene, when the colonists disembark on Zyra and look from ice-capped mountains to an unconvincing lush river valley, was in fact a sketch made by astronomical artist Chesley Bonestell (who also designed the space ark), which was used instead of a matte painting like those Bonestell had so beautifully provided for *Destination Moon* the year before.

X: The Man with the X-Ray Eyes
US, 1963 – 79 mins
Roger Corman

Known as the 'King of the Bs', Roger Corman was a prolific producer and director of low budget genre movies in the 1950s and 60s. Corman worked in a variety of genres, including horror and science fiction, with such movies as *Day the World Ended* (1955), *It Conquered the World* (1956), *Not of This Earth* (1957), *Attack of the Crab Monsters* (1957), *A Bucket of Blood* (1959), *The Wasp Woman* (1959) and *The Little Shop of Horrors* (1960), a cult favourite that generated a successful stage musical and film adaptation. He also made a series of films loosely based on the stories of Edgar Allan Poe, all but one starring Vincent Price and many written by Richard Matheson, including *House of Usher* (1960), *Pit and the Pendulum* (1961) and *The Masque of the Red Death* (1964), the latter photographed by Nicolas Roeg, who would go on to direct *The Man Who Fell to Earth** (1976).

Working frequently with American International Pictures (AIP) and, from 1970, through his own production and distribution company, New World Pictures, Corman served as a mentor to many younger film-makers, including James Cameron (*The Terminator** [1984], *Avatar** [2009]) and John Sayles (*Brother from Another Planet** [1984]), and was the North American distributor of art films by Ingmar Bergman, Akira Kurosawa and others. Corman is legendary for his efficiency and speed of production, reputedly making *The Little Shop of Horrors* and *The Terror* (1963) each in two days. Of all of Corman's science fiction, *X,* shot in only three weeks on a miniscule budget of $300,000, may nonetheless be his most accomplished.

Dr. James Xavier (Milland) develops a drug that increases the range of human visual perception and gives him X-ray vision. Against the advice of his colleague, Dr. Brant (Stone), Xavier decides to experiment with his untested drug on himself because he would be able to provide reliable reports on its effects. At first, Xavier is able to control his newfound visual power, and he saves the life of a girl who has been misdiagnosed by locating the tumour in her body. He also discovers that, as in Russ Meyer's soft-core feature *The Immoral Mr. Teas* (1959), he is able to see through people's clothes at a party, although Corman is disappointingly chaste in comparison with Meyer, Xavier apparently looking only at the dancers' feet and backs.

Wanting to see more, to penetrate the secrets of the universe, Xavier unwisely continues to self-administer the eyedrops, and as a result he grows mentally unstable as he sees things he cannot comprehend. Like so many science fiction scientists since the prototypical Griffin in *The Invisible Man** (1933), he begins to succumb to megalomania. Accidentally killing Brant, Xavier hides out by becoming a mentalist at a carnival and then by posing as a faith healer. In the climax, Xavier stumbles upon a tent revival meeting in the desert where he tells the preacher that he can see to the ends of the universe and that in its centre there is 'an eye that sees us all'. The preacher regards it as the work of the devil and, quoting from *Matthew* 18:9, replies, 'If thine eye offends thee, pluck it out!' – advice which the tortured Xavier follows. The last shot is a quick close-up of Xavier's face with blood-smeared, empty eye sockets.

DIRECTOR Roger Corman
PRODUCER Roger Corman
SCREENPLAY Robert Dillon, Ray Russell
DIRECTOR OF PHOTOGRAPHY Floyd Crosby
EDITOR Anthony Carras
MUSIC Les Baxter
PRODUCTION DESIGN Daniel Haller
MAIN CAST Ray Milland, Diana Van Der Vlis, Harold J. Stone, John Hoyt, Don Rickles
PRODUCTION COMPANY Alta Vista Productions

The special effects showing the incomprehensible depths of the universe as seen from Xavier's perspective are rendered with unimpressive optical effects that, although they prefigure the experience of the Stargate at the end of *2001: A Space Odyssey* (1968), are crude and unconvincing. However, the climactic sight of Xavier's eyes, hidden by sunglasses through most of the film, with blackened whites and copper irises, remains especially effective. Equally surprising is the dramatic performance by acerbic comedian Don Rickles who, as the sleazy carnival barker Crane, all but steals the film from the more stolid Milland.

Zardoz
UK, 1974 – 105 mins
John Boorman

Following the success of *Deliverance* (1972), British film-maker John Boorman's delirious *Zardoz* was a thoroughly personal, if not self-indulgent, film. It remains Boorman's only foray into science fiction, although immediately after it, still working in the modes of the fantastic, he made both *Exorcist II: The Heretic* (1977) and *Excalibur* (1981). Borrowing from the contrast between the Eloi and Morlocks in H.G. Wells's *The Time Machine* (1895), *Zardoz* depicts a post-apocalyptic world in the year 2293 inhabited by an elite group of 'Eternals', immortal humans who live inside the Vortex, a protective force field that separates them from the 'Brutals', including the 'Exterminators', a warrior class that keeps the population of Brutals manageable. Boorman also co-wrote a novelisation of *Zardoz* in 1974 with Bill Stair, credited as consultant on the film, which fleshes out the early life of the film's protagonist, Zed (Connery).

The Exterminators worship the god Zardoz, a huge, flying stone head which supplies the Brutals with weapons in return for the grain that feeds the Eternals. In an attempt to give some sense of meaning to the life of the Eternals, The Tabernacle, the AI that maintains their immortality, punishes them with artificial aging for violating the rules of life in the Vortex. As we eventually discover along with the Brutal Zed (Connery), who enters the Vortex by hiding inside the Zardoz godhead, Zardoz is actually controlled by one of the Eternals, Arthur Frayn (Buggy), who has put into motion an elaborate scheme to manipulate Zed's intelligence so that he would eventually penetrate the Vortex and destroy it, releasing the Eternals from the crushing ennui of their immortality. Frayn's inspiration for creating a deity that would ultimately be rejected as an illusion came from the unlikely yet relevant source of L. Frank Baum's book *The Wonderful Wizard of Oz* (1900).

Recalling John Savage in Aldous Huxley's *Brave New World* (1932), Zed is like a beast to the Eternals. They are curious about him, examining him and assuming his lack of intelligence, trying to exploit him in their internecine politics. In one scene, Zed absent-mindedly pokes a hole in a Van Gogh self-portrait with his finger, completely oblivious to the painting's artistic value. Yet Zed continues to learn, and soon discovers the truth: that Zardoz is not a god but merely a man, as in *The Wizard of Oz*, manipulating events 'behind a curtain'. Eventually, Zed brings his band of Exterminators into the Vortex, where they destroy the Tabernacle after Zed has absorbed all its knowledge. The Eternals then welcome their true death as they are slain by the invading warriors. Zed leaves the destroyed Vortex with a few of the Eternals, including Consuella (Rampling), to begin new lives as mortals in the outside world.

Zardoz was Connery's second film after moving on from James Bond, and the camera, abetted by a somewhat absurd costume design, frequently emphasises his body, especially his hairy chest, as erotic object. The 'Apathetics', near comatose Eternals who have succumbed to the meaninglessness of their eternal existence, taste Zed's sweat as if it were holy communion and regain consciousness, along with a consuming

DIRECTOR John Boorman
PRODUCER John Boorman
SCREENPLAY John Boorman
DIRECTOR OF PHOTOGRAPHY
Geoffrey Unsworth
EDITOR John Merritt
MUSIC David Munrow
PRODUCTION DESIGN Anthony
Pratt
MAIN CAST Sean Connery,
Charlotte Rampling, Sara Kestelman,
John Alderton, Sally Anne Newton,
Niall Buggy, Bosco Hogan
PRODUCTION COMPANY John
Boorman Productions

sexual desire – a humorous reference to Connery's already growing sexual appeal as a star.

The film is beautifully photographed by cinematographer Geoffrey Unsworth, whose extensive credits also include *2001: A Space Odyssey** (1968), *Superman** (1978) and *Superman II* (1980). The final sequence, accompanied by Beethoven's *Seventh Symphony*, is a montage, inspired by a visual gag in Buster Keaton's *Three Ages* (1923), of Zed and Consuella sitting in a cave, shown aging in a series of overlapping dissolves, producing a baby son who grows up and goes off on his own, and then Zed and Consuella die, turning to bones that crumble to dust. The scene is an aptly lyrical conclusion to a wildly imaginative film that explores some of science fiction's most enduring themes such as the conflict between nature and technology, the effects of the mass media, and questions of mortality and the meaning of life.

Notes

1. Mark Bould and Sherryl Vint, *The Routledge Concise History of Science Fiction* (London and New York: Routledge, 2011), p. 1.
2. Edward Buscombe, 'Introduction', *100 Westerns* (London: BFI, 2006), p. ix.
3. Christian Metz, *Film Language: A Semiotics of the Cinema*, trans. Michael Taylor (New York: Oxford University Press, 1974), p. 44.
4. Damon Knight, *In Search of Wonder,* 2nd ed. (Chicago: Advent, 1967), p. 13; Siegfried Kracauer, *Theory of Film: The Redemption of Physical Reality* (New York: Oxford, 1965).
5. Terry Ramsaye, *A Million and One Nights: A History of the Motion Picture through 1925* (New York: Touchstone, 1986), pp. 153–4.
6. Carl Freedman, 'Kubrick's *2001* and the Possibility of a Science Fiction Cinema,' *Science Fiction Studies* 75 (1998), p. 305.
7. Vivian Sobchack, *The Limits of Infinity: The American Science Fiction Film* (New York: A.S. Barnes, 1980), p. 47.
8. Darko Suvin, *Metamorphosis of Science Fiction: On the Poetics and History of a Literary Genre* (New Haven: Yale University Press, 1979), p. 4.
9. Susan Sontag, 'The Aesthetics of Destruction,' in *Against Interpretation* (New York: Delta, 1966), p. 212.

Further Reading

Anderson, Craig W., *Science Fiction Films of the Seventies* (Jefferson, NC: McFarland, 1985).

Atkins, Thomas (ed.), *Science Fiction Films* (New York: Monarch Press, 1976).

Bartkowiak, Mathew J., *Sounds of the Future: Essays on Music in Science Fiction Film* (Jefferson, NC: McFarland, 2010).

Baxter, John, *Science Fiction in the Cinema* (New York: Paperback Library, 1970).

Benson, Michael, *Vintage Science Fiction Films: The Pioneers, 1896–1949* (Jefferson, NC: McFarland, 1985).

Booker, M. Keith, *Historical Dictionary of Science Fiction Cinema* (Lanham, MD: Scarecrow Press, 2010).

———, *Monsters, Mushroom Clouds, and the Cold War: American Science Fiction and the Roots of Postmodernism, 1946–1964* (Westport, CT: Greenwood Press, 2001).

Brosnan, John, *Future Tense: The Cinema of Science Fiction* (New York: St. Martin's Press, 1978).

Bukatman, Scott, *Terminal Identity: The Virtual Subject in Postmodern Science Fiction* (Durham and London: Duke University Press, 1993).

Cartmell, Deborah, I. Q. Hunter, Heidi Kaye, and Imelda Whelehan (eds), *Alien Identities: Exploring Difference in Film and Fiction* (London: Pluto Press, 1999).

Cornea, Christine, *Science Fiction Cinema* (Edinburgh: Edinburgh University Press, 2007).

Everman, Welch D., *Cult Science Fiction Films: From* The Amazing Colossal Man *to* Yog: The Monster from Space (Secaucus, NJ: Birch Lane Press/Carol Publishing, 1995).

Fischer, Dennis, *Science Fiction Film Directors, 1895–1998* (Jefferson, NC: McFarland, 2000).

Frank, Alan, *The Science Fiction and Fantasy Film Handbook* (Totowa, NJ: Barnes and Noble, 1983).

Galbraith, Stuart, IV. *Japanese Science Fiction, Fantasy, and Horror Films: A Critical Analysis and Filmography of 103 Features Released in the United States, 1950–1992* (Jefferson, NC: McFarland, 1994).

Gifford, Denis, *Movie Monsters* (New York: Dutton, 1969).

———, *Science Fiction Films* (New York: Dutton, 1971).

Glassy, Mark C., *The Biology of Science Fiction Cinema* (Jefferson, NC: McFarland, 2001).

Goldberg, Lee, Randy Lofficier, Jean-Marc Lofficier, and William Rabkin, *Science Fiction Filmmaking in the 1980s: Interviews with Actors, Directors, Producers, and Writers* (Jefferson, NC: McFarland, 1995).

Hardy, Phil, *Science Fiction: The Complete Film Sourcebook* (New York: Morrow, 1984).

Hendershot, Cyndy, *Paranoia, the Bomb, and 1950s Science-Fiction Films* (Bowling Green, OH: Bowling Green State University Popular Press, 1999).

Hochscherf, Tobias, and James Leggott, *British Science Fiction Film and Television* (Jefferson, NC: McFarland, 2011).

Holston, Kim R., and Tom Winchester, *Science Fiction, Fantasy, and Horror Film Sequels, Series, and Remakes: An Illustrated Filmography, with Plot Synopses and Critical Commentary* (Jefferson, NC: McFarland, 1997).

Hunter, I. Q. (ed.), *British Science Fiction Cinema.* (New York and London: Routledge, 1999).

Johnson, William (ed.), *Focus on the Science Fiction Film* (Englewood Cliffs, NJ: Prentice-Hall, 1972).

King, Geoff, and Tanya Krzywinska, *Science Fiction Cinema: From Outerspace to Cyberspace* (London: Wallflower Press, 2001).

Kinnard, Roy, *Science Fiction Serials: A Critical Filmography of the 31 Hard SF Cliffhangers* (Jefferson, NC: McFarland, 1998).

Kuhn, Annette (ed.), *Alien Zone: Cultural Theory and Contemporary Science Fiction Cinema* (London and New York: Verso, 1990).

——— (ed.), *Alien Zone II: The Spaces of Science Fiction Cinema* (New York and London: Verso, 1999).

Landon, Brooks, *The Aesthetics of Ambivalence: Rethinking Science Fiction Film in the Age of Electronic (Re)Production* (Westport, CT: Greenwood Press, 1992).

Lee, Walt, *Reference Guide to Fantastic Films: Science Fiction, Fantasy, and Horror.* 3 vols. (Los Angeles: Chelsea-Lee Books, 1972).

Lentz, Harris M., III, *Science Fiction, Horror, and Fantasy Film and Television Credits,* 2d edn, 3 vols (Jefferson, NC: McFarland, 2001).

Lucanio, Patrick, *Them or Us: Archetypal Interpretations of Fifties Alien Invasion Films.* (Bloomington and Indianapolis: Indiana University Press, 1987).

Menville, Douglas, *A Historical and Critical Survey of the Science Fiction Film* (New York: Arno Press, 1975).

Newman, Kim, *Millennium Movies: End of the World Cinema* (London: Titan Books, 1999). Published in the US as *Apocalypse Movies: End of the World Cinema* (New York: St. Martin's Griffin, 2000).

Noonan, Bonnie, *Women Scientists in Fifties Science Fiction Films* (Jefferson, NC: McFarland, 2005).

Parish, James Robert, and Michael R. Pitts, *The Great Science Fiction Pictures* (Metuchen, NJ: Scarecrow Press, 1977).

———, *The Great Science Fiction Pictures II* (Metuchen, NJ: Scarecrow Press, 1990).

Peary, Danny (ed.), *Screen Flights/Screen Fantasies: The Future According to Science Fiction Cinema* (Garden City: Doubleday, 1984).

Penley, Constance, Elizabeth Lyon, Lynn Spigel, and Janet Bergstrom (eds), *Close Encounters: Film, Feminism, and Science Fiction* (Minneapolis and Oxford: University of Minnesota Press, 1991).

Perkowitz, Sidney, *Hollywood Science: Movies, Science, and the End of the World* (New York: Columbia University Press, 2010).

Pitts, Michael R., *Allied Artists Horror, Science Fiction and Fantasy Films* (Jefferson, NC: McFarland, 2011)

Pohl, Frederik, and Frederik Pohl IV, *Science Fiction Studies in Film* (New York: Ace, 1981).

Redmond, Sean (ed.), *Liquid Metal: The Science Fiction Film Reader* (London: Wallflower Press, 2004).

Rickman, Gregg (ed.), *The Science Fiction Film Reader* (New York: Limelight, 2004).

Rovin, Jeff, *A Pictorial History of Science Fiction Films* (Secaucus, NJ: Citadel Press, 1975).

Schelde, Per, *Androids, Humanoids, and Other Science Fiction Monsters: Science and Soul in Science Fiction Films* (New York: New York University Press, 1993).

Schoell, William, *Creature Features: Nature Turned Nasty in the Movies* (Jefferson, NC: McFarland, 2008).

Seed, David (ed.), *A Companion to Science Fiction* (Malden, MA: Blackwell, 2005).

Senn, Bryan, and John Johnson, *Fantastic Subject Guide: A Topical Index to 2,500 Horror, Science Fiction, and Fantasy Films* (Jefferson, NC: McFarland, 1992).

SFE: The Encyclopedia of Science Fiction, http://sf-encyclopedia.com/

Slusser, George E., and Eric S. Rabkin (eds), *Shadows of the Magic Lamp: Fantasy and Science Fiction in Film* (Carbondale: Southern Illinois University Press, 1985).

Sobchack, Vivian, *The Limits of Infinity: The American Science Fiction Film* (South Brunswick, NJ, and London: Barnes/Yoseloff, 1980). Revised as *Screening Space: The American Science Fiction Film* (New York: Ungar, 1987).

Steinbrunner, Chris, and Burt Goldblatt, *Cinema of the Fantastic* (New York: Saturday Review Press, 1972).

Telotte, J. P., *A Distant Technology: Science Fiction Film and the Machine Age* (Middletown, CT: Wesleyan University Press, 1997).

———, *Replications: A Robotic History of the Science Fiction Film* (Urbana and Chicago: University of Illinois Press, 1995).

———, *Science Fiction Film* (New York: Cambridge University Press, 2001).

Telotte, Jay, and Gerald Duchovnay (eds), *Science Fiction Film and Television: Adaptation Across the Screens* (London and New York: Routledge, 2011).

Warren, Bill, *Keep Watching the Skies! American Science Fiction Movies of the Fifties* vol. 1, 1950–1957; vol. 2, 1958–1962 (Jefferson, NC: McFarland, 1982, 1985).

———, *Set Visits: Interviews with 32 Horror and Science Fiction Filmmakers* (Jefferson, NC: McFarland, 1997).

Weaver, Tom, *Interviews with B Science Fiction and Horror Movie Makers: Writers, Producers, Directors, Actors, Moguls, and Makeup* (Jefferson, NC: McFarland, 1988).

———, *It Came from Weaver Five: Interviews with 20 Zany, Glib, and Earnest Moviemakers in the SF and Horror Traditions of the Thirties, Forties, Fifties, and Sixties* (Jefferson, NC: McFarland, 1996).

———, *I Was a Monster Movie Maker: Conversations with 22 SF and Horror Filmmakers* (Jefferson, NC: McFarland, 2001).

———, *Science Fiction and Fantasy Film Flashbacks: Conversations with 24 Actors, Writers, Producers, and Directors from the Golden Age* (Jefferson, NC: McFarland, 1998).

———, *Science Fiction Stars and Horror Heroes: Interviews with Actors, Directors, Producers, and Writers of the 1940s through 1960s* (Jefferson, NC: McFarland, 1991).

———, *They Fought in the Creature Features: Interviews with 23 Classic Horror, Science Fiction, and Serial Stars* (Jefferson, NC: McFarland, 1995).

Wingrove, David, *Science Fiction Source Book* (London: Longman, 1985).

Wright, Bruce L., *Yesterday's Tomorrows: The Golden Age of Science Fiction Movie Posters* (Lanham, MD: Taylor, 1993).

Index

Huxley, Aldous 65, 203
Hyams, Peter 184
Hynek, J. Allen 33

I Am Legend **79–80**, 81
I Married a Witch 113
I, Robot 39
I Walked with a Zombie 180
I Was a Communist for the FBI 159
Imaginarium of Dr. Parnassus, The 25
Immoral Mr. Teas, The 201
In the Dust of the Stars 5
In the Mouth of Madness 161
Incredible Hulk, The 154
Incredible Shrinking Man, The 57, 79, **81–2**, 182
Incredible Shrinking Woman, The 81
Independence Day 17, 105
Innerspace 58
Intolerance 61
Invaders from Mars (1953) 1, **83–4**, 105, 116, 159, 168
Invaders from Mars (1986) 84
Invaders, The 35
Invasion of the Body Snatchers (1956) 83, **85–6**, 185
Invasion of the Body Snatchers (1978) 85
Invasion, The 85
Invisible Agent 88
Invisible Boy, The 65, 66
Invisible Man, The (1933) 4, 67, **87–8**, 125, 179, 201
Invisible Man, The (1958) 88
Invisible Man, The (1975) 88
Invsible Man, The (1984) 88
Invisible Man, The (2000–2) 88
Invisible Man Returns, The 87, 180
Invisible Man's Revenge, The 88
Invisible Woman, The 88
Iron Man 154
Iron Man 2 154
Island of Dr. Moreau, The (1977) 89
Island of Dr. Moreau, The (1996) 89, 127
Island of Lost Souls 68, **89–90**, 200
It Came from Beneath the Sea 17, 159
It Came from Outer Space 4, 43, 82, 83

It Conquered the World 201
It Happened Tomorrow 113
It! The Terror from Beyond Space 7, 57
It's Great to be Alive 95
It's a Wonderful Life 16
Ivens, Joris 114

Jabberwocky 25
Jackson, Peter 48, 77
Jacobs, Arthur P. 117
Jason and the Argonauts 17
Jetée, La 25, **91–2**
Jeunet, Jean-Pierre 7
Jodorowsky, Alejandro 49
John Carter 192
Jones, D. F. 35
Jones, L. Q. 24
Jones, Tom 106
Journey to the Center of the Earth (1959) 181
Journey to the Center of the Earth (2008) 181
Journey, The 194
Journey's End (1930) 67, 87
Juice 28
Jurassic Park 4, 14, 18, 33, **93–4**, 197, 198
Jurassic Park III 94
Just Imagine 61, **95–6**

Karloff, Boris 67
Keaton, Buster 42, 204
Keir, Andrew 119
Kellermann, Bernhard 179
Kenton, Erle C. 68, 89
Kershner, Irvin 125, 147
Keyes, Daniel 188
King Kong (1933) 17, 46
King Kong vs. Godzilla 76
King, Rodney 151–2
Klement, Otto 57
Kneale, Nigel 111, 119
Knight, Damon 2
Knowing 39
Korda, Alexander 113, 167
Kosinski, Joseph 177
Koyaanisqatsi 143
Kracauer, Siegfried 2
Kriemhilds Rache 109

Kronos 65
Kubrick, Stanley 4, 31–2, 35, 42, 65, 106, 131, 134, 139, 178, 183–4
Kurosawa, Akira 1, 76, 201

Lady in the Water 129
Lair of the White Worm, The 11
Lang, Fritz 5, 45, 69–70, 109, 113, 153, 168, 180, 200
Langelaan, George 63
Lantz, Walter 45
Lassie Come Home 66
Last Man on Earth, The 79
Last Night **97–8**
Last Wave, The 101
Laughton, Charles 89–90
Le Guin, Ursula 13, 51–2
Leader, Anton M. 188
Lean, David 117
Leder, Mimi 199
Lee, Spike 28
Legend of the 7 Golden Vampires, The 120
Léger, Fernand 113
Lem, Stanislaw 2, 133, 141–2
Leni, Paul 67
Leone, Sergio 16
Lester, Richard 154
Lewton, Val 129
Ley, Willy 45, 69
Lianna 27
Lifeforce 41
Ligeti, György 184
Liliom 200
Limelight 17
Linklater, Richard 173
Liquid Sky **99–100**
Lisberger, Steven 178
Little Shop of Horrors 201
Little Shop of Horrors, The 201
Lockout 59
Logan's Run (1976) 111, 170
Logan's Run (1977–8) 155
Lom, Herbert 182
Longyear, Barry B. 51
Look Back in Anger 119
Looker 93, 197
Lord of the Rings (2001–3) 77
Losey, Joseph 37

Lost (2004–10) 29
Lost in Space (1965–8) 66
Lost World: Jurassic Park, The 33, 94, 197
Lourié, Eugène 17
Love Boat, The 82
Love and Death 139
Lovecraft, H.P. 29, 161
Lucas, George 2, 53, 132, 147–8, 169, 191
Lugosi, Bela 89, 115
Lumière, Louis and Auguste 2, 10
Luxo Jr 191
Lynch, David 49–50, 158
Lyndon, Barré 196

McCarthy, Cormac 123–4
McCarthy, Joseph R. 159
McDonald, Bruce 97
MacDougall, Ranald 122
McDowall, Roddy 117–18
McG 156
McIntire, Tim 23
McKellar, Don 97
McLuhan, Marshall 186
Mad Max 4, **101–2**
Mad Max 2: The Road Warrior 101
Mad Max Beyond Thunderdome 101
Maetzig, Kurt 133
Magnificent Seven, The 1, 27, 198
Mainwaring, Daniel 85
Man of Steel 153
Man from U.N.C.L.E., The 35
Man Who Could Work Miracles, The 167
Man Who Fell to Earth, The 27, 55, 100, **103–4**, 201
Manchurian Candidate, The (1962), 127
Mankiewicz, Joseph L. 46
Manoir du diable, Le 190
Marker, Chris 25, 91–2
Marquand, Richard 147
Mars Attacks! 17, **105–6**, 194
Martin, Lock 43
Marvin, Lee 51
Mary Shelley's Frankenstein 67
Mason, Tom 115
Masque of the Red Death, The 201
Massey, Raymond 134, 168

List of Illustrations

While considerable effort has been made to correctly identify the copyright holders, this has not been possible in all cases. We apologise for any apparent negligence and any omissions or corrections brought to our attention will be remedied in any future editions.

Aelita, Mezhrabpom-Russ; *Alien*, © Twentieth Century-Fox Film Corporation; *Alphaville*, Chaumiane Productions/Filmstudio; *Altered States*, Warner Bros.; *Avatar*, © Twentieth Century-Fox Film Corporation/Dune Entertainment III LLC; *Back to the Future*, © Universal Pictures/© Amblin Entertainment; *The Beast from 20,000 Fathoms*, Warner Bros./Mutual Productions; *Blade Runner*, © Blade Runner Partnership/The Ladd Company; *Born in Flames*, Lizzie Borden; *A Boy and His Dog*, Third LQJ/LQJaf Productions; *Brazil*, © Embassy International Pictures; *The Brother from Another Planet*, A-Train Films; *The Cabin in the Woods*, © Lions Gate Films, Inc.; *A Clockwork Orange*, © Warner Bros./© Polaris Productions, Inc.; *Close Encounters of the Third Kind*, © Columbia Pictures Industries, Inc.; *Colossus: The Forbin Project*, © Universal Pictures; *The Damned*, © Swallow Productions, Inc.; *Dark City*, New Line Productions/New Line Cinema/Mystery Clock Productions, Inc.; *Dark Star*, Jack H. Harris Enterprises; *The Day the Earth Stood Still*, © Twentieth Century-Fox Film Corporation; *Destination Moon*, © George Pal Productions; *District 9*, © District 9 Ltd; *Dune*, © Dino De Laurentiis Productions; *Enemy Mine*, Kings Road Entertainment/Twentieth Century-Fox Film Corporation; *E.T.: The Extra-Terrestrial*, © Universal City Studios, Inc.; *Fahrenheit 451*, © Vineyard Films Ltd; *Fantastic Voyage*, © Twentieth Century-Fox Film Corporation; *The Fifth Element*, Gaumont; *Flash Gordon* (serial), Universal Productions; *The Fly*, Brooksfilms/Twentieth Century-Fox Film Corporation; *Forbidden Planet*, Loew's Incorporated; *Frankenstein*, Universal Pictures Corporation; *Frau im Mond* (*Woman in the Moon*), Fritz Lang Film/Ufa; *Galaxy Quest*, DreamWorks SKG; *Ghost in the Shell*, © Shirow Masamune/© Kodansha/© Bandai Visual/© Manga Entertainment; *Gojira* (*Godzilla*), Toho Co. Ltd; *The Host*, © Chungeorahm Film; *I Am Legend*, © Warner Bros.; *The Incredible Shrinking Man*, Universal Pictures Company, Inc.; *Invaders from Mars*, Edward L. Alperson Productions; *Invasion of the Body Snatchers*, © Allied Artists Pictures Corporation; *The Invisible Man*, © Universal Pictures Corporation; *Island of Lost Souls*, © Paramount Productions; *La Jetée*, Argos-Films; *Jurassic Park*, © Universal City Studios/© Amblin Entertainment; *Just Imagine*, Fox-Movietone Productions; *Last Night*, © Rhombus Media, Inc.; *Liquid Sky*, Z Films; *Mad Max*, Mad Max; *The Man Who Fell to Earth*, © Houtsnede Maatschappij N.V.; *Mars Attacks!*, © Warner Bros.; *The Matrix*, © Warner Bros./© Village Roadshow Films (BVI) Ltd; *Metropolis*, Ufa; *Nineteen Eighty-Four*, © Virgin Cinema Films Ltd; *Paris qui dort*, Films Diamant; *Plan 9 from Outer Space*, © Reynold Pictures, Inc.; *Planet of the Apes*, © Apjac Productions/© Twentieth Century-Fox Film Corporation; *Quatermass and the Pit*, © Hammer Film Productions; *The Quiet Earth*, Capricorn Films International; *The Road*, © 2929 Productions LLC; *RoboCop*, Orion Pictures Corporation; *Seconds*, © Paramount Pictures Corporation/© Joel Productions/© Gibraltar Productions; *Signs*, © Touchstone Pictures; *Silent Running*, © Universal Pictures; *The Silent Star*, DEFA/Film Polski/Zespól Filmowy "Iluzjon"; *Slaughterhouse-Five*, Universal Pictures/Vanadas Productions; *Sleep Dealer*, This Is That/Likely Story; *Sleeper*, © Metro-Goldwyn-Mayer; *Solaris*, Mosfilm; *Soylent Green*, © Metro-Goldwyn-Mayer; *Star Trek: The Motion Picture*, © Century Associates; *Star Wars*, Lucasfilm Ltd; *Starship Troopers*, TriStar Pictures/Touchstone Pictures; *Strange Days*, Lightstorm Entertainment; *Superman*, © Film Export A.G.; *The Terminator*, © Cinema '84; *Tetsuo: The Iron Man*, Kaijyu Theatre; *Them!*, © Warner Bros.; *They Live*, Alive Films; *The Thing from Another World*, © RKO Radio Pictures, Inc.; *The Thing*, © Universal City Studios, Inc.; *Things to Come*, © London Film Productions Ltd; *THX 1138*, © Warner Bros.; *The Time Machine*, © Galaxy Films; *Total Recall*, Carolco International; *Tribulation 99: Alien Anomalies Under America*, The Other Cinema; *Tron*, © Walt Disney Productions; *The Tunnel*, Gaumont-British Picture Corporation/Gaumont British Distributors Ltd; *20,000 Leagues Under the Sea*, © Walt Disney Productions; *2001: A Space Odyssey*, © Metro-Goldwyn-Mayer; *Videodrome*, Filmplan International/Guardian Trust Company/Canadian Film Development Corporation/Famous Players; *Village of the Damned*, © Metro-Goldwyn-Mayer; *Le Voyage dans la lune*, Star-Film; *WALL-E*, © Disney Enterprises/© Pixar; *The War Game*, BBC; *The War of the Worlds*, © Paramount Pictures Corporation; *Westworld*, Metro-Goldwyn-Mayer; *When Worlds Collide*, © Paramount Pictures Corporation; *X: The Man with the X-Ray Eyes*, © Alta Vista Productions; *Zardoz*, © Twentieth Century-Fox Film Corporation.